W9-BYT-365

WOMEN'S TRAVEL LITERATURE FROM TRAVELERS' TALES

100 Places Every Woman Should Go

100 Places in France Every Woman Should Go

100 Places in Greece Every Woman Should Go

100 Places in Italy Every Woman Should Go

100 Places in Spain Every Woman Should Go

100 Places in the USA Every Woman Should Go

50 Places in Rome, Florence & Venice Every Woman Should Go

Best Women's Travel Writing series

Gutsy Women

Gutsy Mamas

Her Fork in the Road

Kite Strings of the Southern Cross

A Mile in Her Boots

Sand in Her Bra

More Sand in My Bra

A Mother's World

Safety and Security for Women Who Travel

The Thong Also Rises

Unbeaten Tracks in Japan

Whose Panties Are These?

Wild With Child

A Woman's Asia

A Woman's Europe

A Woman's Passion for Travel

A Woman's Path

A Woman's World

A Woman's World Again

Women in the Wild

TRAVELERS' TALES

THE BEST WOMEN'S TRAVEL WRITING
Volume 11

TRUE STORIES
FROM AROUND THE WORLD

The Best Women's Travel Writing

Volume 11

True Stories From Around the World

Edited by
Lavinia Spalding

Travelers' Tales
An imprint of Solas House, Inc.
Palo Alto

Travelers' Tales and Solas House are trademarks of Solas House, Inc., Palo Alto, California 94306. travelerstales.com | solashouse.com

Credits and copyright notices for the individual articles in this collection are given starting on page 298.

Art Direction: Kimberly Coombs
Cover Photograph: Copyright © Shutterstock. Cyclist on a remote road in Xinjang province, China, leading to Western Tibet.
Interior Design and Page Layout: Scribe Inc.
Production Director: Susan Brady

ISBN: 978-1-60952-111-0
ISSN: 1553-054X
E-ISBN: 978-1-60952-112-7

First Edition
Printed in the United States
10 9 8 7 6 5 4 3 2 1

I'm restless. Things are calling me away.
My hair is being pulled by the stars again.

—Anaïs Nin

For Ellis, who has traveled so far to be in this world and has made it a better place.

Table of Contents

Introduction

On the first day of 2017, I sat in a room I love—a small, bright space with green wicker furniture, three neglected but determined ferns, and five slim hardbacks in an old wooden crate. My toddler was napping, my husband was working in another room, and the next two hours were all mine. As winter sunlight streamed through the windows, I sipped coffee and leafed through the stack of books, all collections of poetry by Edna St. Vincent Millay. The pages were old, sepia, and brittle. I paused on the first stanza of a poem called "Exiled."

> *Searching my heart for its true sorrow,*
> *This is the thing I find to be:*
> *That I am weary of words and people,*
> *Sick of the city, wanting the sea;*
> *Wanting the sticky, salty sweetness*
> *Of the strong wind and shattered spray,*
> *Wanting the loud sound and the soft sound*
> *Of the big surf that breaks all day.*

The words didn't exactly apply to me, but they spoke to me and made me think. About sorrow and weariness, words and people, and wanting. And about water.

I'm not a water person, never have been. I can't swim, and I've always been scared of any body of water bigger than a hot tub. I don't even like to drink the stuff. Though I enjoy lying on a beach, I'm not drawn to water the way Millay was and countless others are. I was born near the New Hampshire seacoast, but raised in Arizona. My grounding place is the desert—its perfect stillness and quietude allow my busy mind to settle.

When I travel, however, my life seems to turn aquatic. I've bobbed in the waves of Mexico, Greece, Spain, France, Italy, and Cuba (up to my shoulders, anyway); snorkeled in the Philippines, Indonesia, Costa Rica, and Saipan (I had fins, and sometimes a flotation device); and tried to scuba dive in Guam and the Great Barrier Reef of Australia (both attempts largely unsuccessful).

I've also taken passage on innumerable waterborne vessels: an inflatable raft on the Colorado River in the Grand Canyon; a hastily assembled bamboo contraption in Northern Thailand that wound up sinking (we were rescued by another hastily assembled bamboo contraption); a couple of shaky motorboats and a barge in Nicaragua; a junk on the Mekong in Vietnam; a river boat in Cambodia that got stuck in the mud (we passengers got out and pushed). There was a barf-inducing overnight ferry from Ireland to France, a civilized overnighter from Tunisia to Sicily, and half a dozen jaunts between South Korea and Japan. That's the short list.

So, even as I've habitually rejected water—refusing to jump in lakes or stand beneath waterfalls or dive in pools or even take swimming lessons—water has trickled into my travel life, mesmerizing me with its bioluminescence, its schools of startlingly blue fish, its coolness on a hot island day. I have been lulled by the flutter of an overhead sail, restored by the steam of a natural hot spring, transported while my fingers dipped into the current as I floated downriver. It's hard to deny its power.

Water grew even more difficult to resist when I became a mother two years ago and started traveling with my family. Everywhere we went, Ellis, our son, was happiest and most entertained (meaning we were happiest and most entertained) in the presence of water. In Hawaii, we squatted in tide pools while he gaped at minnows, and one afternoon I carried him into the lagoon to admire a sea turtle swimming amongst the rocks. In Cape Cod, where he took his first wobbly steps, he clutched our hands in terror as the chilly Atlantic tide washed over his feet—but soon delighted in watching it swirl between his tiny toes. In Portugal, fountains abounded, and he splashed in them with unmitigated glee. One evening after eating at a beachfront restaurant, my husband walked him straight into the surf, unconcerned by their soaked pants. Ellis was wary, then thrilled.

I began paying more attention to water, observing how easily this tiny human loved it, how effortlessly he overcame his initial trepidation. I realized I had never fully examined my own fear of water. It took a toddler shrieking in joy, drenching me with his fervent splashing, to turn my focus to it.

It also took editing this anthology. To select the thirty-one essays for *The Best Women's Travel Writing, Volume 11*, I read nearly five hundred. The job was more challenging than ever, as this was the deepest pool of submissions I'd ever stepped into. I dreaded having to pass on literally hundreds of wonderful stories, many by friends I adore and writers I admire.

I based my decisions on answers to the usual questions: Was the piece well written and developed? Original? Personal? Did it evoke a strong sense of place? Were there compelling characters? Did something happen? Did it surprise me? Move me? When at last I chose the finalists, I began putting my table of contents in order, reading and sorting, re-reading and re-sorting, careful as always to separate essays that were similar in theme.

These two stories, I thought at one point, *are about water.* I separated them. *Oh, and so is this one,* I noticed. *And this one. This essay also has water in it. So does this one. And this one. And this one.*

It appeared water had seeped into my travel anthology just as it had my travel life. And so I was obliged, once again, to think about it.

To think, for instance, about Zora O'Neill's remarkable account of stumbling upon refugee camps while vacationing in Greece—her essay a potent reminder that just as water can steal lives, so too can it save them, delivering them to safety and a new beginning.

And to think about Maggie Downs, who signs up to raft in class V rapids at the source of the Nile River in Uganda, unsure of what is ahead, knowing only she has to do it to complete her mother's bucket list.

To think about Sandra Gail Lambert, whose decision to go on a solo pre-dawn kayaking trip in the Florida Everglades requires unusual planning, great resolve, and impressive fortitude.

And Suzanne Kamata, who encounters an art installation in Japan in which small puddles of water inexplicably morph into snakelike shapes, "squiggling toward a larger puddle and joining it." The water, she writes, seems to be alive.

And Anna Vodicka, who overcomes her fears while scuba diving in Palau ("I had experienced the grip of the waves, the buoyant joy that suddenly turns perilous with the change of a tide or an undertow") and witnesses "the most ordinary and extraordinary" thing she has ever seen.

For several writers in this anthology, water becomes a place of healing and release. For Jenna Scatena, it's when she stands in the Arabian Sea at dawn in Oman, gazing at the horizon, that she feels herself finally able to battle an evil spirit that has haunted her. For Lindsey Crittenden, a swimming pool in California helps move her forward through painful memories. And for Pam Mandel, it's the ocean in Hawaii, under a full moon, that receives her grieving heart.

For other writers, water creates a path to understanding. For Yukari Iwatani Kane, a visit to a Japanese hot springs is a surreal experience during which she finds herself grappling with—and uncovering answers to—a lifelong identity crisis. For Holly H. Jones, water is the subject of a Sufi fable that illuminates her days in Pakistan at a time when some consider the country to be the most dangerous place on Earth. In the fable, a stream making its way down the mountains overcomes every barrier. But when it tries to cross the desert, it dries up. I won't reveal the entire tale—you'll have to read the essay—but I'll say the stream discovers it can only progress by allowing itself to be changed.

I reflect on this again and again after reading Jones's essay, and come to the conclusion that to be good travelers, we must embody the qualities of water: its beauty, strength, mutability, fluidity, and determination. We need its capacity to ebb and flow; to permeate the most hidden and unreachable places; to soften and smooth what it moves against; to carve a path through seemingly impenetrable obstacles; to change form, and allow itself to be changed.

And I come also to this: Just as we travelers would be wise to adopt its qualities, perhaps we need them equally in our everyday lives. We are navigating a troubling time when merely watching the news can cause us to sink into anger and sorrow, a time when women's rights are in grave danger, and when xenophobia and intolerance threaten the fabric of our country and the freedoms of so many of its people. In these days, what may be required of conscientious global citizens is nothing short of transformation.

Since becoming a mother, I've learned a lot, and perhaps the most important lesson is that while joy is contagious, so is fear. Thus, as my son watches me to learn how he should behave, I'm increasingly mindful to exhibit as much joy and as little fear as possible. As he grows up, I never want him to perceive me as afraid, at least irrationally so. Instead, I hope he'll witness me facing my fears and working to conquer them.

I have to assume he will become a traveler, and when he someday embarks upon the world by himself, I hope he'll emulate the amazing women writers in this book whose stories tell of reaching out to embrace the unfamiliar and create meaningful cross-cultural connections.

I hope he will be like Maxine Rose Schur, who discovers in Iran that a language barrier is no barrier to warmth and friendship. And like Colette Hannahan, who surrenders her self-appointed mission in France when an eccentric host insists on befriending her. And like Jill K. Robinson in Switzerland, whose immediate kinship with a stranger offers an opportunity to view his country in a whole new way. I want him to learn, like Marcia DeSanctis in Russia, that even when all you crave is solitude, sometimes companionship can be comforting. I trust he'll discover, like Elen Turner in Nepal and Colleen Kinder in Iceland, that love makes everything taste better. And finally, I hope he will take a page from Anna Badkhen in Mali, who journeys to the farthest extremes of the world and returns to generously share the intimate stories of people who live there.

I have no idea who my son will become. All I know is someday I'll give him a copy of this book (it's dedicated to him, after all), and what he'll learn from the stories herein is that whether one travels to Arizona, Bulgaria, the Czech Republic, Ethiopia, Hungary, Italy, Mexico, Montana, Mongolia, or Singapore—it's best to go with an open heart, the inclination to practice human kindness, a sincere intention to build pathways of understanding, and the willingness to be transformed.

As for me, I've decided this is the year I'll learn to swim—in more ways than one. Says Crittenden in her essay, "The laws of swimming are simple: you stop, you'll sink. . . . Swimming is not about memorializing or staying still; it is about moving without thinking about it."

I will not stay still. Like the mysterious water in Kamata's story, I will move and morph and squiggle and become alive. Like the stream in Jones's story, I will allow myself to be changed, in order to make progress. And like the waters that offered understanding and solace to several authors in this collection, I'll do my part to help and heal others. I won't let fear stop me or sink me. I'll swim, forward.

I hope these stories inspire you as they have me. May they remind you of the enduring radiance of other places and people, and the timeless gift of sharing their stories. I invite you to jump in. The water is fine.

— LAVINIA SPALDING
NEW ORLEANS

ZORA O'NEILL

❧ ❧ ❧

On the Migrant Trail

Her holiday, their journey of a lifetime.

*A*t first glance, the crowds outside the train station in Izmir, Turkey, could have been picnickers. In the balmy August night, groups of young men lounged on the grassy medians. Children darted from parent to parent under the yellow glow of streetlights.

Yet the atmosphere was far from festive. The street felt like an airport terminal, abuzz with anxiety and excitement. Some people spoke urgently into phones; others rifled through their backpacks. A man bounced his daughter on his knee, staring out at the passing traffic.

Izmir was the second stop on a summer trip with my husband and my father. The next day, we would take a ferry to the Greek island of Chios, famous for its fortress towns, and then another to nearby Lesvos, where we would meet my mother-in-law for our biennial beach vacation. On each trip we take a different route to Lesvos to see more of Greece and Turkey before settling in for swimming, reading, and *tzatziki*. But this year, the road we'd chosen to relaxation was the same path followed by hundreds of thousands of refugees fleeing Syria, Iraq, and Afghanistan.

Izmir, a midsize port city on Turkey's southwest coast, usually draws tourists interested in its multicultural history; it has a pier designed by Gustave Eiffel and a famously ornate clock tower. It also has excellent bus, train, and plane service, making it a natural staging ground for smugglers moving thousands of people each night.

When I'd boarded my plane from New York, the American media had just begun to cover the situation. There'd been no mention of Izmir as one of the hubs of the crisis, or of the commercialism that had developed as a result. The cash-for-gold shop was packed. A clothing store had outfitted its mannequins with life jackets. A black market of second-hand clothes and household goods had sprung up, consisting mostly of items sold off or jettisoned to speed the trip across the Aegean on an overcrowded rubber dinghy under cover of darkness. My family crossed to Chios in daylight, in an hour and a half, on a regularly scheduled ferry.

More refugees were gathered around the boat harbor when we arrived. Here, people slept on benches or sat staring at the sea. Chios was the end of one trip—out of Syria, across Turkey, and officially into Europe. But it was also a tiny rock in the sea with a free-falling economy and surging unemployment. So it was the starting point for another, even longer journey as well, to the mainland and then farther north, to more prosperous countries such as Germany and Sweden.

I visited Syria three times between 1999 and 2009. I was charmed by the exotic details—the fresh mulberry juice, the sumptuous *hammams*—but I was more fascinated by how familiar and functional the country was. In stark contrast to the American political rhetoric about Syria, Aleppo and Damascus had a cosmopolitan middle class that commuted to work, went to movies, and drank fancy coffee. Axis of evil, really?

People shared meals, posed for goofy photos, and asked about American policy, listening patiently to the bookish Arabic I had learned in college. I felt safe, welcome, and cared for by every stranger. At the end of my first trip, a teenager selling cold drinks at the border gave me a free can of Pepsi and his mother's phone number. "When you come back," he promised, "she will cook for you."

I thought of him now, sixteen years later, as I left a bundle of leftovers from dinner with a group of men sitting outdoors, before I hurried to board the next ferry out of Chios.

Lesvos, the largest island in the Aegean and at some points only six miles from Turkey, is the top destination in Greece for those traveling by sea. At that point in the summer of 2015, more than 50,000 had landed there; by the end of the year, the number would be almost ten times that. When we arrived that August evening, the parking lot of the port was crowded not with the usual brigade of taxi drivers and truckers, but with hundreds of people sleeping on pieces of cardboard and sitting idle in the sticky heat.

Our destination, on the west side of the island, faced away from Turkey. No refugee boats drifted ashore there. It was summer business as usual: grilled octopus, outdoor movies, lazy swims in the clear bay water. Smooth as oil, as the Greeks say.

But I couldn't ignore what I had seen. After a few days, I returned to Lesvos's east coast to see how I could help at Kara Tepe, the designated spot for Syrians and Iraqis to wait for permits to travel off the island. Because of the war in their countries, they were granted passage to Athens automatically. But the bureaucracy, slowed by the economic crisis, could take several days—sometimes even a week. That left people stranded in this makeshift camp, a big parking lot once used for driver training, and the dusty olive grove next door.

Locals who wanted to help joined a small and disorganized effort. The only official aid presence was a tiny trailer staffed by Médecins sans Frontières, and there was no government representative or other leader to delegate or direct volunteers. But it wasn't long before I found myself in an ad-hoc outdoor kitchen with a handful of Greeks, cooking lunch for camp residents. As we hunched over the rickety folding table and started preparing vegetables to fill a knee-high pot for spaghetti, a trio of young Syrian men in tank tops and backward baseball caps approached. "Do you need any help?" one asked politely.

I handed him a flimsy paring knife, and he joked to his friends, *"Yalla nchayyef, ya shabbab!"*—"Let's chef it up, boys!" The men—who it turned out had all cooked in restaurants—snapped on rubber gloves, and within minutes had precision-sliced a large bag of onions and tidied the whole workspace. Once the sauce was simmering on the portable gas burner, the smell of browning onions wafting over the waiting crowd, they planned the most efficient way to serve the finished pasta. When hungry people surged forward for the aluminum trays of noodles, another team of men stepped forward to maintain the line.

To the Syrian palate, this Greek lunch, though cooked from scratch with fresh tomatoes and generous glugs of olive oil, was lacking. Mahmood, a tall young man with thick eyelashes, cast a sad glance toward the Greek lunch table. "Aleppo has the best food in the world," he said, referring to his city's famously refined sweet-savory concoctions, like tiny lamb meatballs simmered in sour-cherry sauce. "But this. . . ." He shook his head. "If the war ended, I would go home tomorrow."

For those with money to spare, there was the *kantina*, a camper-van café set up by the MSF trailer. The pretty young Greek woman at the counter had learned enough Arabic to confirm people's orders: one sandwich, three iced coffees. Her female customers smiled, while the men swooned. One stood to the side of the *kantina* and led an English lesson:

"Say, 'I. Love. You,'" he told his friends. "I. Love. You," they parroted back.

All around, I saw other attempts to live normally. A man sculpted his hair just so in the side mirror of a van. A teenage boy and girl exchanged numbers. People charged their phones on a long daisy chain of power strips, spliced into the base of a streetlight. "Everyone in Syria knows how to do this," a man told me, gesturing at the extemporized wiring. "We learned because of the war."

After having witnessed the migrants in Izmir clutching their life vests and luggage, I was encouraged to see how people had made it one step farther, resourceful and resilient even in the midst of the most grueling trip of their lives. But the positive attitude faded in late afternoon when a Greek police officer arrived to distribute the day's travel permits. A dense crowd quickly formed in the road at the mouth of the camp.

Yelling into a feeble megaphone, the cop bungled the foreign names. "Ma-her Seed-kee?" The people closest by shouted again, with proper Arabic intonation. "Mahir Sidqi!" Those farther out in the crowd strained to hear. *"Uskut!"*— "Shut up!"—they snapped at one another. They repeated the names. Mohammad Sidqi? Maher Siddi? Cicadas droned incessantly in the olive grove. One frustrated girl threw a handful of rocks at a tree, in an attempt to silence them.

Eventually, a few names were matched to people. They emerged from the middle of the crowd, permits held high in triumph, and walked back up the driveway to collect their belongings for the next leg of the trip.

Roughly two thousand migrants remained to wait for their papers at Kara Tepe, ranging from small babies with heat rash on their cheeks to wrinkled grandfathers. But many were men in their late teens and early twenties—prime fighting age.

One was Yaman, a gangly, outgoing engineering student from Aleppo. He was midway through college, he explained, and would surely have been drafted into the army had he stayed in Syria. Now he was bound for Germany with his brother and mother, a doctor who specialized in women's health. (The majority of refugees from Syria are professionals, members of the educated class.)

Yaman hoped to complete his degree there, and his mother hoped to continue supporting the family by joining a local practice. But he worried about racist attacks on Syrian refugees in Europe. "Where do radicals get this idea about the meaning of *jihad*?" he asked. "*Jihad* just means to study hard."

In nearly flawless English, Yaman told me that the war had made it difficult to study. His exam scores had not been as high as they could have been. Did he know the phrase "extenuating circumstances"? I asked. "Yes, of course," he replied, with a wry smile.

I spent four days at Kara Tepe, driving east in the morning with only delivery trucks on the winding roads, squinting into the low sun on the way back in the evening. During those days I met more students like Yaman, along with farmers, former political prisoners, moms with kids of all ages, and an Arabic teacher so excited to encounter an American who spoke his language that he launched into an impromptu lesson, ticking through verb conjugations on his knuckles.

Some moments, I felt the same easy familiarity of travelers meeting in a hostel. At the same time, I was acutely aware of our differences: an hour away across the island, I had a soft bed, a warm shower, and air conditioning. My trip, during which I had sprawled in the sun by choice and swum in the Aegean for fun, would end in another week. Their journeys would go on for months or years.

But in those days at Kara Tepe, travel felt more essential than ever. Travel to Syria when I was younger had shown me

regular life there. Travel had brought me to another side of a
Greek island I thought I already knew well, and introduced
me to Syrians I had not seen written about in newspapers:
the volunteer chefs; the flirting teenagers; and funny, smart
Yaman, the future engineer.

Yaman's family had passed through Izmir only days after
I had. For $1,150 a head, smugglers had packed him and his
family into a boat with forty-five others. Offshore, the engine
failed, and they drifted for hours until the Turkish police took
the boat back. Another night, they tried again, on an equally
packed boat, and succeeded.

The story was not as harrowing as some, but it still shocked
me. Yaman saw my look of worry and grinned.

"Yes, what a story it is," he said, with a hint of pride. "One
day, I can tell my kids about it. They won't believe what their
father did."

❧ ❧ ❧

*Zora O'Neill is a travel and food writer based in Queens, New York.
She is the author of* All Strangers Are Kin: Adventures in Arabic and the Arab World, *about her time studying and traveling in
the Middle East. She also writes guidebooks for Lonely Planet and
Moon, and she is the coauthor, with Tamara Reynolds, of* Forking
Fantastic! Put the Party Back in Dinner Party. *Not long after
this story was first published, Zora learned that Yaman had made
it safely to mainland Greece, then to Germany. After winter in
a camp in Kiel, he and his brother and mother were able to find
an apartment. A year and a half after their arrival, Yaman's asy-
lum application was finally approved, and he had progressed to an
advanced German course, in preparation for enrolling in university
again.*

JILL K. ROBINSON

❧ ❧ ❧

The Interpretation of Sighs

There is more than seeing with the eyes.

Mountain upon mountain upon mountain, the jagged layers of white overlap and stretch into the distance just beyond the train platform in Wengen. A train leaves with passengers headed up to the Jungfrau, one of the most famous peaks in Switzerland. After spending time in the Alps, I am waiting for my ride in the other direction, to begin my long journey home.

"Do you know the time?" asks a blond man wearing sunglasses, khaki pants, and a red shirt. A moment ago, when I last glanced away from the snowy Alps, he wasn't here. It's as if he has appeared silently from nowhere.

I look above my head at the Swiss railway station clock, with its black-and-white face and red second hand that sweeps to the top.

"Ten o'clock," I say.

"Are you sure?" he asks.

At first, I think he's playing games with me. But he seems to be awaiting my answer without a trace of humor on his face.

I check against my watch. "Sure," I answer. "Even my watch says so."

"Good," he says. "The train will come in four minutes."

I wonder why, when there's a clock right here, he asks me for the time. Perhaps it's his way of starting a conversation with a stranger. Before most of my life was filled with travel, when I didn't need to rely on others for directions, cultural insights, or even restaurant recommendations—I kept mostly to myself. Now, anything is a conversation starter, but my first instinct has always been to quietly observe.

"Is your watch Swiss?" he asks.

It happens to be. A Wenger with the red shield and white cross of Switzerland. "It is," I reply.

He smiles, and crow's feet fan out at the edges of his sunglasses. "We are very good with time," he says. "I like asking visitors because you can take these items—a watch or clock—home. But to experience precise time is a very Swiss thing."

I know this, because in my travels here, my guide tapped her watch with a finger when I was one minute late.

He interrupts my thought, telling me the train is coming. I don't see or hear it. He is not looking at the clock. There is no announcement. But sure enough, seconds later, the train pulls in—a regional green-and-yellow train that stands out against the snowy Alps like a slash of sunshine.

As it comes to a stop, my new acquaintance pulls out a white cane from his bag and unfolds it, and I realize he is blind.

"Do you mind if I walk with you to the closest door?" he asks. "My name is Michel. I hope I didn't make you uncomfortable with all my talk about time."

I tell him my name and assure him I'm fine, then take his hand, place it on my elbow, and walk with him up the steps and into the car, where we choose seats together.

The track angles down into the valley, between gigantic rock faces and mountain peaks laden with late May snow, to Lauterbrunnen. For the past two days, I've gazed at this valley from my hotel room window in Wengen. If any one place looks like a fairy tale—or at least what I imagine a fairy tale place would look like—this is it. The valley is carpeted with rich emerald grass sprinkled with wildflowers, and the cliffs are beribboned with gushing waterfalls. Out the window, I see a blackbird dive straight down to the valley floor, as if so overcome by the beauty, it had reached its ultimate goal in life.

"My family once had friends here," says Michel. "We used to visit every summer. A successful day was marked by how many waterfalls we saw while out hiking. But my favorite is Staubbach Falls, which plunges from an overhanging rock face right by the town."

"That's a good goal," I remark. "It seems far better than counting passport stamps. How often do you visit now?"

"When I can," he answers. "But not as much as I'd like to. See? As we get closer to town you can spy Staubbach."

For someone who visits only on occasion, Michel has a knack for knowing the exact train schedule and when landmarks will come into view. I want to know how long he has been blind, but that seems too personal a question for our short friendship.

As if reading my mind, Michel explains that he became blind as a result of a car accident five years ago. "I have been taking this train route for years," he says. "I know every turn, every sight, every smell. I know when the train is late and when it's on time, which is almost always. I know when people are happy to see the beautiful views, like you, and when they are quiet and thinking of something else."

"How do you know I'm happy to see the landscape?" I ask. So far, I have said nothing about the views, even though I'm regretting not spending more time here.

"You have a quiet way of sighing contentedly," he answers. "You don't shift in your seat, like someone who is anxious. You must come back. This is a special place." His voice drifts off, as if, like the blackbird, he's overcome by the scenery. Or at least the memory of it.

We change trains in Lauterbrunnen, and I resist the desire to veer from my itinerary to walk away from the train station, find a new hotel, and take daily hikes to count the waterfalls. On a new train now, heading toward Geneva and away from this fairy tale land and out of the valley, the tracks follow steep fields of purple, gold, and azure wildflowers alongside Alpine homes with viridian shutters and perfectly manicured gardens. Trees' new growth stands out against the deeper green of pines, as if someone has selectively turned up the color saturation.

When Michel rides through the valley, does he remember this place only with summer colors, or does he occasionally recall the veil of white and gray that seems to enhance light and shadow in winter? I hesitate to describe the scenery to him, thinking the act may be too patronizing.

The glare from the train window makes it difficult for me to take photos. Each shot results in a ghostly streak across the image, so I soon give up and put my camera back in my bag. Like Michel, I'll have to rely on remembrance.

The glacial, milky blue color of the Weisse Lütschine River winds down the valley on its own path from Lauterbrunnen. I look up to catch the last glimpse of the Jungfrau before we leave the valley. Before I can stop it, a sigh escapes my lips. My train companion will know why.

I can still see the mountains while we wait for the next train in Interlaken. But now the mountains are farther away, like fading memories.

A man taps Michel on the shoulder. I step away to give them some privacy while they exchange greetings in French, but knowing that Michel has my exact same itinerary, I keep an eye on the Swiss railway station clock. The next train comes into view—this one with a red, blue, and yellow color scheme—and like clockwork, the two men hug, wiping their eyes as they part. Michel and I board, his hand on my elbow.

When we're settled into our seats, we each pull lunch items from our bags. My lunch consists of a baguette and Berner Alpkäse, a cheese made high in the Alps in summer, and one I've craved every day since I first tasted it. Michel's lunch is a similar picnic: bread, cheese, sausage, and strawberries. We unpack all our food items onto the table in front of us, and at Michel's suggestion, arrange them in a clock format with the strawberries at noon, bread at three, cheese at six and sausage at nine. This way, he can grab what he wants without asking me where things are.

"That man is someone who helped me after my accident," he says, with a mouthful of bread. "He used to travel to Geneva often, and I'm friends with his sister. He would visit me to keep me company, bringing small items that make me happy: cheese, fresh fruit, some music."

"Is five minutes enough to catch up with someone who's that important?" I ask.

"No," Michel says. "He was out of town when I called to tell him I would be passing through, so I didn't schedule time to stay in Interlaken. He's coming to Geneva soon, so we can catch up then. He just stopped by the station to say hello."

The quick exchange between the two of them reminds me of friends who have met me at airports around the world, even when I've had a short layover. To visit each of them is worth my trip back through the long security lines between flights. My connection to a place consists of memories strung together, but the people I meet are the pearls that make the entire experience worthwhile.

They seem to be for Michel, too. As we careen through the Swiss countryside, he describes the landscape perfectly, from river to field to mountainside. Even more so, he recounts the reasons his travels bring him to a destination. Here, it's a friend from university who lived on a dairy goat farm. There, it's an old girlfriend who encouraged him to travel between Geneva and her home village in the Bernese Oberland for the better part of a year.

He has connected me to this place more than a solo train trip could have done—merely passing through the landscape like turning the pages of a book. What I'll remember about Michel isn't what he looked like, but how he could interpret a sigh, anticipate the arrival of a silent train, leave the Alpkäse cheese for me after learning how much I loved it. I will see Switzerland differently because of him—a better tour guide than I could have asked for.

I walk Michel home after we arrive in Geneva. Two blocks from his place, we pass a park, overflowing with roses. He squeezes my elbow and nods in its direction.

"When you leave me, go sit on a bench over there," he says. "Don't rush to your hotel. Spend time and smell the sun on the roses."

An hour later, while I am sitting amidst the sun and roses, I spy Michel on a nearby bench. He's facing my direction, but I know he doesn't see me, and I can't possibly sigh that loudly. I pick up a fallen petal, walk over to him, and place it in his hand.

Michel's hand closes over the petal, and he smiles.

"I'll see you next time," he says. And I know that he will.

Jill K. Robinson is a freelance writer and photographer. Her work has appeared in the San Francisco Chronicle, AFAR, National Geographic Traveler, Outside, American Way, Every Day with Rachael Ray, Robb Report, Coastal Living, *Travelers' Tales books (*The Best Travel Writing *and* The Best Women's Travel Writing) *and more. Her sigh interpretation skills need some work. Follow her on Twitter @dangerjr.*

❧ ❧ ❧

Sono Felice

Perhaps the key to happiness is leaving yourself behind.

I'm in Venice and I'm smoking. It's the first time a cigarette has touched my lips in nearly ten years, and it's heavenly. It's like going back in time and grinding with your high school boyfriend. It's like your first ice cream cone.

It's the first time I've been this far from my kids since their birth three years ago. I haven't seen them in 48 hours and I do not miss them. Because, really, how could you when you are standing outside a Venetian bar smoking cigarettes and flirting in extremely broken Italian with a guy name Fulvio who's wearing dress pants and flip-flops. Fulvio! It sounds like a female body part. *My fulvio is inflamed.*

After weeks of worrying about what I would wear in Italy, how I would stand up to their rigorous but mysterious standards of *bella figura*, I am flirting with Fulvio in an oversized men's t-shirt the color of crap and a cheap straw fedora that was crushed in my suitcase and revived only with much scrunching and lowering of standards.

I am dressed like I am, badly even for an American, because I've spent the day rowing an outrigger canoe through the Adriatic with a bunch of Italian outrigger enthusiasts, friends of friends of Hilary's. It was a day you couldn't

invent—a giant seafood lunch, pitcher after pitcher of slightly
fizzy white wine poured from a barrel. Men named Carlo and
Flavio and Mauro who thought we were charming. (Italian
men who think you are charming is, by the way, the quickest
and most effective route to actually being charming.) It was
a whole day in which I didn't know where I was—island or
mainland, no idea. When I was told to row, I rowed. When I
was told to swim, I jumped with everyone else into the green
water and splashed about, letting my coral-colored toenails
peek above the water just for the pleasure of seeing those colors together. It was like being in an Anthropologie catalog,
except we were smiling.

I have been known to say that I can't have a good time when
I feel ugly, but tonight even my hideous outfit (which has the
effect of a fading mosquito bite—vaguely irritating but not
life-ruining) can't keep me from declaring, out loud, clutching the scrawny arm of my friend Hilary, that I am happy. I'm
shining like a sorority girl, lit up with stupid joy. How do you
say it in Italian? I ask. *Sono felice.* And I take another sip of
my prosecco, which, because it costs $1.50 a glass and because
the temperature is perfectly warm in the narrow alley where
we've found this bar, I drink many glasses of.

"*Sono felice*," I say. Baggy brown t-shirt be damned. I am
happy. It could be 8:30. It could be midnight. I don't care.

It's not until later, back at our borrowed apartment and eating the most gorgeously wrapped cookies you've ever seen (I
would wallpaper my bedroom with these cookie wrappers if
I could get away with eating that many), that I realize I haven't
felt this way in a long time. And that I am this happy in part
because my children are not here, because I can afford not to
know the time. Because no one is going to wake me up at 6:30
complaining of urine-soaked sheets or clamoring for cereal.

My father once told me that the pleasure of travel is egolessness. He is a Buddhist and this is how he talks. "When you

are away from your life, you lose the markers of self and you are liberated from your ego." And I think he is right. In Venice I have no minivan. I have no career, failed or otherwise, no family, no shameful fugue-state trips down the aisles of Target, no dog reminding me of my finite capacity for love. This is liberation, the untethering of identity. Plus, you get to eat and drink everything your eyes light upon.

I'm here for a week—eight days if you count all the flying—and I'm pretty sure I'm supposed to feel guilty, that I'm at least supposed to make a show of missing my children. I know people—they are the same ones who know a lot about things like hormones in meat and which preschools are best—who are proud of the fact that they have never spent a night away from their children, people who claim not to be able to enjoy a movie because they can't stand the time away from their kids. These are not my people. When my children were only weeks old what I longed for more than anything was a night alone in a hotel room. I fantasized about the sheets, smooth and cool as marble.

There are moments when I miss my kids in a physical way, the slippery smoothness of their perfect skin when they emerge from the bath, the way their tiny soft hands pat my cheeks sometimes when they are liking me a lot for some reason. But these are only fleeting. The truth is I do not want to share this with them. I want this week to myself, unencumbered by three-year-olds and their wants. I will wipe no asses but my own. Forget egolessness. *This* is liberation.

Except for the bells, which seem to celebrate everything—hurray it's eleven, hurray it's sunny out, hurray the sky is blue—Venice is the quietest city I've ever been in. Seagulls do their frantic calls, some Catholics sing from unseen courtyards, as if they were hired just to make this place even more surreal in its perfection; not only are there Gothic marble palaces sinking into the sea, there is a choral soundtrack to put you in the mood. There are no cars in Venice, so we walk through alleys and over bridges, sometimes with somewhere to go, sometimes aimlessly, to the left because the light is nice, to the right because we can glimpse some perfect garden behind a locked gate. To say it is mazelike is not quite right. A maze implies frustration, repetition—I picture hungry, irritable rats. In Venice the wandering is joyful and light. There is always a *gelateria* around the bend. There is always another pink building sprouting geraniums from its window boxes.

I recently walked through a labyrinth in California. It was a small circle made of stones in the woods near the bank of a creek. I wanted to feel some transformation in the labyrinth but I didn't know what kind to expect. Also, I was in a hurry. My husband, Pete, was keeping the kids occupied with rocks and flowers nearby while I checked it out, but I could hear them plainly—it was just a matter of time before they got wind of my solitude and rushed in to fill the void.

As I began I imagined some mysterious force or energy might materialize from the pattern of the stones; I hoped, but also doubted, there was something to it and that I would feel that something if I just followed directions and gave in to what I normally dismiss as New Age hooey.

What there was, was simple: by following the labyrinth, surrendering to its turns and directions, you triumph over your desire to go straight. You can plainly see your destination—the center of the circle—but you are constantly turning away from it, backtracking and looping. You lose a sense of direction and give up on your own impatience. I was actually getting pretty into it until Oliver picked up one of the labyrinth's stones and hurled it into the bushes and I had to jump over the lines, forsaking the journey for the destination, to scold him.

"Oliver," I said, "you do not throw these rocks. These are special rocks that someone put here."

Oliver looked at me, his eyes almost ridiculously round—he looked like a Kewpie doll—and said, "Mama, you're making me very angry."

Hilary and I are in the museum café with the Communist professor and the book editor. We've just looked at a lot of contemporary art—glass molds of negative space, life-sized headless taxidermied horses sticking out of walls—much of which I don't understand.

Because they are mannered people, the editor and the professor speak English for my sake, and because I am overly enthusiastic and prone to imitation, I speak with my hands for theirs. We are talking about the bourgeoisie, about how Milan is not a city for intellectuals. Or, rather, they are talking about this and I am sitting in a fog of jet lag, breathing through my mouth. But even in my lumbering way, I'm glad to be where I am. It is not often that I sit around in the middle of the day drinking tiny cups of espresso and discussing the Milanese bourgeoisie. In fact, it is never. My life in its current manifestation is not a life for intellectuals.

At a break in the conversation Hilary asks Margarita, the book editor, if she is married, and she emits that wonderfully dismissive Italian "*boh*," as if to say the very idea is ridiculous. Married? What on Earth do you take me for? And she and Hilary laugh a little laugh of solidarity and I look around the bright white museum cafeteria at all the married couples—Italian, French, English, American, Polish—as they silently munch their tiny sandwiches and sip their glasses of prosecco. I love my husband, but I know I am having a better time without him here. Being with Hilary is like being with a new lover, without all that distracting sex. We hold hands as we walk along the canals, she laughs at my jokes until she pees. She tells me my outfits are super cute. Traveling with her is like having a guiltless affair. I am revived and freshened by her new eyes. It's the closest I've ever come to cheating on Pete.

So it is almost a betrayal when, in the next breath, Hilary tells our gorgeous companions that I am the mother of twins. When this moment comes, as it inevitably does in any conversation, there is always a part of me that wants to lean across the table and press my finger to her lips. Because once I am the mother of twins, I am the mother of twins, with all the attending associations of sagging and routine. I am no longer a charming young friend of Hilary's who appeared out of nowhere to drink pitchers of prosecco and waltz through the Piazza San Stefano; I am a sturdy 39-year-old changer of diapers and monitor of table manners. I am someone who regularly clips someone else's toenails. Suddenly, the fact that I'm smoking a cigarette is unseemly. The fact that I am where I am is suspicious. No wonder I don't have much to add to the discussion about the influence François Pinault is having on modern art in Italy. I am too busy wondering if my kids have had their afternoon bowel movement.

And yet, I don't lean across the table. Because—along with the associations of elongated nipples and playground harping—being a mother earns you immediate legitimacy. I am not alone in the world. I am not without purpose. And the mother of twins? Forget about it. I am capable as shit. I have instant position and my belly, which protrudes from my dress like a bulbous scarlet letter, is more easily forgiven.

Still, the professor and the editor don't have much to say about my motherhood. "How old are they?" they ask. "What are their names?" But now, finally, I know what I am talking about, even if I feel less like Sophia Loren as I say it.

The rest of our week is a movie montage. Here we are riding bicycles on Lido. Here we are perusing a flea market. That's us cooling off in the fountain. Us again in the ghetto eating falafel and hummus. And eating, always eating: mortadella and gelato and tiny sea snails. We capture it all in golden-hued photos, self-portrait after self-portrait after self-portrait, our arms stretched as far as they will reach. We document our days as if even we won't be able to believe it was real.

On our last night in Venice we meet up with Fulvio again. Hilary and I have been drinking prosecco since lunch, fortifying ourselves between museum visits with *ombra de vin* (petite pours they call shadows of wine) and some bits of fish on toast. We look at modern art from Iran and blinking light installations set to pounding hip-hop music. We see fourteenth-century painting with all its gilt and purpose. Madonna after Madonna after Madonna with Jesus in her arms like some shrunken old man. I try to pick out the Tintoretto paintings but I am hopeless. I am still getting used to the idea that people were around six hundred years ago, walking upright and making music. My sense of time is all fucked up and I can no longer really blame jet lag.

Fulvio meets us at a bar filled with college students and old men in beautiful shoes. He is wearing dress pants and flip-flops again; his fly is undone and he has a deflated-looking canvas bag over his shoulder. He has just come from practicing his trombone and his upper lip is puffy and red.

I don't know why Fulvio likes us so much. He owns a news-stand next to the Accademia and spends his days selling postcards to tourists (at a 500 percent markup) and playing chess. I imagine he gets his fill of tipsy Americans toting digital cameras and asking questions about where to find that Hemingway bar. Still, he *does* like us. You can see it in the crinkle of his eyes when he locates us in the sudden dimness of the bar.

Hilary and I are maybe five glasses ahead of him, but we are not exactly drunk. Lit might be a fair assessment. We are buoyant and gleaming. Our faces hurt from grinning and I've felt all day as if we are about to fall into a kiss. It's as if we exist at the very best part of a romantic comedy, the jittery, exquisite moment before the climax. I'm pretty sure we have a soundtrack and I'm pretty sure it's by Katrina and the Waves.

Although we like Fulvio immensely, not least because of his disheveled, absent-minded professor helplessness, we can't help wondering if his presence might break our magic.

But even when Hilary starts weeping drunkenly at the lovely outdoor restaurant where we are eating yet more fried fish and drinking a white wine that Fulvio says smells like cat pee, but in a good way, the golden bubble in which we've been floating does not burst.

"Why doesn't he love me?" she hiccups, tears streaming down her face, arms splayed on the shower of crumbs left on our tablecloth. She is speaking of the latest in a string of almost-loves, having been reminded that tomorrow she will return home to take up their troubles where they were suspended when she left. Fulvio and I look at each other over our wine glasses like indulgent parents. Somehow, because he is Italian, I imagine he will be O.K. with this moment in a way an American man would not. Lost love, weeping women—they eat this stuff for breakfast.

For me, her lament is only vaguely familiar. I remember what that yearning feels like, that subsuming bittersweetness. But only sort of. If I were to let the looming return of real life into this moment, it would be filled not with the longings of romantic love, but with the dreaded return to myself. What I see lurking at the edge of the golden bubble on our last night in Venice is the real me: the American wife and mother, suffering as she does from minor but chronic irritation and impatience. At home my husband and I have just started couples therapy, my kids have discovered whining, and my dog has once again chewed his paws into an infected mess.

I turn away from Hilary and look out across the water at the sparkling lights on San Marco and sigh. "*Sono felice*," I say for the thousandth time.

Fulvio, now seated between a weeping woman and one who exclaims her happiness like an obsessive parrot, has no choice but to laugh. "You keep saying that," he says. "And it is funny because you do not need to. We can tell you are happy. We can see it when we look at you."

The evening sun sets the rose-colored buildings aglow. I am sipping my tenth glass of prosecco and tonight my outfit is totally working for me. There is no possible way not to be happy.

Samantha Schoech's fiction, essays, and journalism have appeared in places like The New York Times, The Sun, Glimmer Train, *and* Seventeen. *She is the program director of Independent Bookstore Day and a friend to booksellers everywhere. When she is not living the glamorous life of the mind, she packs lunches, sorts laundry, and ferries her twins around San Francisco while listening to NPR or Beyonce, depending on her mood. She has never been to Asia but it's definitely on her list.*

ℬ ℬ ℬ

Grounded

How far must we go to truly run away?

"This is where the jinn live," Mustafa said softly, as if he could see something on the stark plateau that I could not. We were in Oman, a small country on the southeast tip of the Arabian Peninsula, slinking across a strip of desert highway. As we sat idling behind pickup trucks teeming with camels, I noted tire tracks that veered off the road and disappeared into the sand. Beyond, rose-hued dust gave form and color to the wind, as its ghostly figure pirouetted across the plain.

Mustafa pressed his finger against his SUV's sooty window, pointing to a stand of wizened juniper trees sprouting from the cracked desert floor.

"The *who*?" I asked.

"Shhhhhh," he sneered, as if I were rousing something. "The jinn." He lowered his voice to a whisper and shrank into his seat, hoping to coast through this section of the highway undetected. "The evil spirits."

I scanned the horizon, seeing only earth and shrubs and, in the distance, the Al Hajir mountains that separated us from Saudi Arabia. With no apparent logic to the ridge lines, and almost no flora growing on the slopes, the terrain could be mistaken for a massive rock quarry, with pyramids of loose rock the colors of honey and oxidized silver.

"There are stories of people falling asleep in their beds and waking up the next morning being auctioned off in Saudi Arabia," Mustafa warned. The jinn were folkloric demons that had plagued the Arabian high desert for centuries, he told me. While tales of them extended across the Arabian Peninsula, all the way to Morocco, this was their heartland. The town we were passing through, Bahla, was the center of Oman's power in the medieval ages. Now, thanks to the jinn, it had been reduced to ruins, nearly abandoned.

"Sometimes they haunt the palm oases down the highway too," said Mustafa, "calling to people after dusk, repeating their names until those who follow become hopelessly lost."

It took five seconds to pass the mud-and-cement town. I held my breath for the duration, as if that would keep me safe. On the edge of town, a hitchhiker stood crisping in the raw desert sun.

"The jinn could make a fire combust at any moment here," Mustafa said. I kept my eyes fixed on the empty plain, bracing for the flame.

There were jinn in my life, too. Ones I knew well—not spirits, though a haunting of sorts.

It was September in Manhattan, a place with possibilities as seemingly infinite as its avenues. I had walked through the Lower East Side after a business meeting, admiring the pink cotton-ball clouds that had been tumbling across the sky all afternoon. The air still held the warm dampness of summer.

I remember the gin and tonic in a frosty bucket glass. I remember the mirror behind the bar. I remember checking the time, responding to a text from my boyfriend, David, who was at home in San Francisco, then scrolling through pictures on my phone from earlier that day. The Empire State Building.

Central Park. Those gorgeous puffy clouds. I remember the tonic popping on my tongue in those first two refreshing sips. And then I don't. I don't remember finishing the gin and tonic. I don't remember leaving the bar with the colleague I had come to meet. I don't remember walking, or stumbling, or cabbing. I don't remember arriving at his apartment, or setting down my purse, or deciding to sit on his couch or when he decided to sit so close to me, or how I ended up naked on his living room floor. If that was the sequence of events at all.

I don't remember force. I don't remember being held down or trying to escape his grip. In the back of my mind is only the sensation of being incapable of moving or speaking, and the impression of large clammy hands on my neck and the words, "*Shhhh, it's O.K., it's O.K.,*" repeated over and over and over.

The inflatable air mattress in my cousin's guestroom in Brooklyn at noon the next day: My dress was back on, my jacket over that, my shoes still politely buckled at the sides, my phone resting in my open palm, out of battery. The ceiling twisted clockwise, then counterclockwise, then back again. Warm sunshine and the sound of strollers wheeling down the sidewalk filled the room.

I felt a million miles from all of it, a lone planet spinning through a universe with no orbit.

Like the moment the atmosphere shifts from day to night, the world looked different after that. Everything was cast in a new, dim light. The sky on the horizon at home in San Francisco I had always turned to for inspiration, now a wall. Standing at the kitchen sink, the water filling a tall slender glass seemed to say, "Drown." From the vantage of a fifth-story balcony, a manhole on the sidewalk below looked like a bulls eye.

Psychologists call it *dissociating*; separating from one's own identity. It's a way of saying you've floated away from yourself, drifted out of your skin—a common response to a traumatic event.

For me, it felt more like a spell than a symptom.

The therapist at the Trauma Recovery Center advised me to practice a technique called "grounding." Breathe. Recite your name. Say today's date. Identify the objects in the room. Feel your feet on the ground. "It's important to stay in place, in order to let things go back to normal," she said as I sat in her windowless office, fixated on a sign that read, *Grief dares us to love once more.*

To try to reorient, I went to my mother's farmhouse in Sonoma, half-hoping I might also find the part of me I'd lost. But it was only my mother there, in her same tattered floral dress, thinned by years of wear and heavy wash cycles, waltzing around the kitchen like an elderly Cinderella; expired wrinkle cream in her medicine cabinet, a fridge missing its handle, and the dust on the windowsill that that day looked like ashes.

After I told her what happened, she disappeared into her overgrown garden, and while hastily pruning the hydrangeas with a pair of rusty sheers, split open the skin on her middle finger. It was spring, and the sweet smell of lilac and eucalyptus barreled through the front door as she ran inside, gripping her hand like it was no longer hers, the siren-red blood draining from it.

I wrapped a wad of paper towels around it and squeezed. When the blood raged its way through, I told her she needed stitches. "I'm fine," she said, "just get me a Band-Aid." As I coiled the biggest one I could find around her finger, I stared out the window, keeping pressure on the cut. Weeds had taken over the driveway again.

Instead of going to the ER, we drove to the coast, unsure of what we were looking for. Maybe just an empty beach to walk, or a person who looked like they had something to say.

We drove until the road stopped, pulling the emergency brake at the edge of the continent. When I looked through the windshield at the horizon, I was struck by what I saw—nothing. Not a path or a route for a ship. Just a vast watery emptiness with a great wall of sky at the end.

"Self care is important," my therapist said the next week. But I didn't really know what she meant by "self care," and I didn't bother asking. Instead, I bought a plane ticket. I didn't want to be grounded. Staying put felt like a trap. Stagnancy wouldn't stave off the physiological effects of trauma, the stiffening and cramping of the body, the cooling of blood and the chills that came with it. I needed kinesis, to let the blood move through me again. When I told her my decision to end the sixteen-week therapy program prematurely to leave the country and travel, partly with my boyfriend and partly solo, she set her clipboard aside and said, "That's called running away."

I read somewhere that before the Age of Discovery, when people believed the world was flat, the Azores, a spotting of lush volcanic islands in the mid-Atlantic, were thought to be the last pieces of land before the planet ended. I figured we would start there.

At a thousand miles away from any continent, it was a land defined not by prominence, but obscurity. I found comfort in its unfamiliarity—cartons of whole milk were marked "*gordo lactolus*," and locals stored jars of mayonnaise in the pantry instead of the refrigerator. Rooftops were orange beneath a Windex-blue sky, and music filled the streets, not from car stereos, but squeezed out of accordions. Every word I overheard locals say was veiled in Portuguese's distinctive "*shh*" sounds, as if everything spoken on the island was a secret.

Sure enough, at sunset the wide horizon looked not like a curve, but a thin delicate ledge. David had rented us a stone cottage with a soot-caked fireplace to live in indefinitely, mere feet from a cliff that dropped into the ocean. It was his first attempt to forge a home for us while running away. Over a dinner of bread, cheese, and Portuguese milk whiskey, his gaze across the kitchen table told me this house came with the hope that I would find my way back to him. To our normal life. But after only a week of living there the grief caught up with me, and I told him I needed to go farther.

For a while, I worked on a small Slovenian farm digging potatoes out of the earth. No one asked me why I'd come there, about what had happened in America the year before. I loved that about them. Their reticence. *I could stay here forever,* I thought, filling plastic pails with lumpy potatoes and slurping salty wild boar stew with this nice, slightly inebriated family in Slovenia's bucolic oblivion. How easily I could become a Jelena, or a Franciska, or a Slavka. But eventually, harvest ended.

Before the incident, I had always been an intrepid traveler. Now I was wary and afraid of the world, stumbling through it with my arms crossed and eyes closed, sinking deeper into the wilderness of distrust. Even the places I stayed with David—the sunny studio in Lyon, the beachfront apartment in Split, the artsy loft in Istanbul—I felt walled off from everything. He'd look at me sweetly as we walked down the cobblestone streets of Lisbon and Barcelona, not seeing how heavy the clear blue sky was weighing on me.

David returned to the U.S. to visit family periodically, while I continued traveling by myself. I turned down dinner invitation after dinner invitation from polite strangers, avoided bars or anywhere someone was prone to strike up a conversation, and I would no longer venture out after dark. Alone in Marseille on Bastille Day, I shut myself in my apartment, cursing the booms of the fireworks over the *quai* as I sat with a baguette and a wheel of camembert, slugging an entire bottle of Cotes d'Azur in lonely peace. When it was time for bed, even with the door locked, I wedged beneath it a door stopper rigged with an alarm—one of many products I'd piled in my backpack, purchased from websites that catered to cautious women. Websites with names like Damsel in Defense.

We kept going east, until seven months later David and I ended up in Oman, in the car with Mustafa, our home-stay host, and one of the only people on our trip with whom I had engaged in an actual conversation.

"Don't tell anyone," Mustafa said quietly to me, as I peered out the passenger-side window—his small frame resting in his ivory *dishdasha,* a traditional ankle-length robe.

I turned to hear whatever confidence he was about to reveal.

"I won't," I promised.

Mustafa kept one hand on the steering wheel as the other twirled the loose silk tassel fashioned at his collar—a cologne-soaked accessory Omani men wear so the smell of home travels with them wherever they go. "My favorite musician is Adele."

"In America, the most important part of any road trip is the soundtrack," I said, turning up the music.

"In Islam we aren't really supposed to listen to music," he said bashfully.

But no one was around to hear his secret; beyond the window were only rocks and a round, orange sun in the sky.

I immediately loved the way Mustafa trusted me, and in return, I felt the blood in my body beginning to warm again. "What about movies?" I asked.

"I love movies! Stories of warriors and courage are the best, like *The Last Samurai* and *Braveheart.*"

"And books?"

"Definitely Murakami," the gaze of his wide loam-brown eyes drifted out the window in contemplation. Then suddenly, his expression hardened and he turn up the radio, listening intently.

"What is it?" David asked, leaning in from the back seat.

"A cyclone," he said. "It's supposed to hit Muscat on Monday."

I only saw what rose above the mob: staggered palm trees, a camel's oscillating head, the coruscant dome of a small mosque. I tried to keep up with Mustafa and David as they hurried through Nizwa's Friday market, unable to prevent my hips and shoulders from brushing against strangers as we made our way through a riot of fragrant *dishdashas,* long beards, and vibrant turbans swirled atop heads.

But soon I lost them, so I waded through the market alone. A bull was tied to a date tree by his septum, and people lined up goats to be paraded around the auction. I smiled at the first women I had seen all day, only there was no way to tell if they smiled back; their expressions were veiled in the theater of the jewels that line the masks some Omani women wear in lieu of a *burka*. The nervous goats stomped clouds of dust into the air, filtering the world in sepia tone. The scarf I'd wrapped around my head as a makeshift *hijab* and the baggy dark clothes I wore hoping to "blend in" were instead making me feel unfamiliar to myself. I knew the sweat on my palms was not from the desert heat, nor was the throbbing of my pulse in my temple from dehydration. This was a trigger, and the little confidence I had was dissolving.

I sought a patch of personal space in the refuge of a shaded arbor, around which the throng of white robes circled as if it were the *Tawaf,* the ritual when Muslims circumambulate the most sacred mosque in Mecca. From the platform,

I could see silver rings glinting in the sun, and men with *jezail* muskets—long handmade rifles with brass and mother-of-pearl—slung over their shoulders, and some with a *khanjar*, the curved dagger that's also the insignia of Oman, tucked into their belts. I admired the beauty of their decorated weaponry and feared how they would look in action. I pictured my flimsy self-defense toys, sitting in my pack back at Mustafa's house.

David and Mustafa came up behind me, and Mustafa peeked into the shadow of my scarf.

"Are you nervous?" he asked gently.

I shrugged, wishing I had one of those bejeweled masks to hide my true expressions. "A little," I said.

At this he laughed, entertained that I thought I might be in danger. "All this—it's tradition, like art," he said. "We wear the daggers and rifles on Fridays as a symbol to honor our history, all that we had to fight through to get to the state of peace we are in now."

He gazed over the mass, past the apricot glare of the sun on the Nizwa Fort, toward the sawtooth tips of the Al Hajar mountains, then added, "What Yemen and Syria are going through now, we lived for centuries. Now we treasure peace. Don't worry. You are safe here."

Later that day, in the souks, sunshine seeped into pyramids of dates, making them look as if lit from within. Some were thick and dark, tasting like molasses. Others were light and sweet, like caramel. We sampled them while sipping bitter Yemeni coffee, the halls echoing with shopkeepers tinkering with their wares: silver jewelry, clay water jugs, amber cubes of local frankincense, and piles of myrrh. Mustafa stopped to let me try a piece of Omani bread—stone-ground wheat, water, and salt rubbed onto a hot stone, then scraped off in a thin, crisp sheet that resembled a doily. The spicy smell of peppercorns and turmeric floated through the air, and for a moment I felt like I was back in my mother's kitchen.

In many ways, this was the unlikeliest of places to feel safe: the Middle East in 2015, a time when terrorism was rampant. Yet I felt soothed by Mustafa's genuine warmth. Maybe it was because Oman had recently overcome its own violent history. For hundreds of years, tribal warfare plagued the country, and as the only available trade route connecting the Far East to the Middle East, outside forces were constantly trying to invade and conquer it. But when the current sultan came into power by overthrowing his own corrupt father, he was able to unite the country and inspire peace across it.

At lunch we sat cross-legged on the floor, tearing tender meat off the bones of pit-barbecued beef with our nails, then scooping it into our mouths with our fingers. We were inside a concrete restaurant that looked like a giant cinderblock, with nothing around it but dust. We finished our meal and stepped back into the heat, cooling ourselves with an icy blend of watermelon juice and rose water before we got in the car.

On our return to Nizwa, streets paved on the unsettled mountains pitched and depressed in areas where the road gave way to the shifting earth beneath it. Hills turned into rockslides, tumbling onto our path. Chunks of pavement and rust-colored boulders had to be hauled off the road by forklifts, as we watched from behind the windshield.

"Is it the jinn?" I asked.

"Oh, I don't actually believe in the jinn," Mustafa said. "What good is believing in jinn? If you believe in them, you give them all your power, and that's how they become real."

After leaving Nizwa and Mustafa behind, David and I drove to the coast. There, we hit a dead-end road. It reminded me of the one I'd driven with my mother at the end of California, when the sky had looked impenetrable, but this time, beyond the pavement was a beach made of sand the consistency of baking flour. It was empty and awash with swirls of millions of tiny rubicund seashells. I waded into the warm emerald waters of the Arabian Sea, my feet sinking deep into the untrodden sand. But I stopped when the water hit my ankles, knowing that somewhere beyond the shimmering offing, Cyclone Chapala, the Middle East's second-largest hurricane on record, was inching its way toward me.

"It's time to find home for the night," David said, as he had, unwaveringly, for more than half a year.

Down the beach, we found a patch of sand beside a quiet village with a pink mosque. David set up a tent he'd rented from a man in Muscat and laid out our bed of towels and sheets. Throughout the night I dreamt of hurricanes and tidal waves. The jinn. Great shapeless forces that steal into our lives, infinite yet undetectable. Vast expanses that surround us, that seem unpredictable, insurmountable.

In the morning, the muezzin's call echoed across the beach, waking me. While David slept, I emerged from our makeshift home. The sea was steady and glinting like silver as the sun breached the horizon. Cyclone Chapala had changed course, unexpectedly veering away. I stood in the water, letting it rise up to my knees, the humid breeze and salt air a strange but familiar comfort, the emptiness being filled by warmth and light.

I reflected back to the beginning of our trip, when I'd watched the sun set over the Atlantic in the Azores. For the Portuguese, it was possibility, not promise, that propelled them beyond the Azores, past the point they thought the world ended. They imagined something worth moving toward, built their own ships, and pushed past the breaks into the unseeable. There was no ledge dropping into an abyss.

The world is not a line, but a sphere. There is no end to it. To keep going is to eventually come back to where you started. It took sensing the curve of the planet beneath my feet to feel grounded again. I looked at the horizon. Only this time, instead of a wall, I saw my way home.

Jenna Scatena is an award-winning San Francisco-based writer and editor. She is a contributing editor at Sunset *magazine and a correspondent for* Travel + Leisure. *Her writing has also appeared in* AFAR, BBC Travel, San Francisco Chronicle, Marie Claire, O, the Oprah Magazine, Vogue, SELF, Delta Sky, Mr Porter, Via, *and* C: California Style, *and her stories have been anthologized in* The Best Women's Travel Writing Vol. 9 *and* An Innocent Abroad. *She is a former editor at the National Magazine Award-winning publication,* San Francisco. *Jenna received her BA in Nonfiction Writing from Ithaca College. Visit her at jennascatena.com.*

❧ ❧ ❧

Power, Twenty-Four Hour

She had reason to be hopeful.

I didn't know if what we'd had was just a fling. I was pre-pared for it to be. But when I returned from the riverside to the city—from the eastern Nepali riverside where we'd met, to the capital, Kathmandu—he got in touch. He wanted to meet me again, to go out to dinner.

"Is *dal bhat* O.K.?" he asked.

I thought he wanted to give me a taste of traditional Nepali culture, the chance to eat where locals eat, by taking me down a dusty back alley to a dimly lit place with bare walls but never-ending servings of rice, lentils, potatoes, and vegetable curry. It was cheap, and he graciously paid.

He went away for work but returned a week later. He wanted to take me out to dinner again. He asked if *dal bhat* was O.K., again. I suggested I would like something different this time, perhaps *momos*: bite-sized dumplings served with fiery chutney, or fried and dunked in a soup. He looked a little confused while thinking of a good place to go for *momos*.

"I like *dal bhat*," I explained, "it's just that I can't eat it all the time. I get a little bored. . . ."

He agreed. "Foreigner people can't eat so much *dal bhat*. Not like Nepali people."

We wandered the dark streets of Thamel, Kathmandu's tourist hub, looking for somewhere to eat. He steered me back to the same place we had been before, with the bare walls and endless helpings.

"Sorry, you said you wanted something different, but today I haven't eaten *dal bhat*. I need to eat *dal bhat*. You don't mind?"

Dal bhat it was, then. And this time we split the bill.

I returned "home" for six weeks, to pack up my necessities and the strings of my previous life, before returning to Nepal for good. I wasn't going back only for him, I knew; there were freelance writing opportunities for me there in abundance. But I wanted to give this new relationship a chance, and that meant relocating to his country. The only communication we had during that time was through Facebook Messenger. When it was morning in Nepal, it was evening in the U.S. We checked in with each other almost every day. Most of our conversations were not profound, limited by my then almost non-existent Nepali and his basic English. They went something like this:

"What are you doing?"

"Eating *dal bhat*."

Or:

"What are your plans for this evening?"

"Just making *dal bhat*."

Or my favorite—love talk, abruptly thwarted by *dal bhat*:

"I really miss you, my love."

"I miss you too."

"Not long until I see you. I am counting the days."

"Yeah, I really miss you. I think about you all the time."

"Oh really? What are you thinking?"

"I can't write it down. . . ."

"Oh come on. . . ."

"No, what if someone sees?"

"O.K. My love, I'm very hungry. I'm going to eat *dal bhat.* Talk to you later, *la?*"

To call *dal bhat* a "staple" of Nepali cuisine doesn't express the fact that many Nepalis feel bereft, unfulfilled, and mildly panicked if they don't eat it once a day. Sometimes more than once. At its simplest, the dish is spiced lentil curry served over rice. It's commonly accompanied by a potato curry; another vegetable curry—beans, carrots, spinach, whatever is in season—and a chicken, buffalo, or goat curry for meat-eaters; as well as a pickle; yogurt to cool the chili heat; a crispy, fried *papad*; and some discs of carrot, radish, and cucumber. In the hill regions of Nepal, where Kathmandu sits, black lentils are more commonly used, giving the *dal* a thick, tender texture and muddy brown color. On the plains, red lentils are preferred, resulting in a grainier, vibrant yellow *dal*. Nepal is a very ethnically diverse nation, and Nepalis often proudly and fiercely identify with the ethnic group to which they belong: Newar, Gurung, Tamang, Tharu, Sherpa. But if you ask them what they like to eat, what their favorite food is, they will laugh. "I am Nepali! It is *dal bhat*, of course!"

A common saying that decorates t-shirts sold in Kathmandu's tourist ghetto of Thamel sums up much about Nepal: *Dal bhat power, twenty-four hour.* It's simultaneously a comment on the dish's nutritional benefits and a wry joke about the country's scarce electricity. Last winter, it did feel like the only power in the whole of Nepal came from those potent dried grains and pulses.

An American friend asked, with concern, what kind of gender roles I was getting myself into with my relationship with a Nepali man. She hadn't been to Nepal but knew India; knew the South Asian region's reputation for chauvinistic men and submissive women. I was reluctant to generalize about an entire nation of men, and had reason to be hopeful.

He told me he liked to cook. *I not really good cook, but I can cook.* I told him I'd like him to teach me how to make *dal bhat* with all the trimmings. He agreed happily and assured me, "I like to cook."

I moved into my one-bedroom apartment in Kathmandu five months into a political crisis caused by unrest on the plains bordering India. Supplies of essentials—including petrol and cooking gas—were in short supply in the capital because of disruption at the border. Yet in my flat, I had not one but *two* full canisters of cooking gas. I told a few friends, and they warned me—only half joking—not to tell too many people. My flat might get broken into and my gas stolen.

During the earthquake of April 2015, Ramesh's house fell down. His family lived in a small village in Gorkha District, which was the earthquake's epicenter. As the oldest son, he was traditionally bound to support his aging parents and younger siblings. He'd been working for a decade and accrued some reasonable savings, all of which had to be spent on rebuilding his family home.

"I had no problems before the earthquake," he repeatedly told me, his forehead furrowing. "Me, my parents, no money problems. Now, little bit problem."

We hadn't been together long, and he was embarrassed by his inability to pay for anything. "In my culture, man should pay for his girlfriend."

I told him not to worry; that in my culture, women also pay. I thought of all the exceptions, all the people who wouldn't accept that, but I didn't tell him. I've never subscribed to conventional gender roles anyway. He was reluctant to go out for a drink because he couldn't pay, so I insisted that I would. He couldn't pay the three- to four-dollar taxi fare home after a night out, so I did. It was very little to me, earning dollars as I did, but he said he felt uncomfortable.

I didn't want to get our relationship off to a bad start of dependence and guilt. I told him that in exchange for the occasional cover charge to see a local band together, a few beers, or a cheap lunch date from a hole-in-the-wall, he could be my personal chef. The tongue-in-cheek nature of my suggestion was lost on him, but he was even more excited by the prospect than I was. "I like to cook for you," he said. "I want to see you happy."

The first evening he came to my house to cook me *dal bhat,* I had no running water. I'd had none for several days. There were only about three hours of electricity per day, too, because of the regular load-shedding power cuts that afflict the capital. Kathmandu had welcomed me back with a vengeance; I wondered if it was trying to spit me out, to reject me and tell me I had made poor life choices by moving here. A pipe had burst on my floor and would take more than a week to fix. I had to carry down buckets filled from an upstairs shower to flush my toilet, wash my vegetables, and do the dishes. But I didn't dare complain about the lack of gas, lack of water, lack of power, knowing what Nepalis regularly endured. Many didn't have indoor running water, at least not twenty-four hours a day; most didn't have power inverters or generators to use when the electricity went out. Thousands had lost their homes in the earthquakes of 2015.

Ramesh was unfazed by my lack of water, although he proudly told me that in his village, there was never a power problem. "Only Kathmandu has such big problems," he said. "Too many people." He had learned not to waste a single thing, though. Where I would have run the tap over a colander of dried lentils to clean them, he covered them with just enough water and rubbed them together vigorously. Where I would not have considered how much rice was needed for two people and claimed that whatever was left over would be eaten later (three days afterward throwing away the dried remnants), he judged exactly how much we would eat by placing his out-stretched fingers in the water and measuring along the creases. Two small potatoes for the curry; four green beans.

I asked for a task and he got me peeling potatoes. Then he took one of my slightly blunt knives and deftly chopped the onions and garlic with knife skills never before seen in any kitchen of mine.

"Can many Nepali men cook?" I asked him.

"I don't know about that," he said, reluctant to generalize. "All river guides know how to cook because at river time, we always cook."

I remembered him and the other guides on the Sun Kosi River trip preparing our breakfasts before they'd even prop-erly woken up in the mornings. Ramesh was a senior guide on that trip and wasn't cooking for all guests, but one morning he brought tea, toast, and eggs to my tent and said he'd made them just for me.

Now, here in my kitchen, he chopped onion and garlic and added a sprinkling of curry powder, a pinch of chili, and enough turmeric for color inside my shiny new pres-sure cooker, followed by the lentils. *Turmeric* was a new word for him, one I'd taught him a few days earlier. He was shy about his limited English, not having gone to a "good" school in Kathmandu like many of his friends, and his rather quiet temperament meant he wasn't as cock-sure with the language as a lot of other young Nepali men were. He praised the speed with which I picked up new Nepali words, saying my mind was strong, but he dismissed his own abilities. "Can you please pass me the tum-ric?" he asked without prompt, and I felt proud. I taught him "pride." To feel proud, I feel proud of you, you make me proud.

Next he asked for the salt. I sheepishly admitted that I wasn't sure I had any. I'd struggled in the spice aisle of my supermarket to know what all of the packets were. I could read Nepali fluently, having studied Hindi for several years (the two languages share the Devanagari script). But being able to read the words and being able to understand them are different skills. The white grains didn't look quite like salt, but I'd taken a risk. I passed him the packet and saw that I had made a mistake. "This is . . ." he searched for the word. "Not sugar, but to make sweet."

I'm not a fan of salty food anyway, so I suggested we skip it. He didn't dignify the suggestion with a reply, but picked his wallet up off the table and headed out to one of the small grocery stalls on my street that crammed everything from sanitary pads to fresh vegetables into a space no larger than a walk-in closet. A minute later he returned and, crisis narrowly averted, screwed the lid on the pressure cooker.

The pressure cooker—a staple in any South Asian kitchen, though an alien contraption to me—can be left until it whistles at least four or five times. Then, the lentils should be stirred, more water added, and the lid screwed back on tightly. I would have diced the potatoes, but he cut them into strips and placed them in my small, sturdy iron wok with enough mustard oil to prevent them from burning. He didn't add water, as I would have done with a potato curry. He added mustard seeds, onions, and garlic once the potatoes softened.

He concentrated intensely, and I liked to watch him work. It was a novelty for me to have a man so proficient in the kitchen. He hunched over, as the benches were too low for him. Made for the comfort of an average Nepali, they were too low for me, too. I hadn't realized that Ramesh was tall until his friends joked that I'd caught the only tall man in Nepal, so I should hang onto him. (He was five foot ten, while the average height of a Nepali man is five foot four.)

Everything ready, Ramesh stepped outside to smoke a cigarette while I served the food. I regretted my cheap made-in-China plastic plates, as a simple steel *thali* platter with compartments to divide the different curries would have been more appropriate for this traditional feast.

It was the first of many *dal bhat* dinners at my house, which became our house. These days, Ramesh heads to the kitchen promptly at seven o'clock and opens the fridge to see what he can cook with. He's excited if I have bought paneer cheese or some unusual type of leafy vegetable, like dandelion leaves (which I didn't even know were edible). We eat from my brass and steel *thali* platters now. Ramesh eats the *dal bhat* with his right hand, as most Nepalis do, mixing the rice, curry, and pickle together into little balls and scooping them into his mouth with his thumb. I haven't mastered this yet, but I imagine that with his help, I will.

When I tell him it tastes delicious, he says the same thing, every time.

"I like to cook for you. I like to see you happy."

Elen Turner is a Kathmandu, Nepal-based writer and editor who has lived previous lives in the UK, Sierra Leone, New Zealand, the Czech Republic, Japan, Australia, and the United States. She completed a Ph.D. from the Australian National University in 2012, which examined the contemporary Indian feminist publishing industry. Her biggest travel dilemma is how to see all of the corners of South Asia that she hasn't yet visited, without neglecting the rest of the world. She has eclectic tastes, which all feature in her work: good literature, sparkling Indian textiles, street art, white-water rafting. She prefers her lentil curry Nepali-style.

❧ ❧ ❧

You Teach American Way

A dream realized, with an assist from Dad.

 I am wandering through the Prague airport looking for someone who's looking for me. From a distance I spot a slumped round figure who's a dead ringer for Alfred Hitchcock—if Hitchcock had an affinity for lime-green tracksuits and brown moccasins. He raises his stocky arm and waves me forward. The purple stripes that line the sides of his sweatsuit are bulging and sinking along the contours of his torso. He is holding a rose. He hands me the stem, and I raise it to my nose but detect only a faint trace of smoke. I shyly smile my thanks and stick out my hand while he leans in to kiss my cheek. Like amateurs taking dance lessons, we stumble around each other. He manages a quick peck while my hand flounders in space. A petite woman lingering behind him steps forward. She doesn't brave either a kiss or hand-shake. The man gives her a nod.

"Hi Jenni, I am Hanna, the assistant and translator. This is Pavel Dušek, the manager." Hanna turns toward Pavel. "He says he is happy you to play basketball in Strakonice and to teach us American style." She continues after another encouraging nod from her boss. "He says our team will be number one team and you will like very much."

I glance at Pavel, who has yet to utter a word, and see that he is studying me closely.

I thank him for the opportunity to play professional basketball with his team, and when Hanna relays my gratitude he beams back, revealing a mouthful of yellow-stained teeth.

Pavel and Hanna slide into the front seat of the small powder-blue car and I, the lanky basketball player, fold up my legs and arms like a transformer and wedge myself into the back. I don't have to worry about jamming my luggage into this tiny tin box—my lone, stretched-at-the-seams suitcase is lost somewhere between Helsinki and Prague.

I catch only a few glimpses of Prague as we leave the airport. The distant sepia-toned spires and bustling suburban quarters are quickly replaced by farmhouses and crop fields that remind me of the Midwest, until a road sign appears with some bizarre configuration of letters strung together. Pavel drives quietly, his arm perched on the open windowsill, a cigarette drooping from his fingers. He speaks very little and only to Hanna in hushed tones, as if he's afraid I'll eavesdrop.

We meander through the countryside, and Hanna takes on the role of tour guide—telling me about the breakup of Czechoslovakia just eight months ago in January 1993, how much they hate Russians, and something about a famous castle in Strakonice. I try to be polite, feigning interest by inserting "really" and "uh-huh" in the appropriate places but my mind wanders to my luggage. I make mental notes of what I am missing and wonder how I'm supposed to join my new team without a pair of basketball shoes.

I spot a Strakonice road sign and scooch forward to get a glimpse of my new home. What I see bears no resemblance to the attractive tourist brochures I received months ago: large concrete tenement buildings, drained of any hint of color, stand at attention around the outskirts of town. Pavel winds his way through the narrow city streets but there is no discernible downtown area—just rows of apartment complexes, many in disarray, and a few scattered businesses. There's an industrial feel to Strakonice—smoke chugging and hissing through long metal chutes attached to nondescript stone and brick structures.

Two hours after leaving Prague we ease to a stop in front of a ten-story brown-and-cream-striped building crowned by a weathered iron "hotel" sign. As we walk inside, the velvety couches and floral print rugs that pepper the lobby of the Hotel Bavor are a welcome site.

Hanna checks me in and proudly declares, "Best hotel in Strakonice!" In a few weeks, I'll discover it's the only hotel in Strakonice.

Hanna stands in the doorway of my room and hands me a colorful stack of bills. "Jenni, we will try and get bag tomorrow but maybe next week." Then she says goodbye in Czech: "*Ahoy.*"

I will never see my translator again.

I was eleven and a half years old—an age when birthdays are still marked in quarterly increments—when I ducked into my father's study late one night to make a confession. He was cradling a glass of chardonnay while studying lecture notes for his classes the next day. He took no notice of me as I plopped down in his plush love seat and clasped a stuffed soccer ball to my lap. This was a seat I was familiar with—almost every night we'd talk for hours about my struggles in school or his desire to move to some far-flung destination like New Mexico. But mostly we talked basketball. We would debate who was better—the Boston Celtics or the Los Angeles Lakers, Larry or Magic. We had heated arguments over the merits of the three-point line.

"Dad. Hey Dad," I raised my soft voice to get his attention. "I really want to concentrate on basketball. I think I want to be a professional basketball player." He looked up and reached for the wine bottle—half empty and positioned in its usual spot on his desk between family photos—and clinked the edge of the glass as he poured.

I was worried he wouldn't take me seriously; previous career ambitions had coincided with my latest Halloween costumes. I'd had fleeting dreams of becoming a rock star, a ninja, and a Jedi knight. My closet brimmed with light sabers and swords, a scruffy hair band wig, and a plastic guitar. Now I was declaring my goal of becoming a professional athlete—a flight of fancy, considering that in 1983 only a handful of women earned a living playing sports.

My father didn't flinch. He simply said, in his usual reasoned manner, "O.K., then we need to work on your right hand. And your shooting form could be better."

For the next few years we spent weekends at Barton Hall, an ivy-covered stucco building that was home to Cornell University's gym. Inside, dozens of college students, all men, whizzed up and down the basketball courts, sticky with sweat, barking taunts. The rubber courts were slick with perspiration runoff, and phlegmy spit wads lay like little land mines outside the white lines. My father shepherded me to a free basket where we worked on my jump shot. Always the professor, he expected me to understand why the ball sometimes dropped perfectly through the net and other times clanked off the side of the rim. My elbow? My follow-through? I would guess. He wouldn't throw the ball back to me until I stumbled upon the correct answer. After weeks of analysis, I knew whether the ball was true or not from the moment it left my grasp.

A hundred small faces swivel to greet our arrival as Pavel ushers me into the gym. He swishes by in his satiny red sweatsuit and addresses the crowd with a flurry of gestures and unfamiliar sounds that abruptly end with the words, "Jenni

Kelley." My stomach twists as I realize I am the special guest at a camp. He waves me onto the basketball court.

I stand at center court, self-conscious in the now rank t-shirt and jeans I picked out for the plane ride twenty-four hours ago. I cast my gaze downward and study my sneakers to escape the collective stares. Little arms shoot toward the ceiling. A man suddenly pops out of the audience, sidles up next to me, and scans the faces. He calls on a young girl in a faded Nike t-shirt, and she spits out something in Czech.

The man turns to me. "He wants know if Michael Jordan you friends."

I laugh—both at the absurdity of the question and the mistaken pronoun—and launch into a convoluted answer about not knowing Michael Jordan personally but admiring him very much. The translation back to the kids is a fraction of my ramble.

Another child is selected, this time a boy around ten years old.

"He wants know you where from?"

I tell the man I was born in Chicago but raised in Ithaca, New York. This last part seems to cause excitement.

He translates a follow-up query. "He wants know you having gun?"

No, I have never fired a gun, I tell him with a chuckle.

Then Pavel cuts in to issue instructions, and the kids leap to their feet and line up under the basket. They stare at me expectantly. Pavel grins and taps me on the back. "Jenni. Yes."

I have no idea what he means. I look to the man for clarification.

"You teach American way," he explains, and slips back into the crowd, becoming the second translator to mysteriously disappear.

For two hours I am in constant motion, demonstrating every lay-up, ball-handling, and fast-break drill I have ever learned. I teach them games and gimmicky tricks and how to high five, and they giggle with delight. The kids are eager students, seemingly mesmerized by my instructions, despite— or perhaps because—they are issued in English. Or maybe they are entranced by the unlikely sight of a gangly American from New York who packs heat and hangs out with Michael Jordan.

It was the eve of my high school graduation in the spring of 1989 when my dad opened up an old wound.

"Do you miss playing?" he blurted while sitting at the dinner table.

"I still don't know what I am without it," I answered, batting back tears.

Three years earlier, as a sophomore, I'd torn the meniscus in my right knee. My family did their best to support me through physical rehabilitation setbacks and mood swings that settled into depression. Finally my doctor told me to rest indefinitely. Or take up kayaking. My dream of becoming a professional basketball player was over.

I had no plans to play again when I arrived at a tiny college in Iowa. But for several months my knee had felt spry, so on a whim I walked onto the team. I'd missed the camaraderie of team sports, but mostly, I longed for the closeness I no longer felt with my father. My shredded knee had damaged the bond we once shared.

I didn't play much my freshman season—after years away, I needed to retrain my muscles and relearn the game. But when I became the starting point guard as a sophomore, my father flew out to see me play as much as possible. After games, we huddled in Taco Johns and Subways and schemed about ways to enhance my skills. I took his constructive criticism to heart and improved every year. By graduation I was good enough to resuscitate my dream of turning pro.

My father put me in touch with a former student who had played professionally in New Zealand, and she helped me contact foreign clubs. I waited for snail mail to reveal my fate. Contract offers arrived from Manchester, England; Strakonice, Czech Republic; and Bratislava, Slovakia. Strakonice, only recently open to Westerners after the fall of Communism in Czechoslovakia, was the most intriguing destination. I couldn't wait to immerse myself in a new culture, make new friends, and toast victories with frothy mugs of beer.

I immediately hired an agent: my father. He negotiated a contract with Pavel from Basketbalový Klub Strakonice that stipulated I would make 1,400 koruna per week (the equivalent of $45 U.S, but a large sum, considering that a beer cost 10 koruna) plus incentives and access to a translator. I would report to training camp in early August 1993.

My first few days in Strakonice bring a flurry of activity. Pavel holds a news conference announcing that I am the first American, male or female, to play professional basketball in the Czech Republic. I smile, shake his hand, and hold up my banana-colored #14 jersey while a handful of photographers capture the moment. I move from the comfy Hotel Bavor to a room at the brand new International House that resembles my college dorm with its sparse and simple decor. As a vegetarian, grocery shopping is a game of Russian roulette. American brand names are non-existent, so I randomly toss metal cans into my cart and hope they're edible; my success rate hovers around 50 percent. Before I meet my new team, Pavel brings me his version of athletic wear: a couple of ratty t-shirts and a pair of skimpy shorts best suited for a lone butt cheek.

Inside the Strakonice Sportovní Hala, sponsorship boards hug the perimeter of the court like the layout of a hockey rink. Clattering glasses from an upstairs bar compete with basketballs clanking off metal rims as my teammates begin to warm up. From the bench I study the players: most of the women look to be around my age, early twenties, but there's a smattering of older players. One woman has purple streaks in her hair; another is so formidable she looks to have been plucked from a giant sequoia grove. Many of my teammates wear makeup so heavily caked on that I can see layers of blush highlighting their cheekbones from across the gym. The prevalence of knee braces is striking; almost every player is rebounding and shooting while burdened by a medieval-looking metal contraption. A few teammates steal glances at me. No one approaches.

The coach, Tomas, a fit middle-aged man with moppy gray hair, jogs onto the court and breaks the silence with his whistle. After brief instructions, my teammates start sprinting and I follow, a step behind. But without a translator, I'm confused by each drill and play as tentatively as a less experienced player. Hours pass, and we run and run and sweat and run. There is no water break, and little discussion—not that I would understand—of strategy. We run three-on-two fast breaks, two-on-two, and even play one-on-one full court—a backbreaking exercise by American standards.

When practice finally ends, I slump on the bench and watch perspiration droplets slide off my face and hit my tennis shoes. My feet sting from blisters. Tomas approaches and finally speaks to me.

"Jenni, *jak se máš?* O.K.?"

"O.K." is all I can muster. At least until the next practice, which begins in four hours.

Practice, nap, weights, lunch, practice, ice, dinner, sleep. Repeat. My staccato routine is broken up by the occasional surprise: the return of my lost suitcase a week into my stay, the arrival of a care package containing dozens of boxes of Kraft Macaroni & Cheese courtesy of my parents, and letters

from friends that I read over and over to savor the sounds of
a familiar language.

Each day I look forward to my walk to the Sportovní Hala.
Little kids trail after me like streamers on a kite, jostling for
attention and shouting, "Hello, Jenni!" I follow alongside the
murky Volyňka River that never seems to have much flow.
Sometimes I leave for the gym early so I can lounge in the
straw grass by the river and re-read one of the few books I
brought with me. I stop and watch teenagers with wooden
rackets lob tennis balls over hedges; they pause between points
and wave. Just around the corner from the Sportovní Hala,
the crazy gypsy woman leans out of her second story apartment window and shrieks at me with such force that I jump,
even though by now I'm expecting her wrath. I learn not to
take her outbursts personally as she verbally accosts anyone
who dares to walk down her street.

During my limited free time I explore the town and become
a regular at the only restaurant with a vegetarian item on the
menu: *smažený sýr*, or fried cheese. The chunky cubes sauced
with white slop remind me of grub I've seen in bad prison
movies. After eating dinner alone, I drop into the local bar,
the Pivovar, where my arrival is always greeted with cries of
"Jenni!" from groups of young men soaked in beer. I learn to
get my bottle of Coca-Cola to go. To my delight, the local theater is playing *Jurassic Park* one night, and I go, assuming the
film will be in English with Czech subtitles. After I settle into
my seat with popcorn I notice that not only has Sam Neill's
voice been dubbed into Czech, but the voices of every male and
female character sound remarkably similar.

Within weeks of joining BK Strakonice I realize the international game is more physical and punishing than what
I'm used to back home. The thick Czech players outmuscle
me for rebounds, and when they slap the ball away, I wait
for the whistle that never comes. Team captain Drahomíra

Vondříčková, a slender woman with blond hair pulled back in a ponytail that accentuates her high cheekbones, is the only player on the team who speaks any English. It's Drahou's job to teach me the plays, but because her English is limited to "Jenni," "here," "no," and her favorite, "bad," she resorts to clutching my jersey and tugging me around the court like a pawn on a chess board to demonstrate correct positioning.

The language barrier creates a chasm between my teammates and me. Without a translator I am a spectator to their locker-room camaraderie. They joke and dance before practices and games and leave the gym together, arms linked. Drahou begins to ignore me when I look to her for guidance, and the other players smother me with indifference. The only exception is a guard in her thirties named Lenka Bezděčiková, or Bernie for short.

Perhaps sensing my loneliness, Bernie appears on my doorstep on rest days to conduct her own version of Rosetta Stone. We stroll through town and begin our lesson: "*Most,*" she says, pointing to a bridge over the Otava River. We pass by a little cottage and she blurts out "*Dom!*" "*Ulice,*" she says, stamping her shoes on the street pavement like a petulant child. "Jenni! *Ulice, ulice!*" I take my cue and repeat *ulice* until Bernie smiles. When we enter the busier part of town it's harder to follow her lessons. "*Obchod, dítě, brána, sloup lampy.*" Store, baby, door, lamppost. I repeat each word, butchering the pronunciation. "*Dobje,* Jenni, *dobje!*" Good, good, she crows.

Every couple of nights I walk two blocks to the nearest pay phone to try to call my father. I punch in the numbers but either the line goes dead or I reach a Czech operator without English skills. One night, a month after my arrival in Strakonice, I get lucky. The operator speaks English. He puts me through.

"Dad. Dad." My voice cracks. I've imagined talking to him so many times but now I stumble over the words.

"Jink. We got your letters. What happened to the translator? How are you?" His tone remains steady but the use of my childhood nickname gives away a trace of worry.

And then I unleash a breathless stream of concerns: My translator is missing, we practice too much, I'm losing confidence, the food is weird, I think my teammates hate me. And worse, I spit out, I'm completely alone. One by one my father talks through each grievance. Just hearing his voice allows me to hit the reset button. I resolve to stick it out.

Brilliant red and gold leaves drop from their perch, leaving trees half-naked, and scatter into the streets and sidewalks of Strakonice. It's midway through the season and our record hovers around .500 against other first division Czech teams. On game days I pass families lining up at the Sportovní Hala to watch us play. Parents, still in their dusty brown work clothes, and kids with tinted hair and lively outfits greet me with, "*Ahoy* Jenni!" I catch glimpses of Pavel in the stands, his toothy smile replaced by a stony expression I imagine is a result of my unsatisfactory play. My playing time steadily decreases but, to my astonishment, each time I enter a game and "Jenni Kelleyová" is announced over the PA system, the sold-out crowd applauds wildly.

During phone calls with my dad I always lead with something positive to allay his concerns—a sign of encouragement from a teammate or a good play that restores a flicker of self-confidence. Inevitably I confess to him that this game that's captivated me for so long is losing its shine. When I stubbornly refuse to quit, he prods me to "cut the crap and come home"—his version of tough love. But he understands my decision to stay; he alone knows how hard I worked to realize this dream.

At practice, a core group of players turns on me, and snickers and hoots start to follow each mention of my name. I can only imagine what they are saying; my Czech lessons with Bernie ended weeks ago after my progress stalled. When I look to my teammates for an explanation I see only the backs of their jerseys. Only Bernie offers the occasional pat on the back or smile. My isolation triggers paranoia, and the stares, glares, and comments—real or perceived—take a toll. I hibernate in my room at night and wrap myself in a comforter to muffle my cries. When I wake, I stare at my half-packed suitcase and contemplate leaving.

Respite from loneliness comes one November day when Pavel hands me a trip itinerary. It's in Czech but I recognize key names: Praha-London-Chicago. I re-read this last word a few times. I can hardly believe its presence on the page. Chicago. Home. I piece together that our team is taking a trip to America in three weeks to play a series of exhibition games—an opportunity for my Czech team to learn the American brand of basketball.

I arrive in Prague three days before the rest of my team to enjoy my first vacation in the Czech Republic. I spend days wandering through Old Town and the Jewish Quarter. I amble across the St. Charles Bridge,.watching street performers juggle torches, and I tip the busking guitarist who strums Simon and Garfunkel. Near my hotel I spot the golden arches and break into a full sprint in anticipation of inhaling several orders of McDonalds fries. At night I sit anonymously in bars, drinking Pilsner Urquells and Budvars and watching twenty-somethings groove to Euro techno dance beats. Just when I'm beginning to revel in new discoveries and get my bearings in Prague, my vacation is over. "*Ahoy* Jenni! Good?" Pavel inquires at the airport. "*Dobrý. Krásný,*" I answer. Good. Beautiful.

The Strakonice Basketball Club flock together in the arrivals area of Chicago's O'Hare airport and await instructions from

Eva, the translator from Prague who is joining the team during the American tour. I glide past their bewildered faces and
follow the English signs to baggage claim, where I spot my
dad seated casually in the back of the crowd, nose buried in a
newspaper. He stands as I approach and before he can extend
his arms I lurch onto him. I don't let go. He wraps his right
arm around my back and pats me gently.

We stretch in synchronicity around the Iowa State University logo, but I am acutely aware of my outsider status. My
teammates' banter fills the bare gym, and Tomas and Pavel, in
near matching sweatsuits, huddle in the background waiting
to begin the first practice in America. I sit in silence, endlessly
rewinding and replaying the glorious past two days of laughing and gorging on pizza with friends and family who have
traveled to the Midwest to see me play.

But after tasting familiarity, there's something else. I
feel different. Angry. At the absent translator, the isolation,
my own naiveté. And for the first time in months—now
that we're playing American-style basketball in my own
backyard—I allow my frustration to bubble over, and I whip
balls at teammates and berate myself for bad passes. I shriek
when a teammate elbows me out of a rebound. A dirty play, I
think. I throw an elbow right back.

We do the weave drill down the court, and I flub a right-
handed layup. A layup. This infuriates me. How did I get
this bad? How did things get this bad? I collect the ball and
scream as I punt it into the bleachers. I kick open a side door
to the gym. My leg throbs from the impact. Pacing the hall-
way, I'm unsure of how to contain my rage.

In the locker room I take athletic scissors and hack off the
ends of my hair but Eva, the translator, intervenes before I can
give myself a pixie cut. She says nothing; just sits and holds my
hand as I cry. After a time, we walk back onto the court arm

in arm, and the Czechs avert their eyes. Practice continues. I am determined to help teach them American-style basketball on this tour. But then I know I am done.

My parents and extended family are a constant presence over the next two weeks as we play eight games against Division I teams throughout the Midwest. Our team struggles against American competition—the physical style of play that I found so difficult to adapt to in Strakonice now works against my Czech teammates. Multiple players foul out of every game, their fits of frustration punctuated with loud cries of "*Ježišmarjá!*"—Jesus!—as they storm off the court. After games I sit with my team in fast food joints and watch them quietly peck at their food. Pavel and Tomas look inconsolable.

Near the end of our tour, I finally get meaningful minutes in a game against Western Illinois and play well. After the buzzer, the Western coach strides toward our bench and, seemingly displeased by the poor effort by the Czech team, shouts, "What the hell!" She curtly shakes Tomas's hand and then points at me. "You," she barks, "you're the only one who knows what the hell you're doing out there." She slaps me on the butt and beelines it toward her locker room.

Eva and I sit across from Drahou and Bernie at a Mexican restaurant in Champaign-Urbana. The team is in good spirits, presumably because we've finished our American tour with a win against Illinois and are scheduled to return to Strakonice the following day. Drahou and Bernie huddle together whispering, when Drahou suddenly pulls away and addresses Eva.

"Jenni," says Eva, "they want to know if you have a boyfriend."

"*Ne*," I reply nervously.

After a lengthy back and forth with my teammates, Eva reluctantly addresses me again.

"I am sorry, Jenni, but they think you really must have a boyfriend and they will find one for you in Strakonice."

I turn toward Bernie and Drahou, my cheeks singeing, and am surprised by their smiles. I burst out laughing and, in lieu of declining their matchmaking offer, simply thank them.

With Eva's help, we spend the rest of dinner learning about each other's lives. We pepper one another with questions—curiosities that have accumulated over many months of silence and misperceptions. They grill me on why I refuse to wear makeup, and I ask them what's up with Pavel's track-suits. We talk about family. I find out they are both married and want to have children. When I ask about our team and what they think of coach Tomas, Bernie's dismissive wave leaves little doubt for interpretation.

As we make small talk and share laughs through dessert, Drahou's demeanor becomes serious. She gives me a hard look, swigs her margarita, and begins speaking.

Eva translates for her. "She wants you to know it will be much better when we return."

I smile with a trace of sadness, knowing that the following day I won't be on the plane with them.

"*Na zdravi,*" I say, and clink my glass to theirs. My team-mates, in slightly drunken voices, echo back my toast.

It's a few weeks after the Czech team leaves that I hold a bas-ketball again. Back at my hometown gym, my father shags rebounds as I hoist shot after shot; most drop through the rim and brush the nylon net with a satisfying swoosh. The medi-tative catch, shoot, swish, catch shoot, swish calms my busy mind. I move gingerly around the court, my right knee click-ing with each cut, a souvenir from my season abroad. Aside from his occasional critique of my shooting form, my father and I rarely speak. Neither one of us mentions Basketball Club Strakonice.

Our silent companionship stretches into the evenings when I sit in my father's study and scribble in my journal while he prepares lectures. This room, formerly our sanctum for lively debates, is quiet now except for the bitter Ithaca cold that whistles through the windowpanes. I write entry after entry in an attempt to reconcile the events of the last four months with my dream of becoming a professional basketball player.

One night, a month after my return to Ithaca, my father abruptly pushes back from his desk and looks at me. His face is flush from tipping back his third glass of wine.

"What do you think happened over there?" he asks with a solemnness that makes me think this question has been tormenting him as much as it has me.

I suspect I will never be able to fully explain to either of us what went wrong. I'd been trying to make sense of it for weeks in my journal: filling my pages with rants and regrets. But it is too difficult—or too soon—to untangle my complex reasons for leaving the Czech Republic. Instead, I share with my dad the nuggets I've held close since returning home: the little kids greeting me around Strakonice with high fives, the unconditional support from fans despite my inconsistent play, the kindness of Bernie, and the camp where I taught Czech children how to play American-style basketball.

A half smile from my dad encourages me to continue. I tell him that my disappointment doesn't diminish the pride I have in becoming a professional basketball player—a dream hatched between us in this room all those years ago.

He nods in his stoic way, seemingly satisfied with my answer, and pulls his chair back to his desk. I resign myself to another evening of silence until he throws out a question: "Do you want to catch the Laker-Celtics game tomorrow night? Do you think the Lakers have a chance the way Bird is playing?"

And I know at this moment that my journal and his notes will have to wait. We'll need to hash out this basketball debate. And, as is our custom, it might take all night.

Jennifer Kelley is a freelance writer and video producer. Her most recent work appeared in the San Francisco Chronicle, *and she is a regular contributor to* Women's Sports Watch, *a blog dedicated to venting about the marginalization of female athletes by the national media. Jennifer still plays basketball, albeit at a middle-aged pace, and talks hoops weekly with her father. She proudly holds the whack-a-mole crown in her family, despite much trash talking from her sister. Jennifer lives in San Francisco with her wife Stephanie and daughter Alexandra.*

෴ ෴ ෴

The Ritual

The true mystery of the world
is the visible, not the invisible.

—Oscar Wilde

I was sitting inside a sleeping bag pulled up to my chin in a heaterless Volkswagen van. It was February in Iran, and my husband, Stephen, and I were grinding east through the endless stretches of the valley of the Zanjan Rud. For as far as we could see there was nothing. Only snow fluffed high over the earth merging with the white sky above. Every so often in this void I'd see in the far, far distance a line of the tiniest flea-sized creatures. With binoculars I would make out a long camel caravan and get the eerie sense that it was deliberately placed there to mark the horizon, lest we forget the separateness of Heaven and Earth.

It had stopped snowing, and the weather was cloudy with a chance of wolves, starving wolves that crossed the Russian border into Iran and roamed the villages at night looking for food. From Tabriz to Karaj, as evening fell, we were approached by villagers warning us of this danger and begging us to drive them to their homes, as they were terrified of being attacked.

We had been driving the road east for long winter weeks since leaving Switzerland and were now desperately in need of sunshine. We knew that at the Caspian Sea, the weather was mild. So when we reached Karaj in the late afternoon we turned north toward Chalus, a seaside town known for its moderate winter climate. We planned to spend a week at a campground there, resting and sunbathing before driving on to India. Going to Chalus meant driving in below-freezing temperature through the Elburz Mountains. It meant rolling along the edges of icy cliff roads at night above lonely snow-wrapped valleys. And soon after we began this foolhardy trip, we were flagged down by two cars of Iranian students.

"Much danger in the mountains," they warned. "No petrol stations, no people, no help. We must go together." So, there we were, a convoy of reckless souls inching our way toward the promise of sunshine.

In sharp bends the road north rose steeply, winding us above the icy gorges of the Karaj River. The road was protected by numerous tunnels from whose gaping mouths hung long, malevolent icicle teeth as we rolled inside. On the dimming snow piled at the sides of the hairpin cliffs rode the stretched and gloomy shadow of our van.

When night fell, the starless sky turned murky. The black air was bitter with the kind of cold that invades you and remains. Owls cried, and hundreds of feet below us, panthers and jackals hunted.

A half moon like an ice chip appeared, small and white. Then it began to snow. After several hours, our convoy stopped at a mountainside teahouse above Marzanabad. Around a bubbling samovar we all drank glasses of tea and watched the snowflakes swirl outside. I felt like I was inside a Chinese scroll painting—I was one of those very small, awed travelers aloft in a precariously perched teahouse and dwarfed by mountains that loom menacingly up through a mysterious mist.

Sometime after midnight, we passed through the three thousand-foot-long Kandovan tunnel. The road forked and the students honked goodbye, heading toward the port of Bander-e Shah. We descended to the valley of the Chalus River. The snow became patchy, then completely disappeared. At daybreak we rounded a bend, and there it was—the Caspian Sea into which the Chalus River flows, blue and welcoming.

When we arrived at a campground, we realized immediately that we were the only visitors to the park. We took a nap, and when we awoke, the sea had changed color and a breeze had blown in. The water, now gray, was ruffled like cat fur by the wind.

The wind was a disappointment, but there was no snow, the air was bracing, and we had a forest of pine trees all to ourselves—or so we thought. After a few hours we noticed a coil of smoke rising into the sky. Following it like Hansel and Gretel, we found our way to a log hut.

Assuming it must be the home of the forest ranger, we knocked on the door. We wanted to pay the camping fee, but we were also curious to see what an Iranian forest ranger looked like. The door opened slowly, and a thin young man with dark black eyes stared at us. He spoke no English. Not a single word. And we knew no Farsi, not a single word. So we paid the money and left.

But the next day we had a problem. The supply of propane in our cooking stove was nearly gone. Heating a pot of soup took twenty-five minutes; at this rate we would run out of cooking fuel in two days. The only solution, we decided, was to ask the ranger if we might heat up our soup on his wood stove. So that afternoon, armed with our soup-filled pot, we once again knocked on his door. He seemed to know what we wanted immediately and motioned for us to enter. Then began the strange ritual that was to occur, unchanged, every twilight of that week.

This is how it began. We placed our soup on top of his pot-bellied stove and he, at the same time, put on a large aluminum teakettle. Then he went into a tiny alcove and returned with two small, slightly chipped white teacups, one saucer, one small aluminum teaspoon, one handle broken from a small aluminum tea spoon, a large burlap bag, a hammer, and a pair of pliers. He placed all these objects on the floor. Puzzled, we stood and watched in silence as he went to work. With the hammer he whacked the burlap bag, which contained Russian beet sugar in huge, hard rocks. Then, with the pliers, he cracked a rock into smaller sugar pebbles. He filled a chipped china teapot with the boiling water, and after a few minutes poured tea into the two cups and handed us each a sugar pebble. As he owned neither chairs nor table, he gestured for us to sit atop his bed.

"What will *he* drink from?" I whispered to Stephen.

"I don't know," Stephen whispered back.

I was about to fetch the enamel mugs from our van when the forest ranger solemnly poured tea for himself—into the saucer.

We drank the tea, the three of us sitting cross-legged on his high bed facing the stove. He handed us the small teaspoon for stirring, and he used the broken-off spoon handle. He showed us how to drop the sugar pebble into the tea, stir a bit to soften it and, as it wouldn't dissolve, suck it back into our mouths, catch it between our teeth and hold it there as we sipped the hot tea, letting the tea flow over the sugar like water over a river stone.

We had many cups and he had many saucers of tea. As drinking from a saucer necessitates pouring from the teapot at least twice as often as drinking from a cup, each time he refilled, he made a gesture of apology so we wouldn't think him a bad host for replenishing his own drink so much more frequently than those of his guests. By nodding our heads and smiling, Stephen and I conveyed our complete acceptance of the situation. We sipped together harmoniously, yet never said a word to one another, not even to exchange names.

After a while, the ranger stood up, retrieved a rolled rug from the corner, and spread it on the wood floor in front of us. He knelt in fervent prayer. Then he stopped, rolled up the rug, resumed his stoic cross-legged position, and poured himself another saucer of tea. After taking a sip, he looked at us with his gentle eyes, and a small sigh of contentment escaped from his lips. We nodded in agreement as if to something he had said. He smiled shyly. We smiled. We sighed in sympathy with his contentment. The wind whistled through the pine trees, making the cones fall at intervals on the roof with a loud *clonk*. After an hour or so, we took our soup, thanked him, and left.

Every day for a week, the ceremony was exactly the same: the immediate welcoming, the whacking of the sugar, the two cups, the saucer, the spoon, the spoon handle, the tacit apology and assurances, the prayer, the smiles, the sighs, and the silence. The big, wordless embrace of silence.

The ritual was infused with the peace that comes from a complete language barrier. It held the simple, satisfying communication of people who cannot speak to each other. By not attempting talk, we avoided those pocket-dictionary-size conversations replete with non-sequiturs, embarrassing words, obligatory smiles, head nodding, and hand gesturing. For the trouble with knowing a little of a language is that you are restricted to talking only of things for which you've remembered the vocabulary. But in those afternoons in Iran we were forced to acquire a rapport rather than to express ourselves.

From stillness to devotion and back again, we were part of a wordless play in which we all knew our parts. It occurred to me then that polite ritual, more than anything else, keeps us civilized and, often, safe.

Day after day, between dusk and dinner, we drank tea and found comfort in being together. Then at the end of the week, we left Chalus and never saw him again. We drove away, leaving him alone, entirely alone, with his tea things, his faith, his forest and, for his mosque dome, an arch of blue winter sky.

Maxine Rose Schur's award-winning essays have appeared in numerous publications, including the Los Angeles Times, San Francisco Chronicle, Christian Science Monitor, National Geographic Explorer, *Insight Guides, Travelers' Tales, and* Salon, *as well as several travel literature anthologies. She has twice won the Lowell Thomas Award for excellence in travel journalism. Maxine's travel narrative* Places in Time *was named Best Travel Book of the Year by the North American Travel Journalists Association and took the Gold Award from the Society of American Travel Writers. She is also the author of several critically acclaimed children's books, and she teaches children's book-writing workshops. Her website is maxineroseschur.com*

❧ ❧ ❧

Finding the Words

She wanted to finish her book, not her marriage.

I'm young, but not that young. Cash-poor, but rich in aspirations. I go to Bulgaria for no definitive reason. It's a place, I tell myself, just like any other. I'm a writer so I'll write anywhere. Bulgaria is just a backdrop: an affordable slice of Europe with a little Communist coloring. I'll teach English somewhere. What else is there to plan? I think only about my book—the book I'm determined to finish—and let the rest slip away.

I bring my laptop. My special pens. My shabby yet artsy clothes. My husband, who is also a writer, as well as an excellent cook. I bring my Bulgarian dictionary, which I have barely bothered studying. *Mnogo hoobava voda*, I say to myself. Very much good water. Everything will be fine, I decide. After all, I write in English.

I move into an apartment so small the landlord can't promise there will be room for a bed. My husband and I buy a bed anyway and engage in high-intensity Tetris-style furniture arranging. The bed is made to fit. My husband and I fit ourselves into the bed. We sigh into silence, let our eyes flutter closed. As if on cue, the night begins to shudder with the

accordion shriek of dance club *chalga,* the beseeching howls
of starving stray dogs, and the blast and pop of bottle rockets
sent skyward like distress signals.

I wake up early and write anyway. I write on a tiny TV
tray positioned three feet from my husband because there is
nowhere else to go. I sink deep into my book, lose myself in a
thicket of syntax and synonyms. I show up to my first morning
of teaching still drunk on ideas. A Bulgarian translator deliv-
ers the following message: "You will instruct 324 pupils each
week." I smile as if this sounds wonderful. "Ages thirteen to
eighteen." I keep smiling—or trying to—during my tour of
the school. Most books in the library pre-date the moon landing. On breaks, the other teachers avoid me to go smoke in the
basement. Students graffiti swastikas on paint-peeling walls.
My smile splinters into a grimace. As a distraction, I think
about my book: about sentences unwritten but begging for
birth, the blink of words like stars in the dark. What was it
Virginia Woolf said? There's no gate or bolt that can lock up
a mind. Or—no—was it that a mind locks up many gateways
or doors?

I return to my apartment building, rattle the key in a door
with no handle. My husband has prepared a soup made from
local seasonal produce. I spoon in some cabbage. Later, in bed,
I lie awake and listen to the howling dogs, the *chalga,* the bottle rockets.

I feel a growing sense of trepidation.

The next day, the students show no interest in transitive
verbs, nor even of returning to their desks, and especially not
in discontinuing their own affairs—namely, the ejection of
the smallest among them out an open window. Eventually
one notices my efforts to get their attention, asks in broken
English, "How old are you?" Then another says, "Are you
pregnant?" And a third, "Are you an FBI agent?" I reply
that I am ninety-five; pregnant with septuplets; that my true

identity cannot be disclosed. The students laugh. This is not because they think I'm clever. They laugh at one another's commentary on the weirdness of my hair, the exuberance of my gestures, and my overall lameness. The students all wear tight jeans and black leather jackets and look like the tough crowd in *Grease*. Between classes they pour outside the school to smoke and make out. During this time, I retreat to the bathroom. My reflection reveals that my shabby artsy clothes are actually just shabby. I feel like a frumpy schoolteacher and not a writer.

My thoughts turn toward my husband, who—unable to get a work visa—is at home, his head among books and note-book pages.

Envy buzzes in my ears. I shoo it away.

Weeks pass. A month. I learn that Bulgarians have no word for weekend, and little else about the language. My commu-nication skills remain *mnogo* bad. In restaurants, I order only water and lots of it. On my days off, I ride in diesel-drunk minibuses to other parts of the country. I see the giant stone heads of former Soviet leaders. Sprawling factories gone rust-riddled and smokeless. Rows of old tenements like dominos about to fall. I hear about the Bulgarian mob and the worst corruption in the EU and citizens setting themselves on fire to protest. I hear about the refugee crisis. Most Bulgarians want to close the borders. They speak fearfully of an invasion. Only one man, a red-faced police officer with an interest in foreign-ers, suggests anything different: that the refugees just want to cross through. "After all," he tells me, as we sit in his office, him smoking, me checking my watch, "they are looking for a *better* life."

The police officer chuckles, waits for me to join. But I can only blink, parsing the bizarre reality that for a family fleeing war-torn Syria, Bulgaria might still seem pretty grim.

I wake up later and later each morning. I write less. I try giving my students candy to coerce them into settling down. Sugar, it turns out, has the opposite effect. Rates of defenestration increase. As do the insults lobbed in my direction—first at my appearance, then at my country of origin. America is a place the students both revile and revere. "FUCK USA," a student might scribble on his homework, even while wearing a t-shirt bedecked with stars and stripes. I try to remain compassionate—to remind myself of Bulgaria's poverty, the country's rates of unemployment—but often my compassion loses out to self-pity. I want to be writing. I want to so badly, but the anxiety of daily life mangles my mind. I think of my husband, at home, his day sprawled open. This time I cannot dismiss my envy. I begin to pick fights with him over petty things. Where to position the TV tray desks, for instance. Or who gets to use my special pens. I brood over literature's scorned wives—Vera licking stamps, Zelda going crazy—recounting all the times I have introduced my husband and myself as writers, then stood by as only my husband was asked about his work. I'm just a frumpy schoolteacher.

One night, ever sleepless, I send my manuscript out to every book contest I can find because, at this point, what do I have to lose?

The weather turns cold, the leaves fall away, the trees become skeletal. I buy an enormous black coat big enough to fit another coat underneath. When the heater in my apartment breaks, I put on my coats and turn on the oven to stay warm. Outside, the air thickens with smoke as my neighbors burn brush and trash to heat their homes. I rarely leave mine except to go to school. I casually look up flight prices home. After eating cabbage soup for the hundredth time, I dream of glossily-packaged granola bars and avocado-laden

tacos and non-knock-off M&Ms. I start missing everyone I
ever knew back in the United States, including my worst
enemies. I miss everyone except my husband, who is always
there, right next to me, because in our tiny apartment there
is nowhere else to go.

My resentment grows and grows. Soon there is no room for
anything else. The air between us becomes tight, pressurized.
I hear literature's scorned wives screeching in my ears; Shakespeare's sister rolling in her grave. I go to school, come home,
go to school, say little. At night, I kick my husband out of bed
and shiver until dawn.

It's mid-January, many months after moving to Bulgaria,
when I wake up to the news that my manuscript has won
a prestigious award. My book will be published in the fall.
My book. It takes a moment for the news to sink in, then I
feel the urge to jump and yip and distribute high-fives. I feel
this until I remember there is no one around with whom to
do these things except my husband, and the pair of us are
fighting. I walk to school holding the news tightly inside me
like a golden glowing orb, one that warms my way against
the winter chill, the snapping stray dogs, the dumpster fire
inexplicably roaring in the street. I walk into my school like
a queen.

The students have put sticky stuff on the classroom eraser
that turns my hands black and gooey. They laugh. They
continue using the classroom window like the worshipped
mouth of a volcano: a portal by which to make sacrifices to
their god. I decide not to mention the book to them or to any
of the other teachers. I feel my glow get smaller, denser. But
I hold onto it, tightly.

Then: a call from my husband. The connection is bad. He
says something about an accident. Blood. The need for a hospital. I abandon my students and run out of the school, my

frumpy teacher clothing flapping, my weird hair gone wild. I
find my husband staggering along a sidewalk. His left hand
is wrapped in a matted wad of bloody tissues. There's more
blood on his shirt. He tells me that he fell; that he's in terrible
pain; that he may have scraped off his fingernails. I attempt
serenity. I attempt not to giggle, which I sometimes do in
alarming situations. I rush my husband to a hospital where
there is no waiting area, just assorted medical staff milling
about, gossiping and smoking. Is my husband's care a pro-
ductive use of their time? It takes some convincing, but they
finally agree. We are directed into a gray-walled room featuring a boom box and an examining table held together with
duct tape. I watch my husband turn a pale cabbage-green as
a flinty nurse in four-inch heels removes the matted tissues
from his hand. Blood rivers forth. The doctors become more
interested—so do people from the local neighborhood—and
they gather around to watch the nurse douse the raw red flesh
of my husband's fingers with hydrogen peroxide. The peroxide fizzles and foams. My husband starts to slump against
me, the pain sending his body into shock. I feel a swell of
panic. I feel the desperate need to tell my husband that he is
the one thing that has kept me going these many months, that
I am grateful he has stayed here, with me, in this forgotten
corner of the world, that he is undoubtedly the best thing in
my life.

Instead, I tell the doctors that my husband is going to faint.
This fact seems like a priority. But the doctor waves his hand
dismissively. "There is no problem," he says. "Your husband
will be fine."

He is fine. I am fine. We walk out of the hospital holding
hands—good hands—since my husband's left is wrapped in
a white mitten of gauze. "At least you're a righty," I say. We
both know what I mean: he can still hold a pen. I'm grateful
for this because it reminds me that I can as well. To be a writer

who loves a writer means knowing your work is often best in symbiosis. To be a writer who loves a writer means knowing that support takes many forms: beyond money, beyond time, to share a life with someone who believes in you and your work is a gift both intangible and utterly precious.

Again, I begin waking up early. I work on my book—a new book now—with my first in the hands of my publisher. At school, I increase the students' candy rations until they enter a pre-diabetic stupor. They become too tired to bother with windows. My husband and I even find some Bulgarian friends: a young couple, former professional pianists, who loved their country too much to leave. Now they bake bread for a living. They are always covered in flour. They explain, in great detail, many Bulgarian customs. The belief, for instance, that every meal should start with a salad and—more importantly—that every salad should start with a shot of rakia. I learn to order rakia instead of water in restaurants. *Mnogo hoobava rakia.* Very much good liquor. I tell my new friends I have a book coming out. "That's great," they reply. "Could you please pass the bottle?"

No one really cares about my book and I don't care so much that they don't care. My book doesn't fit in with the howling dogs and the dumpster fires and the throat-burning rakia. My book feels far away. Like another country, a place I'll visit someday, once I've finished with this one.

Born and raised in rural New Hampshire, Allegra Hyde has since lived all over the world, with stints in Singapore, Bulgaria, New Zealand, and elsewhere. Her writing has appeared in numerous publications, including New England Review, Gettysburg Review, Alaska Quarterly Review, The Missouri Review, *and* The Pushcart Prize XL: Best of the Small Presses. *In 2016, her short story collection,* Of This New World, *received*

the 2016 John Simmons Short Fiction Award. She has also been awarded fellowships and grants from The Virginia G. Piper Center for Creative Writing, the National University of Singapore, the Jentel Artist Residency Program, The Island School, and the U.S. Fulbright Commission. For more, visit www.allegrahyde.com.

♫ ♫ ♫

Oscar's Dreamland

One man's dream, one family's revelation.

It was a simple rule: No bribing.

We could wield our powers of persuasion. We could point out the pros and cons of one choice or another. We could try humor and philosophical theorizing. We could even look profoundly sad if we thought guilt was the way to go. But if the chooser refused to be swayed, that was that. We had to go along with his or her choice. *Cheerfully*.

These were our rules of the road one summer when we traveled thousands of miles across the middle of America in an RV, and they applied to everyone equally, parents and kids.

We were the poster family for the Recreational Vehicle Industry Association, crisscrossing the country extolling the virtues of traveling by RV. How my frequently unharmonious family of rebels and independent thinkers, from Manhattan of all places—and I don't mean Kansas—became spokespersons for the RV industry baffled many who knew us. But maybe being a rebel was what it took. I was one of the few New York City magazine editors willing to pack up my family and take to the road to find out firsthand what happened when you crammed three kids, two parents, and a dog into a twenty-nine-foot home on wheels.

What happened were stories, hundreds of them. They became the stuff of family lore, and we were bound in the shared memory of them. This is one of those stories. It's about Oscar. Well, not so much about Oscar, a man we never actually met. It's more about the fact that along back roads and highways, between small towns and big cities, in national parks, state forests and KOA Kampgrounds, we fell in love with America. Oscar was one of the reasons.

The afternoon we rolled into Billings, the sun over Montana was blazing hot and there wasn't a hint of breeze riffling across this city that had an aura of grimness to it. To be fair, we didn't see much of Billings, and the part we saw did little to offer a different picture.

On that day in Billings, the job of deciding what we would do in our free time fell to Hutch, a five-year-old who took his job seriously. We never knew what to expect with him. Kira, fourteen, almost always went for an outdoor adventure—hiking, biking, or horseback riding. Molly, eight, was the family historian. When she chose, we ended up at the Harry S. Truman Home in Missouri and the Eisenhower Presidential Library and Museum in Kansas, for which we drove 140 miles out of our way. My husband, Bill, and I usually opted for the nearest national or state park where we delved into ranger talks on bats, snakes, stars, wildflowers, tarantulas, rivers, and geology. Hutch wasn't so predictable. And that was worrisome to us all.

As usual, I got out the guidebook and was relieved to discover there were some promising choices. Relatively speaking. Just 25 miles outside of Billings, along the Yellowstone River, was Pompeys Pillar, a massive sandstone formation compelling enough to make Captain William Clark get out of his boat and climb to the top 190 years earlier. There, he carved his name and the date: July 25, 1806. Clark's scrawl remains the only physical evidence along the trail of the Lewis and Clark Expedition. Big rock, I thought. That's good. If William Clark couldn't wait to see it, surely Hutch would be intrigued.

There was also a cave, a National Historic Landmark with zillion-year-old Native American pictographs offering clues to the past. That seemed like a good bet. And there were unlikely candidates in the Western Heritage Center and the art museum. I thought the historic cemetery might stand a chance.

But none of these could match the singular draw of Oscar's Dreamland. Just the name made Hutch sit up and smile. And once I read the info, I knew. We were going to Oscar's Dreamland, seventeen acres of old farm equipment, and there wasn't an argument in the world that would change that.

Not that we didn't try. But Hutch wouldn't budge, so we fired up the RV and headed to the edge of town and Oscar's Dreamland. There, behind a ratty white picket fence, acres of parched, patchy grass spread out in an endless sweep of disillusion. The word "WELCOME" arched above us in peeling paint that might have once been bright and cheerful. Now, it had the effect of making everything beyond it seem shabby.

I remember thinking at that moment that it could not get any worse. I was wrong.

"Good God," I muttered as we trooped under the arch. In front of us was the largest piece of molded-plastic poultry I had ever seen. A giant chicken—maybe eight feet tall—stood guard at the gates of Dreamland. It was unclear whether it was there to greet visitors or deter escape.

There was no line to enter Dreamland that day, though perhaps there had once been, back in the late 1960s and early 1970s when it first opened. On the afternoon we arrived, there was hardly a soul around. I was thinking we could call it a day and find something actually fun to do. But then we saw

the young girl sitting behind a lopsided table in the sweltering sun, between the faint shadow of the giant chicken and a
truck-sized root beer mug in the distance behind her. She was
so happy to see us, we just couldn't turn away.

"Welcome," she called wistfully, seeming to echo the sadness of the sign. She wrote something down and added up
our entrance fee in neat print. I don't remember how much it
was, but it was a pittance. And it gave us access to Dreamland
in its stunning entirety—all seventeen acres, three massive
sheds holding Oscar Cooke's vast collection, the chicken, the
root beer mug, and a little town Oscar had created by moving historic buildings from across Montana into Dreamland.
He called it Cookeville. It had a bank, the first schoolhouse
in Yellowstone County, a blacksmith shop, a news office, and
more. The little jail was our family favorite. We wanted to
put Hutch in it.

I can't be certain where the day of dread, of being force-
marched through a five-year-old's hellish idea of a good time,
suddenly changed. But somewhere between the giant chicken
and the platoons of vicious insects chasing us through Coo-
ketown, all we could do was laugh. There we were, running
from old building to old building, batting at our heads and
giggling like lunatics because we couldn't believe that Oscar's
Dreamland was so very much weirder and worse than we had
even imagined. Some of the old buildings were locked, and
that would send us into hysterical fits as we staggered on to
the next one in hopes of getting respite from the bugs, along
with our intermittent dose of Montana history.

That went on for twenty minutes until Hutch, who had
come for a purpose and this was not it, insisted we move on to
the thing that had made his little boy heart beat with excitement. The collection.

It's an understatement to say Oscar was a dedicated col-
lector. There were steam engines. There were hoes and

harvesters, crop dusters, wagons and antique cars. There was every kind of tool you could think of and a whole lot of others whose purpose was a mystery. There was random memorabilia. There were hearses and horse-drawn vehicles, old bicycles and threshers, wheels and piles of eclectic equipment that had come down from centuries of American farming.

But most of all there were tractors. Hundreds of them. Row after row after neat row of them. They were old and older. They were red and green and blue and yellow and rust. They had round fronts and square fronts, sharp angles and sweet curves. They were impossibly tall and they were petite, in that way of petite that defines small tractors, not ballerinas. Tractors took up one of the three buildings entirely, and part of another building, too. In stark contrast to the forsaken desolation outside, each and every one of the tractors was meticulously clean and polished, perpetually waiting, it seemed, for some long-ago farmer to appear and put it to work growling and chugging across America's heartland.

Thirty minutes earlier, four-fifths of us, and by that I mean not Hutch, had been plotting our escape, past the giant chicken and out into something, anything, but old farm equipment. But here, at the epicenter of Oscar's collection, we discovered just how cool old farm equipment could be and how little we knew of the tools farmers used. We strolled, we poked, and we craned our necks to get a better look at some of the biggest machines. We read signs out loud and we called to each other from deep within the rows and nooks of the dark buildings when we found something especially wonderful, which happened over and over.

And we laughed. There wasn't another day that summer on which we laughed as hard or had a better time.

America, it turns out, is filled with quirky corners, and as we wandered around Oscar's place, an unexpected appreciation for them crept up on us and took hold.

I still have a photo of Hutch standing on the seat of one of Oscar's massive tractors, its wheels bigger than some Manhattan apartments, its bright red-orange paint still shiny in places.

To be honest, I was perfectly aware of the signs politely asking visitors not to climb on the equipment, on the carefully preserved remains of a man's dream. But Hutch wanted desperately to get up on just one, to hold its wheel and cranks and shifts in his hands. And the rest of us had behaved so badly for most of the day, I felt I owed it to him. When I look at that photo today, it takes me right back there, and I like to think that perhaps Oscar has forgiven me because he, of all people, is the one who could understand the powerful longing Hutch must have felt standing in front of that tractor.

Old farm equipment was not just Oscar's dream; it was his life's passion. He had amassed his collection over many decades, bringing thousands of items to Billings. He died not long before we arrived at Dreamland, at the age of ninety-five. I'm sorry I never had a chance to talk to him, to tell him how his dream of preserving farm equipment became part of the enduring vacation lore of my definitively non-farming family.

Years later I read a quote from Oscar on a website about the then-defunct Dreamland, parts of which had been sold off for taxes after Oscar's passing.

"To me," Oscar had said, "the collection represents an age we'll never see again, when folks used to get together and help each other at harvest time."

I never saw Dreamland in its heyday, if it even had one. But I want to remember it the way I imagine Oscar dreamed it—a place where families could come to be captivated by the unexpected elegance and beauty of hoes and harvesters and crop dusters, by the grandness of wheels and the rainbow of colors sported by industrial machines in a glorious combination of shapes and sizes. I want to remember it as Oscar's poetic if odd collective ode, not just to the forgotten machines that he loved, but to the American farm and a way of life that has all but disappeared. Oscar is no longer here to care for his dream, but I treasure it for him, if only in a family story that endures, a story that twenty years later still makes us laugh. It's a beloved vignette in our cherished timeline of summer memories, as carefully preserved as any piece of Oscar's own collection.

Christine Loomis is a freelance travel writer and editor currently living in Colorado. She covers the Denver area and parts of the world farther afield for USA Today, 10best, *and other print and online publications. This is her second essay for Travelers' Tales; the first, "Vincent's Room," appeared in* A Mother's World: Journeys of the Heart.

෴ ෴ ෴

The Living Infinite

Island paradise and deep-sea
predators for the uninitiated.

"Could you bring me back a bull shark?" my six-year-old nephew asked. "Bull sharks can live in saltwater *and* freshwater." He pointed to his library book. A menacing beast with wild eyes, crooked fangs, and a burly, muscle-ripped physique snarled back at me.

I was moving to Palau, a Micronesian island in the Pacific Ocean, so my nephew's plan to populate northern Wisconsin's lakes with a new invasive species wasn't unfounded. I laughed the nervous laughter of one who has spent her life land-locked in long johns, whose ocean savvy was limited to vacations and Jules Verne books. I've been swimming since I could toddle off the dock. I was scuba certified in frigid freshwater. But the ocean—that vast blue universe that dictates weather and climate, but remains 95 percent Unexplored Mystery—was another beast, a force that looms supernaturally in mythology for a reason. The Greek god of the sea, Poseidon, was famously moody, calm and benevolent one minute, tempestuous and havoc-wreaking the next. In one of their hymns to him, the Greeks sang, "Poseidon of the golden trident, earth-shaker in the swelling brine, around thee the

finny monsters in a ring swim and dance. . . ." And that was
a song of praise.

I'd never been trapped Captain Nemo-style on a squid-
fighting submarine. But I had seen the chilling red flags—too
dangerous for swimming!—on the beach. I had experienced
the grip of the waves, the buoyant joy that suddenly turns perilous with the change of a tide or an undertow. I wanted nothing to do with swelling brine or finny monsters.

"I'll see what I can do," I said to my nephew, praying to
Poseidon that paradise would be bull-shark-free.

A month later, it appeared Poseidon had answered my
prayers. Palau was blessed with a barrier reef: an eighteen
thousand-foot vertical coral wall that diverted typhoons, tamed
waves, and lulled the water around Palau's Rock Islands into
a soundless, lake-like sleep. This was Ocean Lite, a sea for
beginners.

Then again, banners downtown pronounced Palau "The
World's First Shark Sanctuary." In 2009, the government
realized world-class diving was more sustainably lucrative
than commercial fishing (and illegal shark finning). Sharks
thrived here, in a designated shark heaven.

Like the stingless jellyfish in Palau's marine lakes, I was
promised these sharks would be harmless, too busy perusing the
smorgasbord of the reef, enjoying top-of-the-underwater-food-
chain ranks, to bother with *homo sapiens*. And since work permits gave my husband and me "local" status for the year, and
local perks included diving some of the world's best underwater sites on the cheap, I had to suppress any nascent fears. Brian
and I would stick to the scuba buddy system. I would think of
the sharks as really big fish. I would definitely keep it cool.

On our first sunny Saturday, after motoring through quiet
blue-green inlets and coves, we dropped anchor near Ulong
Island and "Survivor Beach," where the reality TV show had
been filmed. With survival on the brain, I strapped on my fins,

waddled to the boat's edge, flashed a semi-confident O.K. sign, and back-rolled into the water.

Moments later, I saw my first reef sharks at the mouth of Ulong Channel. *It's fine,* I reassured myself. *They're just really big fish off in the distance.* But when one pivoted our way, my breath went berserk through my regulator. I checked my gauge; fear was fast depleting my air supply. *Buck up,* I thought. *The big fish aren't interested.*

Inside the channel, we drifted with a light current. On certain incoming tides, we would learn, Ulong could make you feel like a superhero in space, propelled through a wonderland of hawksbill sea turtles, brown-marbled groupers, and giant clams the size of small cars. You could launch rocket-like from here to there, flip gravity-free handsprings off the sandy bottom, inhale to inflate your lungs—the body's natural flotation device—and sail above approaching corals, then exhale to deflate and sink in time to examine a hot pink sea anemone or a grouchy moray eel.

This time, we hovered, meditating on a school of black-and-yellow striped Moorish idols—fish the Moors believed were "bringers of happiness"—as they meditated on a patch of lettuce coral.

Until a reef shark gunned in my direction.

That big fish, I repeated my inner mantra, *does not care about me.*

Up close, though, the sharkiness of the six-foot reef shark was undeniable. I saw the white-tipped dorsal fin protruding blade-like from his spine. The predatory yellow bead eyes. The ragged arrangement of razor teeth inside a jaw that hinged hungrily open. My higher-thinking neocortex registered these details, along with the creature's proximity to my elbow, while my reptilian brain screamed: "SHARK!"

I kicked. I flailed. I grabbed Brian by his wetsuit and launched myself around him, using his body between me and the shark like it was my personal human shield.

This was decidedly uncool, I realized when I opened my eyes and saw we were still alive. The shark had swum on, more interested in fish than humans after all. I smiled feebly through the bubbles of my regulator, trying to figure out how to sign, "Sorry you landed a selfish freak for a life partner," underwater.

The months passed slowly, as if the equatorial heat cooked everything to a slow simmer. Internet connections were sluggish. We unplugged. We ate coconut and clam meat scooped straight from the shell. We chewed betel nut beneath a palm-thatched roof, laughing with Palauan friends who taught us to spit with enough force that the red juice wouldn't drip down our chins. We swam daily, dove regularly. And while I still had occasional panics that something menacing lurked in the deep, I began to appreciate the weightless ease of swimming in saltwater. Palauans live by the lunar calendar and tides, and I found peace in that natural rhythm. It was another kind of weightlessness, paying more attention to the moon and shoreline than apps and newsfeeds.

Through the ebb and flow of days like these, I gradually warmed up to island life. After six months, I'd come a long way from the freshwater girl who feared the open seas. When I heard a local shop had space on a "unique dive"—a rare chance to see fish aggregates spawning during the full moon—I called. I may have exaggerated, a lot, about our certification levels and experience. We were in.

We met before sunrise and loaded our gear by headlamps. I was nervous. But it wasn't until our guide sped past the usual spots, beyond the outer reef, that I was officially in over my head.

This was the ocean's truer form, Poseidon's domain, Nemo's whirlpool, pitching and rolling the boat, rattling our steel tanks, knocking us off balance as we struggled to don our gear. *I need to get into the water or I'm going to retch*, I thought. But out here, the ocean churned below the surface as well.

We descended eighty feet to a murky, desolate scene—drab foliage, a few rocky outcroppings, everything whirling in the washing machine of the sea. I sought to anchor myself by grabbing tall reeds, but they were slippery ropes. I groped for one after another while the surge sucked at my body like a giant vacuum. Feeling desperate, I looked around, and saw with clarity my own tenuous grasp on life: the reef's edge, the deep blue Philippine Sea. I was clinging to a reed at the end of the Earth, my body flailing toward the abyss.

Our guide signaled, and I swam as fast as I could after him, away from the ledge, kicking hard toward a storm-like cloud in the distance. With proximity, the cloud morphed into thousands of red snappers, spinning, swarming and shifting, a wild underwater tornado.

A female fish erupted from the herd like a bolt of pink lighting, leaving a trail of roe in her wake. The male fish gave chase, cavorting around her, wrangling like bucks in rut, clashing clouds of spermatozoa. (In case we misunderstood, our guide pointed enthusiastically to the fish, then gestured like he was jacking off.) These explosions occurred every few seconds, and we watched, awestruck, as if the whole thing were a well-timed fireworks show. I forgot about the swells and the abyss. We were orbiting the dark universe, pulling the curtain on nature's most basic and private act. It was the most ordinary and extraordinary thing I have ever seen.

A muffled, high-pitched shriek turned my attention to our guide, who gesticulated wildly toward a gray mass on the perimeter. He pantomimed two horns on top of his head: *bull shark*. First, one appeared. Then two. I knew my mask played tricks on perspective, but thanks to my nephew, I also knew these sharks bulked up to twelve feet and five hundred pounds. The aptly named bulls stalked the snapper in tandem with blunt snouts and gnarled fangs out.

I checked in with Brian. I saw that he was O.K. I reminded myself to breathe—the number-one rule of Zen Buddhists, yogis, and divers alike. And I felt the rush of my heart kicking strong. To the sound of my body's own metronomic rhythm, I watched this struggle of creation and destruction, beauty and madness, power and vulnerability—the stuff myths and classic stories are made of. The stuff we're all made of.

When we ascended to our five-meter safety stop, the sun had risen. Shafts of light beamed all around, and the water shimmered with iridescent sparkles, as if a giant glitter jar had spilled into the sea. For a moment, I had the sensation I was floating inside a snow globe, the kind I kept on my windowsill as a child.

I blinked and saw that those snowflakes were scales, thousands of them cast off from the friction of fish mating beneath a full moon. The scales tipped, fell, swirled, quaking all around me as I breathed, suspended below the surface, between worlds, in this realm of earth-shakers and finny monsters.

"The sea," Jules Verne wrote, ". . . is an immense desert, where man is never lonely, for he feels life stirring on all sides. The sea is only the embodiment of a supernatural and wonderful existence. It is nothing but love and emotion; it is the 'Living Infinite.'"

I knew now what he meant, how the sea was both earthly and not, belonging to no one and everyone. How one could stand before the mystery, the Infinite, and not fear. How not fearing felt blessed. The notion of an ocean sanctuary took on new meaning now. Poseidon could take me or leave me, but I would emerge from the water that day as if, by the grace of some god, I, too, had shed my scales, left something I no longer needed behind, and emerged, raw and blinking before a new sun.

Anna Vodicka's essays have appeared in AFAR, Guernica, Harvard Review, Longreads, McSweeney's Internet Tendency, Misadventures, Paste, Wanderlust, *and elsewhere. Her writing has been anthologized in Lonely Planet's* An Innocent Abroad *and Capstone Press's* Love & Profanity, *and have earned* The Missouri Review *audio prize, Best American Essays notables, and Pushcart Prize Special Mention. She has been a resident fellow at Vermont Studio Center and Hedgebrook, and currently teaches and writes in Seattle.*

ട്ട ട്ട ട്ട

Rerouted

"The whole future of art is to be
found in the South of France."

— *Vincent van Gogh*

She peeled around the corner at the train station with her
head out the window, waving like she was drowning.

Oh my God. This is her. I waved back and smiled, walking
toward the curb.

The car looked like it had been dragged from the bottom
of an ocean. Rust binged on the bottom of the doors. Dents
everywhere. She swerved, parked on the wrong side of the
road, and tumbled out, leaving the door wide open.

"Oh Colette!" She walked like she'd driven straight
through the night. Billowy shirt and jeans. Laughing. Erup-
tions then aftershocks. It was contagious—I started laughing
too, though I wasn't sure why.

There is no way this woman is French.

"I'm Marilyn," she announced, pulling me in for a crushing bear hug. Her halo of hair smelled like roasted meat and
onions. She sounded Irish. "I'm so sorry I'm this late. I hope
I didn't worry you." She grabbed my backpack and slung it
over her shoulder.

I hadn't been worried until now.

"It's O.K.," I said. "Thank you so much for picking me up. How far did you have to drive?"

"Oh Lord." She opened the back door, peered into the car, turned to me, and broke into laughter again.

The back seat contained a summer's worth of projects and errands. Damp, droopy bags full of recycling and laundry. Power tools and extension cords. A sack of soil the size of a slumbering lamb, and a heap of drapes that could have outfitted the Von Trapps well into their golden years. Swaddled in wet paper towels, a bouquet of wilted purple flowers baked in the back window.

"Your irises!" Marilyn lunged for them. "They look tired, don't they?" She handed me the drunk, swaying flowers, and I propped them up in my arm so she wouldn't be embarrassed.

"They're beautiful. Thank you."

"Ha!" she boomed. "They're pathetic!" She shoved my bag into the back seat then slammed the door before it could spill out. "Shall we?"

I cranked open the passenger side door and got in. It smelled like the windows had been left down in every storm. Marilyn fired up the engine, and together we jiggled to the beat of the sputtering engine as she barreled onto the road.

A few months earlier, I had quit my pencil-skirt job in San Francisco. I was a receptionist for an enormous tech company. For over a year, I ordered shelled pistachios and energy bars for the break room, learned about *big-boy money* and *low-hanging fruit,* and snuck the word *love* into pie charts and graphs on abandoned white boards. I'd taken the job so I could stay in the city and paint—after work, before work, on weekends and vacations. For the first time in my adult life I hadn't needed to worry about money. Instead, I worried about sitting in a rocking chair at age eighty-nine watching the Animal Channel, filled with regret. I wanted to paint for a living, not as a hobby.

Soon being at the office felt like sitting in a hot tub too long. I needed out. I started wearing a nonfunctioning headset so I'd look busy and no one would ask me if their Geico rebate had arrived yet or if Chad was using the corner meeting room as his office again. But it wasn't until the day a bigwig from the Boston office handed me a balled-up gum wrapper, telling me it was my tip, that I lost it. Within a couple weeks, I found a subletter for my apartment, took an editing job that allowed me to work from anywhere, and bought a ticket to Paris. All I could think about was being in that city, standing inches from all the art I'd only seen on overhead projectors in classrooms. I wanted to paint in the same place that had shaped the minds, dreams, and careers of my favorite artists—the artists who made the paintings that pulled me in, that whispered to me, *do this, do this, do this.*

Three months in Europe flew by. Red wine was my elixir. I never got hung over. Not once.

Is this place magical?

I was living someone else's life—out until four A.M., sleeping till noon, wandering all day, visiting museums again and again and again, dancing most nights. One evening, I read one of my stories to a crowd sardined on wooden benches in the basement of a bar called Le Chat Noir—lit under strands of colored lights, drinking goblets of house Bordeaux. I hardly recognized myself. And then I went back. Same basement, different night, another story.

And there was a man—Thiebaud. A perfumer with more than forty pairs of shoes lining his closet. Round face. Crow's feet were starbursts around his eyes from years of laughing, I imagined. I smiled when I first saw him on the dance floor—I couldn't help it. He came over.

"You smiled. You are not French," he leaned in, kissing each cheek with a huge grin.

"I'm sorry, I don't understand. I don't speak French," I said.

"But I am speaking English."

We laughed. I told him I'd never heard the name T-bone before, and we laughed more. At some point he held my hips and pulled me close. We danced. And kissed. He wanted to show me his favorite spots in the city so that's what we did—smooching all over Paris. In doorways, on dance floors, in cabs. This sort of thing didn't happen back home. There, I was early to bed, early to rise. I didn't overdo affection in public because I thought it was terrible for other people to have to see. But for some reason, there, with him, I didn't care. I knew it would end, and I was soaking it up. Thiebaud traveled around the world for his job, staying in his apartment for just a few months a year. And he was leaving again.

What the hell have I been doing? I thought, watching him pack one afternoon. Only a week left of my trip, and I hadn't painted anything. *Is this what self-sabotage looks like? What is wrong with me?*

For the last week, I was on a mission to paint, determined to return to San Francisco with some paintings for my show in the fall, to justify my trip. I'd been hearing about the endless lavender fields, the lush vineyards, the intoxicating light that Cézanne, Bonnard, Monet, and Matisse had chased in the South of France. It was time to find it.

Waiters, cab drivers, friends—I began to ask everyone the same question: "Where should I go?"

They invariably rattled off a few places then concluded with something like, "You're in France. Everywhere is beautiful. You can't go wrong."

It was late. I was so tired, my eyes were watering. It was hours into my search, and I still hadn't found the perfect place to

go paint. My computer was slow-cooking my lap, and in the
process of weighing my options, I had opened so many tabs
I thought it might explode: accommodation websites, travel
blogs, maps, reviews, train schedules, Google translate, and
a meditation website playing "singing whales" on a loop to
make it all go smoothly.

I had sent out a handful of emails inquiring about potential rentals in the South of France, but hadn't heard back
from one, and now time was running out. I moved my search
up to central France. *Maybe it's the up-and-coming South of
France?* Scrolling through more listings, I found an inexpen-
sive cottage—"a charming, cozy retreat"—with a patio, in a
remote part of an area called Allier. Zooming out on the map,
it became clear it was not at all in the South of France, but
smack dab in the middle of the country. A tourism website
described it as "a largely rural area with a unique, quiet charm,
neglected by many visitors." Sold. I sent the owner of the cottage an email. Was it possible to reach her property without a
car? I inquired.

Then I turned off my lamp and was about to shut down my
computer when a message popped up. I could take a train the
next day, the owner said, and she'd be happy to pick me up at
the station. The cottage was far from shops and cafés, but she
could take me to buy groceries.

I booked it. *Allier.* It rolled right off the tongue.

As Marilyn barreled through the countryside, I was struck
by how familiar it seemed. Sprawling farmland, some hills
but pretty flat. Maple trees, oaks too, dirt roads branching out
every few miles, a stream, cows. Kind of humid.

Wait, am I in northern Wisconsin?

"So what's this region known for?" I asked, praying that
central France had intoxicating rays of light, too.

"Let me see. Well, cattle for one and . . . drones. Actually,
drones for your military. People don't really know that."

I could have chosen anywhere in France, and I'd picked a place that manufactured flying, armed robots for the U.S. military and looked identical to Wisconsin. And sure, I loved Wisconsin; it was beautiful. I grew up in Minnesota and spent summers with my family renting cabins on lakes there—but I'd traveled to France to see something new.

Holy shit. I totally blew it.

We drove for nearly an hour, and Marilyn missed our turn two times. At one point we were blinded by the sun.

"I can't see a thing!" she burst out, amused, still firing down the road. She plowed up a steep, rocky path that looked like a drainage trench, slowed down just past a droopy barn, and hit the brakes.

"Here we are!" she announced.

There was only one other cottage on the hill, with no sign of anyone else in any direction.

"An old lady lives there," Marilyn said tapping her window. "She keeps to herself, though. You may never see her."

Marilyn's cottage was built entirely from huge stones, with thick walls and just four tiny windows, iron bars on all but one. Inside, it smelled like the cavern behind a waterfall. I could only see shapes of things. Marilyn's watch ticked. I blinked as my eyes adjusted.

"Even with a fire," she said, chuckling, "it never really gets too warm in here."

When Marilyn and her husband had bought the land, she told me, the cottage was covered in brush and overgrowth, so they had no clue it was there. Her husband had been looking for a barn in which to store his old-timey cars, and the land was cheap. Then they stumbled upon the cottage one day, and after discovering it was built in 1588, decided to restore it and invite people to come and stay.

"It was built during the time of the salt trade, you know," Marilyn said as she fed splintered kindling to the woodburning stove. "The windows were so small because homeowners were charged a tax back then depending upon their size."

I must have looked confused.

"Oh, every society has crazy laws," she shrugged.

After she got the fire going, Marilyn arranged the irises in a vase and gave them a couple fluffs and a mumbled pep talk. Then she spread a map of the area on the burly, wooden table to orient me. "O.K., O.K. . . . let me see," she spun the map around.

"Yes, we are here. No, here." She tapped the table about eight inches outside the map and laughed. "I should get a better map. But really, it's not that difficult."

She began drawing her own map on an envelope. "To get to the town, you take this road, to this road, to this road." She drew three pieces of angel hair pasta and an outline of a prune. "Just make sure the lake is always on your left," she pointed to the prune. "It will take about an hour."

"What's in the town?" I asked, already sure there was no way I would venture out due to my horrific sense of direction.

"A baker . . . but he's rarely open," she said, sounding disappointed. I could tell she didn't want me to regret my eleventh-hour decision to stay there.

"But how will you pass your time?" she asked, pulling out wrinkled brochures from a side table. "I can take you to an art exhibit this week in a town not too far, or I can show you the historic markers in the area—it's quite interesting, really—or to my friend's vineyard?"

I told her I'd be just fine, she didn't need to worry, I knew she was busy. I said the cottage was perfect for some downtime, which I was looking forward to. And I was.

I had exactly one week to hunker down and paint.

Over the week, Marilyn dropped by almost daily to check on me. She brought jugs of water, bundles of wood, tall loaves of sweet bread wrapped in foil, and jams she had made with fruit from her yard: strawberry, blackberry cardamom ginger, peach whisky. Often, she showed up with wine or tea and stayed to swap stories. The irises she'd given me had perked up, and occasionally she cast a sidelong look at them as we chatted, as if expecting them to chime in.

It turned out Marilyn was in fact Irish and had a Ph.D. in molecular biology. As a young woman, she'd fallen for a Dutchman, gotten married and moved to France for his job. Eventually she decided she wanted out of the research lab, so she taught English at a community college. Then her husband died. A few years later, she met and married her current husband and had a family. Now she dabbled in acting while hosting people from around the world in the cottage. She liked the social aspect of visiting with guests, she said, the company and connections.

And normally, I would, too. I enjoyed Marilyn, her million curve-ball stories and quirks, but the retreat I was after wasn't happening. I never knew when I'd hear a knock on the door.

One afternoon, I had finally started painting on the patio when I heard a car approaching. I hoped it wasn't her. The rattling grew louder. And louder. Then her Peugeot flew up the driveway.

Damn it.

With the car idling, Marilyn shouted out the window, "Get your things! We're going wine tasting!"

She was transformed. She wore a fresh white blouse, a silk scarf knotted to the side, and oversized sunglasses. As we drove to the vineyard, she told me about her friend, Guillaume, the winemaker with no insurance.

"People in town call him an outsider, *le marginal,* not in the margins," she said. "This region has strict rules for farming but he just does what he wants."

"Are they after him?"

"Probably!" she bellowed, nearly choking on her own laughter. "Oh, but he doesn't care. It's his love. I think he probably even loses money."

We arrived to find a small group of people standing around a tall man wearing a dark fitted suit, a starched white shirt with a popped collar, and an ascot. His slicked-back, mid-length gray hair could cut glass. This was Guillaume. Marilyn introduced us as she picked a piece of cat hair off his lapel. Guillaume and I leaned in and kissed the air with our cheeks touching. His one-size-fits-most veneers didn't reach his gums and petered out before his smile ended. They looked like they could pop off at any moment.

I was the only one who didn't speak French, so during the tour, Marilyn translated for me in a voice ranging from an aggressive whisper to making sure a microphone was on. At first I was embarrassed, certain we were disturbing the others, but soon I realized no one seemed bothered. The man across from us held his glass to his face like it was an oxygen mask and he was about to go down. Marilyn looked at me with raised eyebrows and smiled. I noticed everyone was pouring out the rest of their wine after the first sip, so I was about to follow suit when I saw Marilyn bang hers back.

As the sun dipped over the vineyards, light poured in through the barn door. I looked over at Guillaume—an underdog so passionate about his craft that he was determined to keep it afloat so he could share it—and then back to Marilyn: bold, endearing, always creating opportunities for herself. The warmth from the wine filled my chest and throat and swirled up to the top of my head. I smiled. Maybe I hadn't gone so wrong after all. Maybe an important part of the creative process was collecting moments that made you come alive—like the moment I saw the Bonnard exhibit at the Musée d'Orsay for the first time and started bawling, then laughed because I couldn't stop crying. Or like losing time, dancing with Thibaud until the lights came on and cool spring air flooded the dance floor. Or the moment my heart stopped racing and I eased into telling my story at Le Chat Noir, or right now, this very instant, recognizing that Marilyn might have more to teach me about being an artist than isolating myself ever could. All these moments would fill a part of me that I could draw from when it was time to paint again. But now I was with Marilyn. I downed my wine and shot her a wink.

Colette Hannahan has had more jobs than birthdays. She delivered mail at a retreat center in the woods of the Hudson Valley; taught Tae Bo to immigrant and refugee teens in a school basement in Portland, Oregon; applied makeup on brides-to-be at a salon in Brooklyn; steamed blouses for models in Manhattan; taught art and yoga to adults with autism in Chicago; held a boom on a film crew in Uganda; and sold knives out of a Camaro in Minnesota. These days she makes her home in San Francisco, where she is an artist, illustrator, editor, and writer. In between jobs she likes to travel. Her favorite nights in new countries always seem to involve unexpected dancing. So far the three A.M. slow dance to "Sexual Healing" with an elderly Portuguese woman takes the cake. Her website is colettehannahan.com.

ఌ ఌ ఌ

Claustrophilia

Do wide-open lands bring us closer together?

I can see a spark of tired panic in Jo's eyes as they meet mine. Our narrow Purgon—a Russian-made UAZ van that resembles a jacked-up VW bus—is bursting with people. The rigid seats, which face each other like those in a diner booth, are crammed with butts, and our knees interlock like a human zipper. In the back, where baggage and boxes of supplies serve as yet more seats, two weathered old men hunch below the ceiling. In the front passenger seat, a woman settles on the lap of the standby driver.

And yet here we are, picking up another passenger. She looks like she weighs maybe 100 pounds soaking wet, but where will she fit? There's a slim gap between Jo and her neighbor; the newcomer clambers over and wedges in sideways. Finally, finally, after six hours of waiting, the driver decides that we're full. He grinds into gear and we chug free of Murun, Mongolia—capital of the country's northernmost province—toward the remote village of Tsagaan Nuur, near the Russian border.

After thirty minutes of paved road, we veer abruptly onto a dirt two-track winding into the hills. Jo's husband, Sean, who finished a Peace Corps assignment here in 2007, grins knowingly at Jo and me. "*Jiiinkheeene*," he comments wryly, drawing out the Mongolian word. *Jinkhene* translates roughly as authentic, or old school. But it can best be defined by what follows.

The Purgon bounces and shudders: the passengers brace arms against seats and one another's knees, occasionally knocking heads.

The Purgon grows steadily chillier: the passengers produce a laptop and memory stick and put together a compilation of Mongolian power ballads that the driver plays on repeat for the next twelve hours.

The Purgon bogs in the mud: the passengers tumble out and push, sprinting in all directions when it lurches free at high speed.

Through it all, everyone smiles, everyone laughs. There's something almost tender about the ease with which strangers drowse on one another's shoulders through the night. Shepherd slumps against meaty policeman; meaty policeman slumps against Sean; Sean, wincing, flattens his six-foot-four-inch frame against the Purgon wall and my feet, which I had propped up to keep my knees from cramping.

The Mongolians are better at this than us.

In my early twenties, I was in a similar situation on a Greyhound bus between Kansas City and Denver. When the sleeping teenage girl next to me began drooling on my shoulder, I felt not tenderness but silent, half-homicidal rage.

Now, though, watching these strangers touch each other as casually as friends, I feel differently. Beyond the smeared windows stretches one of the most sparsely populated landscapes in the world. There are no fences, and little interrupts the gentle roll of the steppe besides patches of dark trees and congregations of plump sheep, yaks, and horses. Felt roundhouses called *gers*—the traditional homes of pastoral nomads—appear now and then like white buttons stitched haphazardly onto rumpled green fabric. Sean has told us about the nomads' generosity, how they will offer even unexpected visitors salted yak-milk tea, food, a bed. And I've read of the blizzards and subzero cold that pummel people here each winter. Maybe, I think, in all this beautiful, brutal vastness, a tiny enclosure that brings the world to a human scale is to be shared, not defended. How else would anyone survive in such a place?

When I left for the three-week summer trip to Mongolia, my friend Rob—who had been in the Peace Corps there with Sean—joked that I'd love it, since I basically already lived in Mongolia. He was referring to Paonia, Colorado, a town of fifteen hundred on the rural Western Slope of the Rockies, where I had spent the past six years. While Jo and other friends I grew up with in Boulder, Colorado, moved on to New York or Los Angeles, Boston or Seattle, I had edged downward in town size and upward in acres of open space, from Walla Walla, Washington, to a series of small mountain towns back in our home state.

I was chasing a feeling I had one summer during college, when Jo and I took a day trip to Rocky Mountain National Park. We pulled off the road above treeline and sprinted to an overlook, racing a thunderstorm. Staring across the tundra-velveted swaybacks of retreating peaks, I knew with uncharacteristic certainty that I wanted to settle in their midst. When a permanent job opened in Paonia a few years later, I saw my chance at last.

I imagined my new life would resemble the 1990s TV show *Northern Exposure*, about the quirky fictional town of Cicely, Alaska. Maybe I was Maggie, the hot-yet-rough-around-the-edges bush pilot, self-sufficient to a fault. True to my fantasy, I spent my free time exploring desert buttes, wandering solo through aspen groves and canyons with a heavy pack, picking my way up to the Continental Divide to peer into glacier-hewn drainages. Once, I looked up from washing dishes to see a moose wander past my kitchen window, smack in the middle of town, just like in the show's opening credits. She was loose-jointed and gangly in that way moose have, and I followed her down the alley, ducking out of sight when her head swiveled my way.

Unlike my fantasy, though, I was desperately lonely. I worked late and came home to an empty house. The isolation of my cat, locked indoors to keep her from murdering birds, seemed a bleak metaphor for my own life. "Give it a year," my parents said helpfully when, curled in a ball on the porch swing, I called them one night. "Maybe it will get better."

Better, I repeated to myself, hiking alone to the highest point on the rim of the Black Canyon southwest of town. Storms brewed over the piñon-studded horizon, unreachable across the canyon's steep maw and its faint roar of whitewater. Who was I kidding? I wasn't *Northern Exposure's* Maggie. I was the show's Dr. Fleischman—a citified know-it-all, bumbling through a working-class community and a landscape he didn't understand. As thunder rumbled closer, I hurried toward lower ground. There was a crack, an explosion of stars, and I found myself sprawled in the trail, blinking stupidly up at a fat juniper branch. Lightning? No. With my head bent in thought, I had run straight into a tree. I gingerly touched my scalp; my fingers came back smeared with blood.

Anthropologists say Euro-Americans like me tend to expect more personal space than people from many other cultures. But far from crowded cities, lost in western Colorado's wild jumble of mountains and mesas, I'd begun to want *less* personal space, not more. I wanted someone to share it with me.

It's veiled, white-lit dawn when Jo, Sean, and I spill blinking from the Purgon in Tsagaan Nuur, where our hostess, Ulzii, greets us at her compound of tourist *gers*. Some other Peace Corps contacts told us she could arrange for us to travel even farther north, into some of Mongolia's remotest country. We have our hearts set on the taiga, where an ethnically distinct people called the Dukha, also known as the Tsaatan, make their living herding reindeer and, increasingly, accommodating visitors like us. We wander blearily around Tsagaan Nuur's scatter of buildings, buying food for the week from rickety log cabin groceries, securing the last of our permits from a military outpost. It takes a few hours and another cross-country Purgon ride for Ulzii to find the guide she has in mind.

He's a wiry fellow named Batdelger, with steep cheekbones shaded under a ball cap. Ulzii says we'll be able to stay with his aunt in the eastern taiga. But first, he has to wrap up the day with his sheep. An hour passes, then two. His children practice their English on us and demonstrate how to bottle-feed a spindly-legged foal. We ask Batdelger's wife how we will make the long horseback ride to the Dukha camp before dark, and she gently ribs us about our impatience—*tourists!*—then pours more tea.

The horses that Batdelger finally rounds up are tiny and strong-headed, and Sean, atop a chestnut stallion, resembles a top-heavy centaur with a small and rebellious set of horse parts. My horse isn't much more accommodating. For his clumsiness, I name him Mr. Umbles, after the symptoms of hypothermia you learn in wilderness medicine—mumbles, fumbles, tumbles. In revenge, Mr. Umbles drops suddenly to his front knees in a marsh, nearly pitching me headfirst into the mosquito-clouded shrubbery. I call him "Utaa" after that—"smoke" in Mongolian, for his dappled gray coloring—hoping this show of respect will dampen his urge to kill me.

Sometime around nine P.M., Batdelger points out a low, doorless building where we can rest for the night. Sean asks in Mongolian if there's shelter farther on. Batdelger says yes. We still feel good, and so continue up a valley shaggy with high grass and willow. Black stands of conifer climb its slopes to the noses and knuckles of mountaintops, which peek down like poorly concealed spies. The low sun paints Jo's face gold as she turns in the saddle to smile at me.

We dismount on a spit where two streams meet. I glance around—there's a well-used fire ring, but no structures. Before I left the States, I complained to Sean that I was having trouble finding room in my pack for camping equipment. He told me I could leave that gear behind: We would be staying with families in their homes. But that is not how things will work tonight. "Does he know we don't have sleeping bags?" I ask Sean. Sean turns to Batdelger, and they speak briefly. Sean turns back to us. "This is it," he says.

Batdelger looks exasperated. Had he known we were so poorly provisioned, he could have brought a tent, he explains calmly. Or pots to cook our dehydrated food. But somehow those details got lost in Ulzii's negotiations, or in the gap between Sean's days as a fluent speaker and the considerable amount of Mongolian words that have come back to him since his return. We settle down for a poor meal around a handful of blazing twigs. The bread we bought turns out to be rancid, but with enough Nutella on it, you almost can't tell. We pass around peas, spooning directly from the can. I collect our plastic bottles and fill them in the stream, then pull out our SteriPEN to purify the water. It feels awfully light. I test the button. Nothing. Then I check the. . . . I smile meekly at my friends. "No batteries," I say, holding up the empty chamber.

As the last light fades, Batdelger stalks off with his short saddle pad to find a place to sleep. We collect our own pads in tense silence, then poke through the trees until we settle on a lumpy but soft deposit of needles. Even wrapped in every piece of clothing we have, it is a cold and miserable night. Jo is the smallest, so we sandwich her in the middle. She attaches to my back like a hungry lamprey, and Sean to hers. When we turn over, we do so in unison, unwilling to give up each other's heat. My feet grow numb, and I flex my stiff hands. I imagine Utaa, hobbled in the meadow below, laughing. *Who's Mr. Umbles now*, he would say in Mongolian.

How do we come to belong anywhere? One answer is that we find each other.

In stressful alpine environments, plants grow and reproduce better near other plants. Some animals, when threatened by predators, clump together in larger groups. Humans are among the most spectacularly social species on the planet, perhaps in part because the more cooperative among our ancestors were more likely to thrive in a difficult and dangerous world. Life is "not just a struggle for survival," as mathematician and biologist Martin Nowak put it. "It is also, one might say, a snuggle for survival."

And in Paonia, I began to piece together a sort of tribe—at work, at pickup ultimate Frisbee games. A new roommate quickly became a dear friend. An intern waded with me to an islanded bridge in the town's flooded river to see the stars. A man asked me to dance at a bar, kept ahold of me the whole night, then surprised me with a kiss when I moved to leave.

My folks were right: These small accumulations of welcome can and do happen wherever we land, if given time. But with time, I also learned how different they can feel in a small town. In that ocean of open country, Paonia came to seem a sort of life raft—sharpening and clarifying the connections I had, and forging new ones I would never have had otherwise. The passengers aboard were who they were; I could not silo in only with people who shared my interests, my age, my background. I still wandered in the hills, but my sense of hopeless drift stopped. These were the shoulders I could sleep on, the knees I could brace against. And I would not have chosen different ones.

The curly-haired clerk at the hardware store, a man in his sixties, let me split his firewood, more for the company than out of necessity. He made me lasagna in return, told me about trails where I could see more moose, and showed me how to use a chainsaw so I could help him buck rounds from blown-down aspens on the mesa north of town. I fell in love with the rogue kisser from the bar—a talented carpenter who was as broken-hearted as he was dear. He took me swimming in the river, tattooed one of my drawings on his skin, invited me to hard-drinking parties with local kids who opened their doors to me as if I weren't an outsider. One day, he showed up unannounced at my office, covered head to toe in concrete dust, and gave me a flower he'd twisted out of baling wire on his break.

There was the friend who hadn't learned to read until he was a teenager, and yet could make his own biodiesel and fix anything, who never charged you what his labor was worth and always had wine and chocolate in his truck in case you wanted to watch a movie. The former large-animal vet who tenderly handled your pets and never charged enough, either. The volunteers who ran the ambulance service, ferrying wheezing old ladies thirty miles down the two-lane highway to the nearest hospital. The friends who hunted and shared their bounty. The single moms who watched each other's kids. The head of the local environmental group who seemed to take on everyone else's wounds—including mine, when my carpenter's broken heart broke my own.

There was darkness in that bright place, too—alcoholism, drugs, deep political divides, crippling poverty, unacknowledged racism. People died or were terribly injured in drunk-driving accidents. During one quarrel, a man threatened his inebriated friend with a shotgun, accidentally firing it into his belly. An ugly divorce ended in a violent murder on the train tracks, just blocks from my house.

The night before that happened, the not-yet-murderer had bought drinks for some of my friends at the local brewery—a tiny former church that filled to standing-room-only on cold winter nights. It was a macabre twist on Paonia's stewpot closeness: With so few places to gather, everyone went to the same places, the same potlucks, the same Thursday-night dance parties and concerts in the park.

It was not that these things were good, though they often were. It was that we craved their energy, craved other people: The emptiness around us pushed us into one another's arms. Once there, I discovered just how many different kinds of people I could love—both for their weaknesses and their strengths.

Eventually, the light returns, first blue, then the same honey-eyed hue that lit Jo's face the previous evening, turning each glossy willow leaf into a candle flame. Sean creaks up from our row of saddle pads and starts a new campfire at the edge of the forest. I follow its smoke down the hill past where Batdelger tends the horses, and fill the same plastic bottles from the same stream. We smile and nod our heads in greeting, and he follows me back to the others. There is the same rancid bread and Nutella, the same dried fruit and nuts. But things have shifted somehow. Today, we have the empty pea can, and I fill it with water and place it in the coals to boil, then brew black tea in my thermos. As the sun climbs, we pass it from hand to hand, each cradling it for a moment to warm our fingers, our faces. Then a long sip, and on to the next person. Outside our tiny circle of warmth, the taiga spreads away, gorgeous and aloof; inside, the long night's chill melts from our bones.

The Dukha village, when we finally arrive, is like something from a dream. The lichen grows spongy and ankle deep. Canvas teepees called *urts* spread across the basin, and reindeer the color of snow and earth meander past errant satellite dishes, their tendons clicking over their anklebones like those of their caribou cousins. When it rains, people watch Korean soap operas. When it doesn't, the kids stand in a circle outside listening to "Moves Like Jagger" and other pop music while punting a volleyball, or ride out on reindeer to herd the rest of the reindeer back to camp. The women milk the animals multiple times a day, using pails of the thick, white liquid for cheese and tea. They roll out their own noodles, make bread in the coals of their fires. The men throw guns on their backs and ride off for days. Their resourcefulness, their practical use of both tradition and tech, is both utterly foreign and strangely familiar.

Punsal, Batdelger's wizened aunt, cackles over our shyness, our wide-eyed appraisal of the place, and, with the three of us sharing her extra bed, her own joking speculation about which of us women is the real wife. We carry water and cook for her, and she chain-smokes cigarettes rolled on pages torn from a book that Sean surmises is a Mongolian play. My birthday falls in that week, and after Jo and I have returned from a hike, Punsal taps me on the shoulder with a wide, toothless grin, and produces a bouquet of tiny orange poppies from behind her back. She gestures at the paperback I'm reading, then helps me spread each bloom between its pages with her shaking, deeply lined hands.

A couple of days later, Batdelger collects our horses at dawn to avoid another frigid campout. As we begin to ascend the steep pass that marks the beginning of our journey in reverse, I'm startled to find myself weeping. The taiga mountains, rolling away in broken waves toward Russia, bear a heartbreaking resemblance to the peaks that first called me into

Colorado's rural backwaters. This trip marks the end of my time there: In my last years in Paonia, I had realized that I was still on my way someplace else, though I wasn't sure where. Once home in the U.S., I will try life in a big city, in a different state. The choice feels right, but the knowledge of what I will lose has suddenly cut through me like a knife.

Late that evening, as we pile into the Land Rover that will take us back to Murun, we are mostly quiet. Too exhausted and saddle-sore to contend with another night in an overfull van, we've paid the drivers enough to ensure that we have it to ourselves. Jo and Sean take one bench seat, I take another, and we toast each other with Tiger Beer, a weak, American-style lager that seems to fit this final surrender to our weak, Euro-American constitutions. I use mine to wash down a Dramamine tablet, and we retreat into our separate cubbies and ourselves.

As I float in a druggy stupor, I smile through the rear window at the long line of peaks, which cradle the sunset sky in their jagged fingers. But something still isn't right, and at a petrol stop, we fix it. It takes only a few minutes to fold the back seats flat. Then, we curl up beside each other with Jo in the middle, and go to sleep at last.

Sarah Gilman is a freelance writer and editor based in Portland, Oregon, where she still has plenty of awkward, bumbling Dr. Fleischman moments despite leaving the hinterlands. Her work has appeared in High Country News, Hakai Magazine, Smithsonian *and others.*

♬ ♬ ♬

Stray Cat Strut

Two sisters slink down Cuba's alleys, looking for cats.

*I*t's January and I'm in Havana for a week, sipping moji-tos by a rooftop pool, dancing in the streets to *son* music, and eating *ropa vieja*, which literally means "old clothes" but tastes delicious. Fidel is still alive, though everyone is discussing how he'll surely die sooner than later. "As will we," joke my travel companions, who are all thirty to forty years older than me. They are especially intrigued by the crumbling Jewish cemeteries our tour guide keeps tak-ing us to. "Look, David! That's what I want," says a New Yorker named Barbara, pointing to a simple white marble headstone.

I've come to Cuba with my sister, Julie, and our dad—and the Siegels and the Rosenblatts and the Rosenthals: it's a bus tour of seniors from the Boca JCC, and I have my mom's fear of cats to thank for it.

There are cat people and there are dog people—and then there is my mother. She once brought home an aging Wheaten Terrier and tried to be a dog person, but it didn't really pan out. The rest of her life she's spent being actively anti-cat.

Not in a pro-bird way. But, like the Kiwi economists who call for the elimination of cats to protect New Zealand's wildlife, or those freaks who want to poison stray kittens with Tylenol, my mother, too, wants a world free of felines.

As for the proliferation of cat cafés from Osaka to Oakland, my mother would never enter, let alone order take-out from, these establishments if they were the last food source on Earth.

It's not that she's worried about being mauled or scratched or even sneezy. The sixty-six-year-old woman is *terrified* that a little kitty will "rub up against [her] leg."

Or worse: land next to her schnitzel at an outdoor restaurant in Tel Aviv. I remember it clearly. My mother standing on her chair, arms flailing, tears gushing, mascara smearing. "Do something, Danny!" she frantically screamed at my father. *"Do something!!!!!!"* I was fifteen and wanted to skulk away.

Nothing objectively traumatic ever transpired between my mother and cats. It all started, she says, with the hedges in Jersey City, New Jersey, where she grew up. "I'd be walking home from school, and the alley cats would jump out of nowhere!" she recalls. "At night, their screeches sounded like wailing babies."

By high school, her fear had unfurled into a full-on phobia. Her best friend had two cats. "Get this," my mom tells me now. "One was named Pussen. And the other was Boots. You know, like Puss 'N Boots. *How gross is that?*"

"Ughh. Disgusting," agrees her mom, my ninety-four-year-old grandmother. "I can't even watch them on commercials," she says, wincing. I recently learned that *her* mother, my great-grandmother, felt the same way. Turns out, *ailurophobia* is the closest thing we have to a family heirloom.

My mother was a real estate broker. I remember listening to her make appointments to show houses. "Now, are there any *cats?*" she'd routinely ask, twisting the kitchen phone cord around her finger. She lost more than a few listings.

Finally, in 1992, she went to see a shrink, who tried his best, but unfortunately he wasn't as successful as the Russian hypnotist who'd cured her addiction to cigarettes.

Which is why I got to go to Cuba.

My parents were packed and ready to go—until Mom Googled "Cuba and cats" and discovered that Havana has a "severe" stray cat problem.

In the Bahamas, they crept outside her vacation condo. In Marbella, Spain, she'd seen "*hundreds* of cats *dripping* from the roof" of her hotel.

"I will not go through that again, Rachel," she said, when I told her she was being ridiculous.

"Now you're not going to travel?" I asked, totally annoyed.

"Just not to Cuba," she said. "Or to Puerto Rico. I won't go anywhere with narrow streets. Then there's no escape," she explained.

But wandering narrow streets in foreign countries is *the best*, I explained to my mother. Not if you encounter *a cat*, she countered.

"It's typically the Spanish-speaking countries that have the cats," she continued.

Uh, O.K. What about San Francisco, where, I remind her, a homeless man cares for dozens of feral cats in the woods across the street from my house, where her grandchildren also live?

"Well, I still have to visit you. But I'm always watchful. Ever vigilant." (Homeland Security, new hire?)

"You really should see someone," I said. "Your phobia has officially taken over your life."

"No it hasn't," she said. "I'm fine. So what if I walk in the middle of the street instead of the sidewalk? So what if I don't go into antique stores? So I miss Havana. There's always Helsinki. I Googled it. No cats."

So Julie and I joined the JCC senior bus tour while Mom happily stayed at home, secure in her Florida gated golf community where she occasionally sits on her back patio with a squirt gun "just in case a cat comes by."

"I understand your mother," says her friend Estelle Siegel as we stand in Plaza Vieja surrounded by pigeons pecking at breadcrumbs. "I feel the same way about birds." She pinches her face and inches closer to her husband. "It's the flapping."

As we wander Havana's (indeed narrow) streets, inhaling the scent of cigars and eating in al fresco *paladares*, we're on the lookout for cats. Motivated not by fear, but by *schadenfreude*. Look, mom! No cats! We want to come home gloating.

And, lo and behold, we see not one. Instead we see a shell of a once-regal Caribbean capital, gorgeous Baroque architecture begging to be restored. A moving museum of '57 Chevys and '54 Fords; peeling billboards advertising the perks of socialism; butt-length skirts paired with six-inch heels; bored expressions and blasé servers; leathery men smoking on stoops and lipsticked ladies topped in tangles of fake flowers. And dancers and artists and musicians, so many musicians, shaking maracas, banging on drums, belting "Guantanamera."

But, serves me right, we see plenty of stray dogs. Scrappy, ugly, hungry strays. They're everywhere. Tottering along the Prado. Creeping out from decrepit tenements. Sprawling, nipples-up, on sun-beat sidewalks. *Stalking* me on my morning runs along the *malecón*. I spot one lurking ahead and dart across the multi-lane street, weaving between old pink convertible Buicks with barely functioning brakes.

I realize I might feel the same way about stray dogs overseas as my mother does about house cats across the street. In Costa Rica, I was once chased by a muscular mutt while on a run. I was scared out of my mind but ducked into a local shop and survived. In Mexico, we pulled over to pee in an empty dirt lot—and all of a sudden a herd of lean, mean stray dogs came charging at us from all corners. We got in and slammed the doors of the rental car just in time. But Bhutan was the worst. I believe I saw more dogs than people. One terrifying creature, spotted like a leopard, nipped at my heels and still haunts me in my sleep.

But my thing about stray dogs is justified, right? I mean, dogs are *dogs*. And cats are just . . . *cats*. My fear isn't something that interferes with my life. I admit, I haven't been back to Costa Rica since The Chase, but that's only because I discovered Nicaragua is better.

On our final morning in Cuba, Julie and I stroll back to Plaza Vieja for the best coffee in town. School kids run around squealing, and tourists funnel paper cones of peanuts into their mouths. A bassist sets up with her band. A curvy woman sporting bright blue spandex and a head full of plastic curlers struts by.

As my sister and I swat flies and sip our *café caliente,* we laugh about how ridiculous it is that our mom's cat phobia landed us in Cuba.

A black-and-white kitten with cloudy gray eyes and a thimble-sized nose tiptoes toward us. Soon, a fat cat appears out of nowhere, as if it rose from beneath the cobblestone, and crawls over to its baby.

"Look, they're cuddling," Julie points out. "That's cute," she says, shifting her chair to the left. The cats nuzzle and purr and move closer. As we rehash the highlights of our trip, I feel soft fur gently graze my ankle. Like grass in a summer breeze. I sling my camera over my shoulder, and without saying a word, my sister and I stand in unison, leaving our glass mugs half full, and slowly walk away.

☙ ☙ ☙

Rachel Levin is a San Francisco-based journalist. Her work has been published in The New Yorker, The New York Times, Lucky Peach, Outside, *and* Sunset, *where she was a senior travel editor. Her book* Look Big: And Other Tips for Surviving Elephant Encounters of All Kinds *will be published by TenSpeed/Random House in Spring 2018.*

LINDSEY CRITTENDEN

Pool of Memories

She swims through the past.

Every day I follow a narrow, black line. Up and back, sixty times. I swim the length of the Phoebe Apperson Hearst Memorial Gymnasium for Women on the U.C. Berkeley campus. It's a circle lane so the line seems one, continuous, a strip of black marble streaked with orange and gold veins, the same marble that climbs the walls at either end, so black that at dusk I have to lift my head a few strokes before the wall so I don't slam into it. As I touch one end of the pool and the other, as I pull myself up one side of the lane and back the other, I think about what it means to love a place and leave it, and to come back and love it for entirely new reasons.

I was worried, moving back to Berkeley after twelve years, because I have a tendency to memorialize places, enshrining them so that they become more about the past than the present. As a child, I would wait until we were all packed for home and everyone else was in the car, and then I'd make up some excuse to go back into an empty vacation cabin or rental condo so that I could walk through the rooms my family had inhabited for a week (or two days) and freeze them in memory. Berkeley had meant so much to me—my college years, close friendships, falling in love—that I'd expected to find it the same as I'd left it, fixed by nostalgia. I expected to find a ghost of myself still here, haunting my old boarding house and apartments, the corner in Doe Library where I liked to study, Café Roma. I expected to see Wurster Hall still as the Other Woman—a name I'd given the building for the nights my boyfriend, an architecture major, chose the company of its ninth-floor drafting tables over mine. Instead, I found Hearst Pool. And as I come here every day, to swim back and forth, I see that leaving a place doesn't have to mean leaving myself behind.

For most of my years away from Berkeley, I lived in New York City, where the place that came to mean the most to me was the West Village at dusk. It was there I fell in love with the city, walking home from my first job through the late-afternoon light that warmed the cobblestone streets and the brick townhouses. When I was leaving New York, I would stop in the middle of packing to sit in front of my window, my feet propped on the sill, and watch the Hudson River go silver and then gunmetal and then black, the warehouses a few blocks uptown turning ruddy from the setting sun. I needed to take the memory of that view with me, so that after I left I could pull it out like a snapshot and remind myself of the independence and adulthood I'd found in New York, as if these things belonged more to the city than to me.

As it turned out, I would worry very little about adulthood and independence because my brother died a few months after I left New York, and grief took up all the space it could find. I was back in California then, living in Davis, and in those moments when the walls of my apartment could not contain me, I would walk the fields along the road running west of town, screened by a row of walnut trees, so that no one could see my face or hear my screams.

I walked those fields every day, as the moon climbed higher and grew fatter and thinned again, as the sun stayed up longer so I could leave later and still see it set, as I traded my parka and wool hat for a Levi's jacket and then no wrap at all, as over my head geese honked and crows whirred and cawed. I walked through tule fog so thick it was like being inside a Monet painting, all grays and mauves, and then the wet muck of winter gave way to small purple wildflowers, lush miner's lettuce, and the parched, cracked dirt of summer, and I walked past yellow bands of sunflowers shimmering in heat that still radiated from the road at eight P.M. I walked as grief lifted from me, and I felt excitement at teaching my first class and joy at a story going well and eagerness at meeting a man I liked, and I walked when grief dropped over me again. I rushed around all afternoon my last day in Davis, not as much because the movers were arriving the next morning at nine but so I'd be home in time to go for my last walk when the light was best. The fields had become as important to me as the Hudson River, a reliquary to the emotions they'd witnessed, and I could not leave without saying goodbye.

Back in 1984, one week before I left Berkeley, on one of those perfect September evenings, I went with three friends to hear James Taylor at the Greek Theater. I didn't want any of it—the friendships, the sunset, the music—to end. But the reason I love Berkeley now isn't because the view from the Greek Theater is unchanged, or because I can point out the parking lot where my boyfriend and I first held hands or the window of the frat house where I lost my virginity. If you were to ask me why I love Berkeley now, I would tell you about swimming at Hearst Pool.

For those of us who grow up klutzy and awkward, afraid of the ball and chosen last for every team, who spent recess hiding in the rest room or the back corner of the library, swimming holds a special power. Noncompetitive in nature—at least in sports—and aliens in the land of hand-eye coordination, we at last find a place where our arms and legs belong to us, where we can move with grace and even something like athleticism. This makes of us swimming fiends, awed and a little in love with our newly capable bodies, and we come to the pool each day rain or shine with the ardor of the converted. Last spring, after surgery, it wasn't until I was back in the pool that I felt I was starting to heal.

Swimming has given me something I take with me wherever I go, from the Ys of Park Slope and midtown Manhattan to the overheated public pool in Rome where I needed a notarized letter from my physician to enter to the serene, marbled luxury of Hearst—where, if I've timed it right, the bells of the Campanile are pealing as I step out on the deck. The laws of swimming are simple: you stop, you'll sink. Breathe at the wrong time, and you'll get water up your nose. Swimming is not about memorializing or staying still; it is about moving without thinking about it. I'm going in a circle, over and over, yes—but I'm progressing from lap number one to lap number thirty, and when I'm done, I've been somewhere.

I will never see a walnut tree without thinking of my brother's death or turn the deadbolt on a vacated apartment without one last peek inside. But now I see the danger of investing too much identity and emotional life in a place. When I heard that a certain fraternity had lost its lease on the grand brick house where I spent many hours I felt shock but also relief, as if the part of me that was still in that small room upstairs could finally get up and go, too. Swimming in Hearst Pool has shown me that moving on doesn't mean abandoning the past as much as claiming the present. Home has meant the Hudson River and the Davis fields, and right now it means a narrow black line I follow up and back, sixty times.

Lindsey Crittenden is the author of The Water Will Hold You: A Skeptic Learns to Pray *and* The View from Below: Stories.

Her essays, articles, and short fiction have appeared and are forthcoming in Cimarron Review, Best American Spiritual Writing, The Washington Post, The New York Times, Image, Bon Appétit, Real Simple, Glimmer Train, *and elsewhere. She lives in San Francisco and has recently traveled to the Sacramento Delta, Tecate (Mexico), Stinson Beach, and the Big Island of Hawaii.*

HOLLY H. JONES

ᘓ ᘓ ᘓ

Spinning in Lahore

She learned the distance between fear and reality.

*B*y the time I realize just how crowded the enclosed courtyard of Babu Shah Jamal shrine is, it's too late to leave. It was too late long before I reached Lahore and this night. Ever since I first read Rumi's poetry, penned a thriller set in Pakistan, and booked my ticket for a five-city trip around this country some call the most dangerous place on Earth, turning back ceased to be an option. I have come alone but, for the evening, I'm with two Pakistani women, their military father, and his four guards. I have a Thursday night date with Pakistan's celebrated *dhol* player Pappu Saeen and, as it turns out, several hundred male fans. Seven chaperones seem about seven hundred too few.

Pappu Saeen has been beating the *dhol*, a double-sided barrel drum, and helping Sufis sink into a trancelike state for years. Once in this ecstatic state, these mystical followers of Islam can achieve a closer connection to Allah. Letting go of earthly concerns and self-consciousness, they may even begin to spin. I can't turn a single circle without stumbling but I love the Sufi tales I've been reading, so I asked my hosts if we could see Pappu Saeen. But as we enter the courtyard, I'm no longer sure he, or anything, is worth the risk I believe I'm taking.

Bodies clog the steps climbing to a cemetery where even more men gather. I see no light-haired people or, aside from my friends, women. I also find no exits save the doorway now behind me. I stumble under the weight of the crowd's gaze and touch my bare head. I left my headscarf in my hotel room, assured by my friend I wouldn't need it. Many in Pakistan will tell me the same. Hyper-aware of the stereotypes set forth about Pakistan and Islam, they want me to see how modern they are. Even as she reassures me head coverings are no longer relevant, the *dupatta* that shields my friend's head flutters in the late night breeze.

She presses me forward. We are heading toward a square of elevated and exposed dirt on the other side of the staring faces. A VIP area, next to the legendary performer, has been reserved for us.

Two men flank Pappu Saeen. As we approach, they step aside. Absent their lateral support, he teeters. I'm reminded of spinning tops, steadiest when in motion or held in place by others.

"When will you begin?" my friend's father asks.

"When the spirit moves me," Pappu Saeen tells him. It's already 12:30.

My friend's father insists on a picture of us. He won't take no for an answer. Because of his top-ranking military status, Pappu Saeen won't either.

The flash goes off. For one merciful moment, I can't see the expressions of the men watching. I can't read what I imagine they're thinking: that I'm the American who gets to stand beside their idol simply because of my nationality. That I'm the American delaying his drumming and their ascent to ecstasy. The day before, the U.S. led a strike in the north-western province and gunned down twenty-one Pakistani innocents instead of the Taliban they were seeking. I'm the American who's invaded yet another cherished space within their country.

My trip began in Karachi. I told people I was staying at the Marriott. They said I was staying in the triangle of diplomatic ties gone bad.

The Marriott is housed in one tip of the triangle. At another tip is Frere Park. Across from it stands a modern concrete, clean-lined structure, undisturbed by cars or people. This is the American Consulate. Once upon a time, these three points cradled a book fair that drew crowds every weekend.

In the aftermath of 9/11, American consulate officials deemed the book fair a potential gathering spot for anti-American interests and insisted it be moved and the surrounding roadways secured for their further protection. Karachi officials complied and redirected the book fair and the traffic away from the triangle its citizens' tax dollars had funded. Not a day of my trip would pass when someone wouldn't speak of the Americans having demanded a beloved institution be moved and gotten their way, despite a complete lack of violence, unrest, or even reckless drivers in the area. Just because they were Americans.

Pappu Saeen and the two men begin striking their *dhols*. The beat and its counter rhythm start slowly. Cheers rise up as the tempo quickens. It is almost one A.M. and the fifth day of Ramadan is upon us.

Some Sufis have complained that these gatherings encourage drugs, not spiritual connections. Spinning should occur when people feel connected enough to Allah to shed their ego and the trappings of an externally focused life. I consider the men sitting on the courtyard walls, lining the stairs from upper quadrangle to lower. How many have come to shed those trappings? How many have come for the far more mundane, earthly pleasure of a show and hashish? Pappu Saeen has reportedly stopped mid-performance when he felt the men had come for the wrong reasons. Tonight, though, he continues to play.

The music moves in waves, daring anyone alive to resist swaying to the beat. A man steps from behind Pappu Saeen and lifts a horn to his mouth. The sound, high and sharp, pierces the *dhol* rhythm to drive it faster. The men around us stand.

Our guards show no concern that they're laughably outnumbered in the event we truly need guarding. I tell myself to trust in their knowledge of the place and people. I have no choice, really.

The horn wails and the *dhols* are sounded ever faster. The audience steps back from Pappu Saeen. Long-haired men in *hoppi* coats step forward.

Each finds his way into the rhythm. Some warm to it with hand twitches. Others bob their heads in time. Soon a dozen men are shuffling and spinning. Never in my life have I seen men such as them.

I begin to nod to the beat and my hair clip pops. It's held my long blond hair in a tight knot. My hair spills around my face like the rhythm spilling in wave after wave over this crowd. I long for the headscarf I should have brought, even though my friend said I didn't need to cover my head.

I landed in Karachi on a Sunday when most everything was closed. Guidebooks had recommended Clifton Beach, and it never closes, so I asked a Stanford classmate's driver, on loan during my visit, to take me there. He told me to cover my head.

We parked at the water's edge, near fishermen. My white headscarf flapped in the wind, and I stumbled as I climbed onto the seawall. The driver offered me a hand and didn't let go until I was steady on my feet by his side and looking down at the waves crashing into the rocks.

In June 2003, a tanker sank off the coast of Clifton Beach. Fifty thousand tons of crude oil spilled from its hold before the Pakistani authorities could contain the problem. The boat was never retrieved from the sea. Now it was 2008, and oil still leaked through its seams into the city's water.

A wave slammed into the seawall with enough force to shake it beneath our feet. Water splashed black specks onto my arms. My driver began trying to wipe away the black with his hand. I almost drew back in shock, but then remembered he worked for my classmate. Sense of duty trumped the reserve Pakistani men would typically show a woman outside their family.

"Don't worry," I told him.

He swiped at another glob on my wrist, making sure only the edge of his hand touched my skin.

With my white headscarf, I wiped away what I could of the streaks. "It's fine. See?" It wasn't, but I felt bad. For him, for all of us.

Farther down the beach, seven rows of empty chairs—the metal kind with a vinyl cover—lost their legs to the oil-streaked surf again and again. A man stood nearby, waiting to sell seats to those wishing to view the sunset. Boys darted between the rows, never thinking to sit down, never pausing to watch the sun set.

Pappu Saeen and the men in *hoppi* coats shuffle around each other. They spin, he plays, the crowd sways, and the hashish smoke grows thick. Round and round they go. *Tap tap tap* goes my foot.

The electricity dies.

The fans emit a last gasp, and faces remain illuminated in the memory of light just extinguished. When they fade into darkness, my heart stops.

Our guards spring forward.

I freeze.

Everyone else continues swaying.

After an eternity, noise returns in the form of the crowd's roar. They are cheering as the next beat sounds.

One guard places a call and learns this was a planned outage. Load shedding, the cutting off of power by city officials, takes place at various hours throughout Lahore. Most homes and offices have backup generators. This shrine does not.

The crowd doesn't care. They've brought torches, candles, and cigarette lighters. Within minutes, dots of light fill the courtyard. In the flames' light, the hashish smoke cloud can be seen atop the dust cloud the dancers kick up. I can't tell where one ends and the other begins.

There's a Sufi fable, the "Tale of the Sands," I've come to love. A stream making its way from the mountains successfully overcomes every barrier until it reaches the desert. Each time it tries to broach this expanse, the water dries up. A voice inside the stream's depths suggests it can't cross the desert unless it becomes one with the wind. Convinced that crossing the desert in the same way it's crossed every other obstacle is its destiny, the stream ignores the voice.

Pappu Saeen spins faster and stirs the lowest wisps. A man in a *hoppi* coat the color of forest dances toward him. Hair in face, eyes closed, their collision seems fated. At the last second, they spin in opposite directions.

In the dervishes' tale, the stream's internal voice insists it must allow itself to be absorbed by the wind if it wishes to cross the desert. The stream, having never before been absorbed, wishes to remain as it has always been. To give up its individuality is incomprehensible and, once lost, how could it ever be reclaimed? How could the river ever be the same again? But, to its questions, a whisper replies that, otherwise, the earth would soak up its water at the desert's edge. The stream cannot remain the same, unchanged, regardless.

To my left, men pass a smoking Coca-Cola bottle. Several holes in the glass hold cigarettes, and the glow reminds me of the 1970s Coca-Cola commercial. Thousands of Americans held candles, stood in a Christmas-tree formation, and sang about wanting to teach the world to sing. The lyrics loop over and over in my head. I draw in a breath of hashish. I crave a drag on that bottle to mute the American commercial in my mind.

"Who is the terrorist—the Pakistani farmer minding his own business or the American soldier who flies five thousand miles, comes into our country, and shoots our women and children? The American. That's who."

Hearing these words, my armed guide sat back and crossed his arms. We were in the Peshawar Pearl Continental with my escort, a farmer who had been recruited to help me—the American friend of a boss's nephew's boss. It was my eighth day in Pakistan. The day before, a suicide bomber had detonated his explosives nearby. Days before that, a U.S. drone had been dropped not much farther away.

This farmer had shown me the utmost courtesy as he escorted me through Peshawar at his friend's request. He had called ahead to every place we would pass, alerting locals that he was bringing an American but she was O.K. He had gotten me into a gun bazaar after hours and calmed the guards bearing AK-47s. Now he wanted to engage in a discussion about American-Pakistani relations. To engage in a calm, dispassionate discussion was the least I could do.

"Who is the terrorist?" he asked again, tapping his empty plate.

The other two men—my guards—stared at the remains of their lunches. Though Muslim, they claimed a traveler's exemption from Ramadan's rules. I was trying to fast.

"Am I making sense?" he asked.

I'd told people back home that it was the one "crazy" about whom I'd have to worry. Not petty crimes and not mugging. Now, in the hotel known as Spy Central, where every nook and cranny could be bugged and every move observed, I felt the presence of danger more surely than anywhere else in Pakistan. Perhaps I'd met my "crazy." Perhaps he felt he'd met his, in me.

"The Americans—and, of course, by that I mean your leaders and not you personally."

"Of course," I retorted. That my mouth worked surprised me.

"The Americans are not just terrorists. But bullies, don't you think?"

"Perhaps."

"What do you mean by 'perhaps'?"

"Just that—"

"What?"

The thing I didn't want to say flew out of my mouth. "We may be the bully, but isn't it better to be on good terms with the bully than not?"

It was the wrong thing to say. Wrong, and as pointless as some back home called my curiosity to see up close this country in which I had set a book.

I tried to tell myself I was overly tired and this man was argumentative. I assured myself that, of course, I couldn't think straight for the hair clip that had pressed against my skull for the last eight days, folding my hair over and over itself until it was no more than a suggestion of blond length. If I were thinking straight, I would have kept my mouth shut. But, like the stream that couldn't cross the desert in the Sufi tale, keeping quiet would have been as much an answer as the retort I'd delivered.

My guide chuckled in the way people do when nothing remotely funny has transpired. I reached for my wallet and asked for the check. The man who would not break his fast would not let me pay.

In the hour Pappu Saeen performs without electricity, a boy fans the smoke and heat off us. My friend begs her father to give him some rupees.

"He must be tired," she tells him. "He's so young."

The boy's expression reveals no fatigue or expectation of money. My friend's father's hands remain tucked in his pocket. The boy continues to fan our faces.

At least twenty men spin and shuffle in the courtyard's center. *Hoppi* coats billow around them, and an image of the Southern belles dancing like there's no Civil War afoot in *Gone With the Wind* comes to mind.

Light flares nearby. I see another empty Coca-Cola bottle, its soda long gone, aglow. A young man places his mouth over the bottle, and his cheekbones stand out, shadow against light, as he inhales. He lifts his head from the bottle. Our eyes meet. I look away first.

After visiting Clifton Beach my first afternoon in Pakistan, I wound up in the living room of a friend's friend's friend. She and others drank beers and smoked while I nursed a coffee and tried to stay awake. They talked about Pakistan for my benefit. I considered the oil tanker's residue on my skin and focused as best I could.

My hostess, a Pakistani writer of some renown, told me she'd published her recent book in English only.

"Why not Urdu as well?" I asked.

"Why bother?" She grinned at the others and lit another cigarette. "I ended my decade-long boycott of the United States last year."

I opened my mouth to ask why, but thought better of it. I was missing too many pieces of this puzzle to risk offending with a bad question that first day.

"Be prepared to bear witness," she told me. "You'll have to. For your country."

I wasn't yet tired of bearing witness. The tales of Pakistanis who'd repatriated after one too many encounters with an overzealous American police officer hadn't yet sickened me. And I'd not yet learned of the Pakistani who broke down and wept in the U.S. embassy after they refused him the visa needed to complete his doctoral work at the American university where he'd already spent six years. I wanted to bear witness. "I don't mind."

They fell silent. Cigarettes were smoked down to stubs. New ones were lit.

"Expect questions from the people you meet," she told me. "Lots of them."

I hadn't yet been questioned in the Peshawar Pearl Continental and begun to wrestle so acutely with the answers.

We are moving back through the crowd we navigated hours before. The dancers continue spinning and Pappu Saeen continues drumming. No longer scared or perhaps too high on secondhand smoke to care, I want to stay. As the tide of the group carries me away from the swirling *hoppi* coats and drumbeats, my eyes search for something on which to focus in the blur the night has become.

A man standing still amidst the now frenzied dancing.

His beard is shot with gray, and his *shalwar kameez* glows white. His hands are clasped over his heart, and he stares up at the night sky. The dancers shuffle around him, but never draw his gaze.

Sufis believe that the elements—air, water, fire, and earth—constitute four pillars holding the roof of heaven in place even as they destroy each other. The pillar of water can ruin that of fire. Air can banish earth. Creation is thus built on opposites. The man whose eyes reach for the night sky while his hands hold his heart seems encircled by these opposing elements. Can he, standing still and uniting opposites, create some truth that those of us spinning at three A.M. and those of us traveling halfway around the world in search of the story behind their story can't?

Through breaks in the crowd, we move. My friends marvel at how wonderful this was. I reconsider my anxiety, flaring as often as the cigarette lighters did in the last three hours. While Pappu Saeen was letting the spirit move him, I'd been waiting for everything bad that could happen to happen.

These men who watched me so intently earlier don't even notice me now. Their eyes follow Pappu Saeen. The still man's eyes hold the moon. I am the one staring this time.

Some of them hate Americans. More believe Americans hate and misunderstand them. But no one wants me to bear witness to their stories this night. I am the one now truly ready to bear witness.

The still man's hands remain clasped at his heart as if what he sees in the moon might otherwise burst it and him into a million glowing embers. Does he believe he holds up the roof of heaven by not spinning and letting fly the elements, the body, and the consciousness? Would he, like too many of us, stand at the edge of the desert and refuse to believe his resistance to change was about to transform him as surely as allowing himself to be lifted and carried above it would?

The drums. They continue to draw in the crowd, even as my hosts believe we are leaving their call, the people, and the night behind us. Even as I understand all too clearly, with no head covering to shield my gaze and no fear left to cloud my mind, that none of us ever truly leaves a people or country behind.

Holly H. Jones has been published in several print and online journals, and has written two column series, "Dispatches from the Anacostia" and "Dispatches from the Capital," for McSweeney's

Internet Tendency. *Working closely with Dave Eggers, she co-founded Washington's 826DC (initially known as Capitol Letters Writing Center) in 2008 and remains very close to the larger 826 National family and its network. She was awarded the TED Challenge Prize for her work to fulfill Dave's TED Prize wish and is a long-standing member of that community as well. She holds an MBA from Stanford and an MFA from Vermont College, and she is the only Chicago-based member of the San Francisco Writers' Grotto.*

♫ ♫ ♫

The End of Something

The best goodbyes are the quickest.

"Mom?" my eighteen-year-old son says from the passenger seat of our rental car. "Have you ever driven drunk?"

I glance over at him, phone perpetually in hand, light brown hair hanging into his gray-colored eyes.

"Well," I begin, insanely about to give him an honest answer, "when I was eighteen, it was legal to drink in New Jersey. So it's possible."

"Oh. My. God," he says, thumbs working overtime on his phone. "I'm telling Dad."

I turn my attention back to the bug-spattered window of the rental and wonder what my ex-husband, a man I count as one of my closest friends, will make of this information.

"While you're at it," I toss Alex my phone, "why don't you text *my* dad and tell him?"

As we drive through the sun-struck landscape of the Arizona desert—a place so arid, I can feel my contact lenses drying up even inside the air-conditioned car—my son lectures me on the dangers of drunk driving. After twenty or so uninterrupted miles, I turn to him.

"You realize we're talking about something that *might* have happened forty years ago," I say. "I think the statute of limitations is up on this one."

I pull off the highway into the nearest rest stop.

And though I do not actually have to use the squat adobe restroom on the other side of the blindingly bright parking lot, and the temperature gauge on the rental's dashboard reads 115, making me fear that the moment I step outside my hair will catch on fire, I open the door and get out of the nice cool car. Because I need five—no ten—minutes away from my son.

Inside the stifling restroom, I cannot for the life of me remember why I thought driving Alex to college, a fourteen-hour journey from San Francisco to Tucson, was a good idea. I might have been operating under the delusion that the trip would give me the opportunity to impart some final wisdom to him. Provide us with a last chance to do some mother-son bonding.

Instead, my usually charming and witty son has used this time to point out every character flaw and personal failing I possess. Leaving me with an unmotherly desire to push him out of the rental's passenger-side door, stranding him in this parched and barren landscape.

Unable to remain inside the suffocating women's rest room any longer, I return to the car, where I discover that Alex has changed the wallpaper and most of the settings on my phone.

"You're too close to that truck!" my son screams at me, the second we are back on the road.

"That's why my foot is already *on* the brake," I tell him.

For the next fifty miles Alex keeps up a running commentary on my driving. From the position of my hands on the

wheel—"too low"—to the way I turn my head when changing lanes—"too weird," too weird?—to the speed at which
I'm driving—"too fast *and* too slow"—which, considering the
fact we've been on cruise control this entire time seems to defy
some fundamental law of physics.

As we approach the outskirts of Tucson, the bossy voice
of the navigation app on my phone begins to direct us to our
downtown hotel—though to be fair, by this point, that voice
sounds a lot less bossy than it used to. The route is a series of
quick lefts and rights, and I've got the phone propped up in
the cup holder so I can glance at the map.

"Stop that!" Alex says, grabbing the phone up and out of
my line of sight. "It's dangerous."

We miss a left, and then a right. It takes us an extra half-
hour to find our hotel. When we do, I go directly to the bar
and down two margaritas in quick succession.

The next day, we drop Alex's duffle bags in his new dorm
room and head out to buy him a bike to ride around campus.
Because I have suggested we try one of the bicycle shops near
the university, my son insists we go to Target.

Everyone, apparently, has had this idea. The most adult-
looking bicycle left on Target's rack has a piece of cardboard
stapled to its spokes that reads, *For riders 5'4" and under.* My
son, who is 5'10", takes the bike off the rack and begins riding
it up and down the toy aisle.

"It's perfect," he calls out as he whizzes by.

His knees splay out to his elbows as he pedals. The only
way he would look normal on this bike is if he were wearing
a clown suit.

"Maybe you want something a little bigger," I venture.

Continuing to ride up and down the aisle, Alex points out
that I know nothing about sizing bicycles, that I have never
known anything about sizing bicycles, and that most likely, I

am incapable of acquiring this skill. As he informs me of this, his eyes appear in danger of rolling out of his head.

The only reason we leave Target without that bike is because I have possession of both the credit card and the car keys.

At the bike shop closest to campus, my son sits on a chair sullenly staring into his phone while I pick out his bike, his helmet, and his lock. It's possible he's sulking about not buying the clown-sized bike. Or it's possible he is sulking about one of the other very many things of which I have no understanding. Either way, I ramble on in a bright, cheery voice that in no way resembles my own to the middle-aged man who is helping me, as if that will somehow prove to him that I am not the mother of the rudest eighteen-year-old on the planet. As my son appears to be glued to both the chair and his phone, the nice bike shop man helps me wrestle Alex's new bicycle into the trunk of the rental.

There is no parking near Alex's dorm, so I drop him off with a pile of the things we bought at Target—clothes rack, hangers, standing lamp.

"I'll go park," I tell him, "and ride back on your bike."

"Thanks so much," he says *in my mind.* "I really appreciate it."

Day Three is a visit to Bed, Bath & Beyond—a trial under any circumstances. But truly unbearable when you are lost somewhere among the fitted sheets and someone is explaining to you that you know nothing about plastic storage bins, are totally clueless when it comes to hampers, and seem to be completely hopeless about shower shoes. Three items, by the way, I would have sworn my son possessed zero information about himself—particularly hampers.

Behind a display of microfiber blankets I spot the sign for the ladies room and again seek refuge in the one place my son cannot follow me.

This, I think, hiding out in a stall, *is the worst trip I have ever taken.* But I know I am wrong about that. The worst trip I have ever taken was the one my ex-husband and I took exactly seventeen years ago when we traveled to Russia to retrieve Alex from a Moscow orphanage.

We probably never should have left for Moscow in the first place. But we already had twenty-five of the twenty-six Russian signatures we needed on our adoption paperwork, and we were eager to hold the little boy we'd first seen in that Moscow orphanage seven months before. The little boy in the blurry Polaroid we'd stuck to our refrigerator with a magnet shaped like St. Basil's Cathedral. A Polaroid I touched every day for luck.

But this was the summer of Russia's first democratic election, and anyone who could have provided that twenty-sixth signature was out of the city, campaigning for Boris Yeltsin. So for nearly a month, we stayed in Moscow. First in a western hotel. Then, as our money ran out, in a Soviet-era hotel. And finally, camping out in our translator's apartment, while she vacationed in Spain on what we'd paid her until we'd been forced to give up her services to save money.

Each day we took the metro to Alex's orphanage, which always smelled of boiling cabbage, and stayed as long as Irina, his caretaker, would allow. Irina dressed in a white lab coat and men's ankle socks, and was responsible for twelve children under the age of two. After we gave up our translator, she took to shouting at us in Russian, seeming to believe that if she spoke loudly and slowly enough, we—like the children in her care—would eventually understand her.

Alex was sixteen months old when we arrived in Moscow. He had dark circles under his eyes and the wispy hair of a cancer patient. I could see that the clothes I'd brought for him—clothes Baby Gap described as for children twelve to eighteen months old—would be much too big.

Most days, when we arrived at the orphanage, we'd find Alex wandering around the big playpen with the other children. Children who had for company only each other and the radio Irina left tuned to a Russian news station. Children who were eerily quiet, who made no sound, even when they fell. Watching them play was like watching television with the sound on mute.

Every afternoon, we left voicemail messages for Yuri, our Russian adoption coordinator. Yuri never answered his phone. He said he was hiding from the Russian mafia, said they were after his money. Although, the way he looked the few mornings we did see him—bleary-eyed and stubble-faced—made us believe it might have been because he was drunk. We'd ask if he'd gotten that twenty-sixth signature yet. If there was someone else we needed to bribe. He'd call back days later to tell us to keep waiting. To say we should have stayed home.

One day, the metro line we took to the orphanage was bombed. Another day, a government official had his fingers blown off in a car explosion. "I hope it wasn't his signing hand," my husband told me. He did not say it like a joke.

The English language newspapers were full of stories about a rival candidate for president—a man who wanted to stop American adoptions of Russian children. Every day he gained a little more in the polls. A few of the papers started predicting he would win.

One night in our hotel room, I tried to convince my husband to kidnap Alex from the orphanage. By that time, Irina was letting us take him into the weedy garden behind the orphanage where we would sit on a rusted-out swing set.

My plan involved a rental car and drugging with cough medicine and driving to Finland. And I think if the uncertainty had gone on any longer, we would have attempted it. Because by then, it wouldn't have felt like kidnapping, it would have felt like rescuing our own child.

But a couple of days later, close to midnight, Yuri called to tell us we'd gotten the twenty-sixth signature. His words were slurred, making it almost impossible to understand him.

The next morning, when Irina made the sign of the cross over Alex's naked body—the orphanage couldn't afford to give away any clothes—and put him in my arms, I told myself, *I am never letting him go.*

But now, seventeen years later, I am letting him go.

I come out of the Bed, Bath & Beyond ladies room and go in search of my son. As I wander the aisles of juicers and duvet covers, I see other eighteen-year-olds rolling their eyes at their parents, telling them they know nothing about thread count or bathroom scales. And it dawns on me that this is yet another rite of passage, as natural—if somewhat less endearing—as when your five-year-old clings to your hand on the first day of kindergarten.

My son is near the registers, pushing a shopping cart filled with plastic drawers.

I see him before he sees me, and for a few seconds I hold back, thinking how nearly impossible it seems that the small boy we taught to walk in the weedy garden of the orphanage has grown into this lanky, gray-eyed almost-man, this person who is more capable than he yet understands. And I suppose that if pointing out all the things I do not know will help him to realize this, I'm willing to allow it.

For exactly twenty minutes more.

We load up the rental with Alex's plastic drawers. Then, because I learned on the first day of kindergarten that the best goodbyes are the quickest, I drive close to Alex's dorm and pull into a bus stop.

"You know you're going to miss me," I say.

"I know," my son replies. It sounds like the most sincere thing he's said since we left San Francisco.

We get out of the car, and I pile the plastic drawers into his arms. Then I reach around them to give him a hug.

The grief hits me ten miles outside of Phoenix. It's as sudden and swift as the thunderstorms that sweep across this desert. And it does not feel very different from Alex's first day of kindergarten, when I sat in a coffee shop for an hour, stunned into silence by how watching my five-year-old walk into his brightly painted classroom without me felt like the end of something.

I drive for ten minutes or so, tears spilling down my face—probably the moistest my skin has been in days—until it occurs to me that what I'm grieving is some version of myself, that woman who spent so much of her life being a mother.

I look over at the empty passenger seat where no one is lecturing me about transgressions I might have committed forty years ago or changing the ringtones on my phone. Then, I wipe my face dry, place my hands wherever I damn well please on the steering wheel, and head home to California.

Janis Cooke Newman is the author of the novel, A Master Plan for Rescue, *a* San Francisco Chronicle *Best Book of 2015, and the novel,* Mary: Mrs. A. Lincoln, *a* Los Angeles Times *Book Prize Finalist and* USA Today's *Historical Novel of the Year, as well as the memoir,* The Russian Word for Snow. *She is also the founder of the Lit Camp writers conference. Her travel stories have appeared in* The New York Times, Los Angeles Times, San Francisco Chronicle, *and* Travelers' Tales.

♫ ♫ ♫

Goodnight, Sweetheart

On trust in the sleeping compartment.

When traveling alone, my preference is to keep it that way. I'm not one for chatting people up in hotel bars or reeling out my anecdotes or listening to theirs. Which is why, when a man entered my chamber just as the overnight train left Moscow bound for St. Petersberg, my heart sank.

I thought I had reserved both beds in my first-class compartment—a private suite, so to speak. The day before, I had paid with cash at my hotel service desk. When I got to Leningradsky Station, the woman at the ticket kiosk, annoyed and clearly ready to call it a day, nevertheless barked me a confirmation through the glass.

The purpose of my voyage, after all, was contemplation. I had spent much of my twenties in Russia back when it was the Soviet Union, and traveled this train route countless times. I always loved to head north in the nighttime, across the Volga River, toward the Gulf of Finland and the Baltic Sea. But I hadn't been back for years, during which time life simply did what it did: it carried on, through ecstasy, heartbreak and usually, everything in between. I had spent much of the prior week retracing my younger footsteps. I wanted to reflect in the sleeping car and do it in solitude.

I unfolded the sheet and draped it on the bunk, making hospital corners as if it mattered. I unpacked a nightie and my toothbrush. I kicked off my flats, sat on the bed, rearranged my skirt, and studied my feet for a minute. They were smudged with a day's worth of urban grime, and my pedicure—which had been painted Beach Party pink in a packed New York nail spa—was showing signs of wear. The linen felt cool under my sticky legs. It was 10:30 on a June evening and it was still hot in Moscow when the train pushed off.

Still sitting up, the gentle vibration of the wheels beneath me caused my head to get heavy as the rest of me grew weightless. As I began to drift off, a man walked in. He looked at me with what was surely a reflection of my own expression, which said roughly, "This isn't happening."

"I don't think this is your room," I said. My displeasure was unambiguous. I looked over at the other bunk. It was a foot from mine. I stood, and together we examined his ticket, then the number on the door, and finally each other.

Damn, I thought. *Damn damn damn*. He was a hulking tree of a man, easily six and a half feet tall, red face, shaved head, wearing a scarlet warm-up jacket that was covered with writing and numbers that had no theme or point. I guessed he grunted or worse in his sleep, probably had foul breath too. And I was stuck with him. Tantalizing fantasies about strangers on trains were the furthest thing from my mind. My night passage, my meditation on where all those years had gone, my sentimental journey: all dead on arrival.

He was as flustered as I was.

"I didn't think they'd put me with a woman," he said.

"Tell me about it," I replied.

We puttered about awkwardly. I stuck my nightie under the pillow. He checked his phone. And then we sat and looked at each other. Our knees touched briefly, and we both scooted a touch in the opposite direction. He had a kind face.

"I'm Marcia," I said.

"I'm Igor," he said. *No kidding*, I thought.

"Where are you from?" he asked.

"The USA," I said. "What about you?"

"Vladivostok," he answered.

"From Siberia," I remarked.

"No." He smiled. "From the Russian Far East."

"Got it," I said, and asked, "Do you have a family?" But I misspoke, using the word *familia,* which means "surname," instead of *cemya,* which means "family."

"Umm, yes," he answered, looking slightly panicked.

"I mean, a *family*," I said, correcting myself.

"Yes!" he said. He took out his phone and displayed a shot of his wife and kids, tall and smiling—a girl, twelve, and a boy, fifteen. Just the same as I had.

So I fired up my laptop and showed him photos of my own tall, smiling son and daughter.

The attendant brought us tea in glass mugs, and we drank in silence. Then, our dinner came: chicken, noodles, a chunk of rye bread wrapped in plastic. He ordered water, not beer, to drink. I was relieved and, I confess, surprised.

Our dishes were crammed on the tiny, shared table. We spoke between bites about our kids, sports, work, his travels, and mine. He had taken an eight-hour plane ride from Vladivostok that morning. Four days earlier, I had boarded an eight-hour flight from JFK Airport. Igor was exactly as far from home as I was.

"I'll let you change," he said. He stepped out of the compartment and closed the door. The nightie was a tad inappropriate, considering, so I dug out some sweatpants and a tank top. Igor returned in his version of pajamas—basketball shorts and a t-shirt—and shut the door behind him.

"It's better to lock it," he said, turning the bolt. A polite look passed over his face, which soothed the panicked one on mine.

I thought of my husband, who at that moment was probably picking up our daughter from school in Connecticut.

"Nudge me if I snore," he said, covering himself with his sheet and blanket.

"Oh, I know the drill."

"Good night. Sweet dreams."

"You too."

I didn't get much shut-eye that night, between the intermittent squeals of drunks somewhere nearby, the wide-awake children, and a man who paced the corridor talking loudly on the phone or to himself. Being June, darkness never fell, and even though our blinds were drawn, the compartment was doused in half-light. Mostly there was the steady hum of the train against the rails, the shadows that moved and shifted, the crisp pillowcase under my head. There was the rustle of sheets as I shifted restlessly, memories churning through my mind, my sense of Russia that, like me on the train, was fluid and also stood still. Through it all, there was Igor's breathing, not loud, but present, rhythmic, and safe.

In the morning when the attendant came to rouse us, I jumped to unlock the door. She delivered bread and tea again in the lovely glasses, and we both looked down at our trays as we stirred in sugar for longer than was necessary.

"Did you sleep well?" he finally asked.

"Yes," I lied. "Very."

"Let's look at the scenery," he said. "It's beautiful."

"Of course," I agreed, and rose.

"Sit, sit," Igor almost whispered. He stood, grabbed the curtain and shoved it to one side. The rush of white light pierced my eyes, causing a flash of sightlessness.

Condensation glazed the windows. Outside, a million birch trees stood deep and wide along the train tracks. We sped past them, through the Russian forest.

In St. Petersburg, Igor held my elbow as I negotiated the chasm between the train and platform. A driver from my hotel stood waiting for me, and I greeted him and handed over my bags. I immediately turned to say goodbye to Igor, with my arms half-opened, to embrace him, and thank him. But he was already gone, disappeared into the crowd.

Marcia DeSanctis is The New York Times *bestselling author of* 100 Places in France Every Woman Should Go. *She is a regular contributor to* Vogue *and* Town & Country *magazines and has also contributed to* Marie Claire, The New York Times, Creative Nonfiction, O, the Oprah Magazine, Architectural Digest, The Sunday Telegraph, National Geographic Traveler, Tin House, *and many other publications. She is the recipient of two Solas award for best travel writing and five Lowell Thomas Awards for her travel journalism, including one for Travel Journalist of the Year for her essays from Rwanda, Haiti, France, and Russia.*

☙ ☙ ☙

The Bad Place

If she turned back now, she'd always doubt herself.

It takes more than two hours by bus to fully escape the frenetic crowds and wild streets of Kampala, Uganda. Finally, the asphalt is exhausted, becoming firmly packed roads of red clay. Dense, shoulder-to-shoulder buildings disappear, replaced by green trees and modest houses. Each time the bus shudders to a stop, hawkers run to the windows selling skewers of meat, bags of fruit, or warm *chapati* bread rolled around a thin egg omelet, what they call a "Rolex."

Men zip through the streets on motorbikes, bare-chested, not slowed at all by the long, yellow kayaks that balance perpendicularly across the backs of their bikes. When I see them, that's how I know we've reached Jinja, a bucolic town that has become East Africa's hub for adventure sports. People from all over the world travel here for the kayaking, the all-terrain-vehicle safaris, and the epic bungee jumping. I'm here to go whitewater rafting at the source of the Nile River.

My backpacker hostel is situated on a hill that overlooks sinuous curves of water. This is where the tour company will pick us up in the morning. I'm staying in a dorm room with several other adventure seekers, all more experienced than I am. I've never been whitewater rafting before but my favorite amusement park ride as a kid was White Water Canyon at Kings Island in Mason, Ohio, and for some reason, I imagine this real-life experience will be essentially the same thing: a refreshing float on some burbling water through woodland scenery, a height requirement of at least forty-six inches, possibly a funnel cake afterward.

As the sun sets, I open a cold Tusker lager and carefully read the waiver for the next day's rafting trip. The paper says the rapids in Jinja are "Grade V on a scale that runs from I to VI." Grade I means mild rocking and rolling, suitable for beginners. Grade VI presents extreme danger and barely navigable rapids, even for professionals.

So. grade V? Holy mother of paddling. This requires skillful maneuvering of choppy water, huge hazards, steep drops, and crashing waves. It also means that as a first-timer, I am suddenly terrified. The *chapati* bread I ate on my arrival now churns uncomfortably in my stomach. My throat burns and tastes acidic. I knew the rapids were a V before I signed up—I just thought the scale ran from I to X.

That night I call my husband via Skype. He's in California, and I've been traveling without him for about six months, with another six months of solo travel on the horizon. Jason has been an unfailing supporter of my backpacking dream. He understands I'm in search of something that has no name, and that I must make this journey alone.

When he answers the call, I tell him what I'm about to do. I expect him to be proud of me. We met skydiving—he was my instructor, the guy who literally pushed me out of a plane. He knows my desire to live big and boldly, and he's always stoked that fire.

"So this might be goodbye," I laugh.

"Then why are you doing this?" he snaps. He's angry, so different from the man who held my hand on a skydiving aircraft during the ride to altitude. "Nobody's forcing you to go rafting."

"I don't know why. I just need to do it," I finally say.

We don't discuss the real inspiration for my yearlong backpacking trip around the world. My mother is suffering from early-onset Alzheimer's disease. She was diagnosed in 2001. I had already graduated from college and moved away from home. By the time I returned for Thanksgiving that year, she couldn't tell time, remember the president's name, or distinguish my sister from me. With each visit, my mother retreated further, like a secret code I couldn't quite crack.

The grief that followed was the slippery kind, ebbing and flowing over the next several years. Some days I was hardly conscious of the sad, relentless undercurrent that tugged at my heart. Other times I dreamt about the mom I used to know, the one who left handwritten notes in my lunch bag and baked cherry cake for my birthday. I screamed for her in my sleep, then jolted awake, my face slick with tears.

The only redemptive thing about the disease is how it has transformed me. My mom's slow-motion descent toward death has motivated me to see the world she never did, gathering my own memories while I'm able, honoring her life by making the most of my own. I also know there's a genetic component to Alzheimer's, and I might already carry the markers for the disease. That's why, ten years after my mother's diagnosis, I quit my job, left my home, and set off to complete her bucket list, which included dancing the tango in Buenos Aires, going on safari in South Africa, and seeing the pyramids of Giza.

In my hostel room in Jinja, I tell my husband, "People always say when you grow old, you'll regret the things you didn't do, not the things you did."

"That's *if* you grow old," he replies.

It's a joke, but the rest of the conversation is strained. I wish I knew how to comfort him, but it's hard to do over a jumpy internet connection, especially when I am equally apprehensive.

I think about my mother in her quiet yellow room at the nursing home, where she was admitted after she became too violent to stay at home with my dad. The remainder of her life will be spent in that hushed and sterile room, a thought that leaves me cold and afraid. My mom hasn't recognized me in years. She no longer has the ability to speak, walk, or feed herself, and she doesn't respond to her own name. But I know she'd rather be facing rapids than losing more of herself each day. I sign the waiver.

The next morning twenty of us are taken by bus from the hostel to the launch point. My heartbeat is pounding so hard I barely hear the employee who asks for my payment. In return for fifty dollars, I'm handed a long paddle. I have no idea how to hold it, even on steady ground. The paddle is awkward and cumbersome, like I've been gifted a third arm.

Here at the launch point, the Nile River is jagged, a silver expanse that slices through the morning mist. I slip my toes into the river, the longest in the world. The water I see now will flow north from this point all the way to the Mediterranean Sea, a journey of three months and 6,800 kilometers.

From the dock, the rafts look as tiny as poppy seeds floating in an Olympic-sized pool. My boat, which carries four other passengers—all strangers to me—is the last to launch into the river.

Our captain is Jane, a long-limbed, muscular blonde with hair braided into taut cornrows that reveal tanned strips of scalp. Her Australian accent gives the impression of someone who guzzles stocky cans of Foster's Lager and wrestles crocodiles, which is soothing since there are, in fact, crocodiles around us.

Jane barks, "Wild or mild?"

Our group is divided. Half want the more aggressive experience, while the others want something more subdued. Jane narrows her eyes and shakes her head with disapproval. She looks feral, and I'm certain we're in store for something fierce.

The air is hot and stagnant, and the rubbery smell coming from the red raft is strong and medicinal. The shore appears far and unreachable, like a distant mirage on the horizon. Insects skim the Nile with grace.

Jane teaches us how to hold the paddle and scoop the water, propelling us forward. She chastises me for not digging deep, merely skimming the surface. Then, after ten minutes of calm, placid rafting, she suddenly—and deliberately—tips the boat, forcing us to swim through a set of small, milky rapids.

I am plunged into both the river and the memory of the last time I was overpowered by water. My mother, a German immigrant to the United States, never learned to swim, and she wanted me to seize every opportunity she didn't have. So I dutifully attended classes at the YMCA in Dayton, Ohio. And even while I maintained a weak stroke and a strong fear of drowning, I dog-paddled my way through each level: polliwog, guppy, minnow, fish. Up I climbed through the aquatic food chain. When I finally attained shark, I was tested on my ability to tread water while fully clothed. The goal was to last a half hour in the deep section of the pool, and toward the end I gave out. My memory of it is more like a montage of film clips: sinking, inhaling water, struggling to the surface, coughing, chlorine tears burning my cheeks, and my mom on the side of the pool, howling for help. I remember she was beautiful even in her panic, her short, curly blond hair teased into a halo around her head, her poppy-colored lips frozen into an O. I don't recall a single word she said, only that she looked perfect as usual, while I flailed.

But that was many years ago. Now, here in eastern Uganda, it is baptism by boulders. I emerge on the other side of the rocks, bruised and with a stomach full of Nile water. I bob to the surface, white-knuckling my life jacket. I'm O.K., but I'm frightened. I've put myself in the hands of this Jane woman, and she didn't think twice about tossing me from the boat.

After the raft is righted, I hoist myself in again. Jane gives our group the option to bail out now and float down another part of the river in a safety boat instead of tackling more rapids. *Go, fool, go!* yells the sane part of my brain. But I can't. If I turn back now, I'll always doubt myself. I'll forever be the eleven-year-old girl sinking in the deep end at the Y in Dayton.

It's a shock when I discover the first few rapids are actually fun. Each time we approach rocks and roaring water, Jane cries, "Paddle-paddle-paddle!" followed by a quick, "Get down!" We dutifully obey her commands. Our raft successfully skims rapids and slides down waterfalls.

We reach a treacherous spot—a series of rapids in quick succession—known as Itanda, or "the bad place." I dig my paddle in—Jane would be proud if she were paying attention—but the raft spirals as though we're not even tending to it. As I heave and grunt, I peek at the other people in my boat and see we're all grappling with this thing. I see the sturdy, brute determination to survive.

On the other side, I'm surprised to find myself aloft. We've made it through.

Then we meet the rapids called Silverback, a name Jane speaks with such reverence that I know we're in for it. I can hear it coming. The green river churns and crashes against pointed rocks like a terrible, bubbling stew. I close my eyes. I don't want to see what's coming.

My last visit home before leaving on my backpacking trip, my dad brought me to the nursing home, and we entered the elevator. He knew the security code to make the doors close—a safety feature to prevent the Alzheimer's patients from wandering onto another floor or out of the building—and he paused before hitting the button.

"You might not recognize your mother anymore," he said. "The disease has taken a real physical toll in the past few months."

I braced myself for the worst, my stomach hard with dread. I closed my eyes.

When the elevator opened, my dad gestured across the room. "There she is."

I forced my eyes to open, and saw the skeleton of a woman arranged on a recliner. Her eyes were sunken and her cheeks were two dark hollows. I gasped.

"No, no, no," I cried, the words rushing forth before I could stop them.

The waves swallow the boat whole, and I'm still not looking. In an instant I feel the raft drop out from under me, and I am airborne for a brief moment before I am submerged and chewed by raging water.

"That's not your mother," my dad said gently. "Look behind her."

She wore no makeup, and her hair was gray and limp. Her shirt was nothing pretty, and the elastic band of her pants was pulled far too high. But there was no doubt. This was my mother, the woman who birthed me, who nurtured me, who challenged me to become everything she couldn't. She didn't know me enough anymore to love me, but every part of me remembered her.

My head barely breaks the surface before the swells hammer me again. When I open my mouth, it is partially underwater, partially above. I inhale a mixture of sweet air and frothy, murky foam. Above, there's muck and dirt and a kaleidoscopic shimmer of waves.

Sour river water slides through my nose, cutting a raw path down my throat. I splash around and somehow my right hand makes contact with the raft. My shoulder feels hot and heavy as I grab the rope and cling to it.

My arm is fiercely yanked one way, while my body is pulled another. More rapids. In the chaos of rocks and waves, the raft is torn from my grasp.

Crocodiles, I think. *Oh my God, what about the crocodiles?*

I curl into a ball, some kind of animal instinct, then I'm rolling, tumbling downstream, whisked through a channel of noise and turbulence, the container inside a pneumatic tube. If the crocs are nearby, I'm surely moving too fast for any of them to catch me. When my head breaks the surface again, I don't know how much time or distance has passed. But the water is calm, the boat is gone, and I am alone.

I wipe water from my eyes and float for a few minutes, looking up at the vast sky, the river holding me like a hand. Then a safety kayak glides toward me and tows me to a larger safety boat. After I pull myself inside, I cough, but not productively. I try to summon enough muscle to bark out the water in my lungs.

A paddle bobs on the surface nearby, and I heave it into the boat with me. Several minutes later, my sinuses clear. My ears pop. I catch my breath. My heartbeat slows to a normal rate. And it's a relief when more heads bob up nearby—the rest of my group. They swim to the safety boat, and I help tug them inside. Only one girl is bloody, but her cuts are shallow, and our nervous conversation gives way to excited hugs. We are all O.K., and the river has offered us solidarity. Swapping stories about our rapids, adrenaline flowing like a geyser, we don't feel like strangers anymore.

When Jane appears, unscathed, from an inlet with our boat, we all cheer. I'm one of the first to leap into the water and swim to the raft, and I'm genuinely happy to be back in it. We drift for about an hour on a placid portion of river. Jane hands me an orange, and I drop the peel into the water. It curls and floats lazily for a moment, until it catches a current and is torn away. I imagine it gliding from here through the newly formed country of South Sudan, mingling with sediment from the Blue Nile and White Nile tributaries, sweeping past Egypt's farmlands and tombs, washing ashore somewhere in the Mediterranean. Maybe somebody will find this proof of my existence and wonder where it came from.

I think about the letter I wrote to my family years ago, when I was an active skydiver—a letter to be given to them in the event of the worst-case scenario. I kept it in my desk. It explained how my life was richer for them being a part of it, and offered assurance that I wanted it to end this way—that death while soaring is both noble and true.

I didn't write any letters before leaving for this backpacking trip, and I realize now it's because I fully expect to survive. I've hauled my way through the bad place, and I'm traveling the route that will bring me home again.

My legs are tired and my skin is sunburned. When I look to the horizon, I see churning water. It's time to paddle again. I sit erect in the boat and stare down the whirlpools and rocks. When the waves strike I refuse to close my eyes. This time I approach them on my own terms. The raft remains steady.

The last few rapids, I don't even need to hear Jane's instructions to know what to do. Our boat never capsizes again, and my group successfully finishes twenty-five kilometers from where we began.

It's early evening when I jump from the raft for the last time. The sun sinks behind the tangle of scruffy mvule trees, and the river is broad and black, open as a wound. The air has cooled considerably, and the water is chilly. I keep my limbs warm with a few head-high freestyle strokes, making shimmery waves with each movement. My new friends call for me from the muddy bank, but I'm not ready to head for shore yet.

I remember from school that the Nile is shaped like the lotus flower, a symbol of renewal for the ancient Egyptians. Right now I am in the stem, pulling myself toward the blossom.

Maggie Downs is a writer based in Palm Springs, California. Her work has appeared in The New York Times, Washington Post, Los Angeles Times, Roads & Kingdoms, *and* Smithsonian.com, *among many other publications. She holds an MFA in creative nonfiction from the University of California Riverside-Palm Desert.*

❧ ❧ ❧

A Long Night's Journey into Spring

Savoring Iceland's rancid winter feast.

I have a pact with Ragga. When I point my fork at things on my dinner plate, she will tell me what they are. She will say "sheep's head" or "blood sausage" or "sour shark" or "whale." She will do this until I point to a thing she doubts I can swallow. In that case, we've agreed that Ragga will say nothing at all.

We've just found seats at Thorrablot, a banquet dinner held in towns all over Iceland. It's a late-winter feast that harkens back to the cruelest chapters in Iceland's history, when volcanoes blackened the sky with ash, when famines swept the land, and deforestation was so complete you couldn't even warm your hands by a fire.

The menu at Thorrablot—a nauseating list of whey-soaked meats and near-rotten fish—explains how early Icelanders made it through the grim homestretch of winter. They squirreled away the dregs of the fall harvest, buried shark meat underground, and when spring still felt like a far-off dream, swallowed them down. It's some of the worst food in the history of eating.

Alcohol, I'm told, helps. I believe the people who tell me this. I've had two gin and tonics by the time I arrive at Thorrablot, thanks to Ragga and her husband, Biggi, who invited me to their pre-party. It was around their coffee table, over pretzel sticks and tall cocktails, that I announced to my hosts and their friends that I was going to be "adventurous" at Thorrablot. I will swallow that word with a forkful of sheep and a shot called Black Death.

Nobody goes to Iceland for the food. Even less of a draw: winter. In December, the sun arrives as late as 11:20 A.M. and flees as early as 3:30. The darkest day of the year is a mere *four hours* long. You can track the amount of sunlight Iceland gets—and many Icelanders do, down to the second—on the web. That's how I know that there were seven hours, nine minutes, and fifty-eight seconds of sunlight on the early February day I set out for Thorrablot in Kirkjubæjarklaustur.

Kirkjubæjarklaustur sits on the southern fringe of Iceland, three hours east of Reykjavik. There isn't much to the town—its name means "church-farm-cloister" and that about covers it. Only if you were a natural-disaster geek would you pull off the highway here: Kirkjubæjarklaustur is sandwiched by a fearsome volcano and the largest icecap in Europe. Laki, the volcano, once erupted so passionately that its ash blotted out the moon for months. Vatnajökull, the giant glacier, is ungirded by volcanoes. If there's a more calamity prone place on Earth than Kirkjubæjarklaustur, nobody lives there.

I drove east from Reykjavik midday, anxious to see Iceland's hinterlands while the sun was making a showing. But the sky was a thick gray cap: no layers, no nuance, no *movement*. I pulled over a few times to take photos but deleted them. I might as well have been shooting a cement room featuring cardboard boxes.

Something strange happens in the mind of a person deep in the interior of Iceland. It begins with the color problem. The palette of the land gives you no assurance of life. In fact, its mold-green moss and straw-yellow grass and the vast blackness of the fields that lava made all suggest this place either drains life or ends it. Which explains why I quit taking photos. Not just because the images were pathetically grim, but because I was having trouble getting out of the car.

Outside, I felt bare in a way that had nothing to do with clothing. It was cold, but no more so than New York in winter. There were no people to stare me off, let alone predators. So why did I know in my bones that it was unwise to walk more than three feet from my car? How could a place this quiet and static and uncreatured, the very antithesis of jungle, tell a person with such force to keep inside?

And then it got dark. And radio signals vanished. And even the monster jeeps I kept spotting, racing back from the glaciers, were gone now. Deep in the noiseless dark, glacial melt oozed over their tracks. I drove with both hands on the wheel and stared into a blackness flecked on either side by yellow reflectors—a long, unchanging tunnel—and made the mistake of glancing in my rearview mirror: a chasm, all black. It began to feel possible that none of this was happening. Possible that this blackness was not a real place. Possible, then, that I was not *here*, that I could just vanish like a character in some late-morning dream that suddenly drops off.

That's when I began taking great heed of my GPS.

It promised just fifty miles more. I was fifty miles from Kirkjubæjarklaustur. In fifty miles, I might hear noise, see a face, speak. I looked many times at the screen, at this word, the promise. Kirkjubæjarklaustur: It had a silent *j*, just like Reykjavik. The *a* and *e* were melded Icelandically. On screen at least, it looked like a real place.

The phone rings in my hotel room, and I give it a look. Bullshit. Who could be calling me in Kirkjubæjarklaustur? I'm not even certain *I'm* here, yet; how could anyone else be?

The phone rings again. "Hel-*lo*?"

"There's a gentleman here to see you," an Icelandic voice claims. I promise the voice I'll be right down, which isn't true. First, I need to blow-dry more heat into my socks and shoot some tea and find the tiny notebook where I've written the name of the gentleman I believe is here to see me: Birgir Thorisson, husband to Ragnhildur Ragnarsdottir.

I've gotten permission to call them Biggi and Ragga, from their daughter, Brynhildur, a woman I've known for five years as Bryn.

I met Bryn on the cusp of my maiden voyage to Iceland. I was waiting to board the red-eye that would deliver me to Reykjavik and tensed with desire to say that aloud, to feel the new reality: *Iceland*. There was a pretty brunette with an upturned nose standing at our gate on steep heels, her bangs cut boldly short. I wanted her to be Icelandic, and she was.

Across the ocean, Bryn's boyfriend awaited her in the bright dawn. He offered to drive me to my new flat, knowing that Icelandic prices could break a scrappy traveler in days. It was the island's economic peak, three-and-a-half months before the financial meltdown, and mere days before the solstice, when the light vivified everything.

There was a throb to the light, a thrust in it. Crack light, I called it, disoriented to a degree I didn't know possible. I stayed all summer, subletting a room in a creaky yellow house on a street called Lindargata, where the pull-down shades did a laughable job muting the most ebullient blast of light I'd ever seen.

When people told me what time it was that summer, my usual response was a long, doubting "noooo." I talked back to clocks, too. "You've *got* to be kidding me." The hour always sounded made-up, so blatantly mismatching the shade of the sky. There was a clock store up on Sólavördustígur and one day I stood there, shaking my head at all those clock faces in the window.

Nine P.M. They *agreed*. Nine P.M., and I hadn't even thought about dinner.

Light, Iceland taught me, did not fall evenly on all the world's places.

I slept little that summer. I filled wide, white pages with notes, biked to the harbor, said yes to every invitation. I went to a party on an island called Videy where beautiful women wore capes and Björk's son showed up in a helicopter. I got the hang of sulfur-scented showers, electrical outlets that carried the force of geysers. I bought sagas and believed I'd read them. Instead, I read the phone book, its long columns of Ingibjörgs, daring Iceland to be that strange—a land without last names.

I night jogged. I night cleaned. I night wrote. I did all of the above under a sky that also suggested: Why not picnic?

I pored over early Icelandic history books, grew obsessed with the story of Floki, a disgruntled Norwegian who believed he'd found paradise when he landed on the shore of west Iceland in summer. Floki fished late into the bright June nights, oblivious that this was a *season,* not an Eden. Misery awaited Floki: His animals died; Floki gave up. You can find traces of Floki in the menu at Thorrablot: *prepare for winter, bury your shark meat, dark times ahead.*

My summer in Iceland was the second brightest on record, when polar bears were washing up on melting ice floes from Greenland. The island's wealth was also at its height—poised for a phenomenal crash in October. But in June, all through July, people left work early. They made pacts to hike the faint mountain at Reykjavik's back. I'd never experienced a season so dominant and it fascinated me—the way it told a nation of people what to do (renew) and when (right now) and where (outside). Björk threw a free concert. Sigur Rós joined. The whole country showed. We all jumped up and down to a song called "Hoppípolla." The light never quit. It put an entire society in a heightened, hyperactive mood.

Of course, winter played a role in this. There was a preface to summer's glory that I'd missed entirely—a reason the people around me seemed newly switched on. The lead-up to the brightest summer on record was Iceland's standard, brutal winter.

I'd have to come back in that other season, Icelanders told me. I'd hung out in the greenhouse, but Iceland was also a cave. I wouldn't really know this place unless I saw the flip side, they said.

To call me light sensitive would be like calling shark meat unsavory. In winter, I feel like a plant, ready to contort and bend toward any source of light. I'll change seats in cafés three times to get the most sun-lavished seat, leap over snow mounds to reach the side of the street where the sidewalk glows. By February my eyes feel squinty, half-open. I don't take a multivitamin; I pop vitamin D.

One winter, though, I withered long before February. My home had just come apart: My partner and I had just split, in what felt like a fortnight. I kept our place and he dragged off his things, leaving the rooms hollow and haunted with memories of painting their walls as a team. I got skinny in the way that announces something's up. Close friends asked whether I was eating, and I was—predominantly green apples. My face had a new chisel in it—the cheekbone cut straight down to the chin. I checked mirrors for the chisel, wanting beauty in a way I never had before. Thin felt like a power and I was desperate for any new power, alone now and significantly older.

Every weekend was a full-on battle to not feel terrible. I threw parties because I wanted invitations to parties. Old friends were delivering babies, turning their attention to strollers; I needed to refill my ranks with people alone enough to make room for me. Dating often meant hard drinking, and usually on an empty stomach: one cocktail, then another, while I had the body mass of a high-school cross-country runner. I worried about the long stretch of winter ahead. The year already felt dark.

And cold. I'd never felt the chill of winter that acutely. I felt like a person who'd lost her coat.

One morning, I hurried aboard a commuter train, on my way to work. No sooner had I plunked down in an empty seat did I look up at a bright, blown-up photo. An airline ad. I froze, staring at the image like I would a portrait of my family, hung in public with no explanation. What was *Iceland* doing here?

I knew the spot so well: Jökulsárlón. It was the lagoon, way in the eastern corner of Iceland, where calving glaciers break off into hundreds of pieces, cutting every possible silhouette—hooks, ramps, claws, domes. They float in mesmerizing stillness, like razor-edged clouds, gleaming. It has to be the most sublime vista in Iceland.

I got in touch with Bryn—did I remember right? Was there a party called Thorra-something? Rancid food in the dead of February? Yes, Bryn wrote: It's a dreadful affair—why? Thorrablot: Winter Survival Night. I pitched an editor. Send me to Thorrablot. Other people had Christmas parties and snuggly lovers and twinkly-eyed kids. I wanted to sit in a room with strangers just barely enduring winter.

It's bright like a hair salon just inside the banquet hall in Kirkjubæjarklaustur, making it impossible not to notice how dressed up everyone is. I look around the foyer of the banquet hall and see sequins, bowties, stilettos, heels no one should dance on. You can smell the hairspray.

There's an unmistakably bridal feel to this Thorrablot. There's a receiving line, where eight or so townspeople stand, beaming and shaking our hands. Icelanders get tapped at random to serve on their local Thorrablot committee; it's a passing, shared duty, and from the looks of it, an honor. The committee women hold the posture of hens; the men look like they personally slaughtered tonight's sheep. They stand in the blast of light, roses pinned to their breasts, like all eight of their daughters just got married.

It's brilliant, the more I think about it: a wedding with no bride, no groom, no priest, no planner. It's a party everyone can come to, put on their Sunday best for, split the bill for. There are tickets, just forty dollars a pop, and a date everyone agrees upon—late winter—because everyone's stuck in the same dark cave and jonesing for a party. Nobody carries any pressure to impress with food. The food is supposed to be dreadful. If the food tasted *good*, in fact, someone would be pissed.

It strikes me how very awkward it is for me to be here. Even my hosts, Bryn's parents, suddenly look a little sheepish about my presence as their guest. It was so much smoother in their home, where we were faint, glowing faces to one another in the dim den, and I warmed so fast to their friends, Birgir and Hrafnhildur. Birgir and Hrafnhildur, who so kindly renamed themselves for me Biggi (II) and Habba.

Habba! My face crumples with fondness every time it's Habba's turn to talk. A tiny woman with ponytailed gray hair, Habba's favorite topic is whatever delights her. And many, many things delight Habba. Someone once told me that in Icelandic you don't love *things*, just people. Habba's English is choppy, but she has full command of the verb "to love." Habba loves Thorrablot. And Habba *loves* rams' testicles. She tells me this with the gusto of an American woman in a commercial for chocolate-truffle ice cream.

Habba boils Thorrablot down to this: In a winter this dark, in a cold this severe, in a season in which rising from bed is the national challenge, you need something to *look forward to.* Over and over, Habba repeats these words like she's passing on an age-old secret.

The problem with Habba is that, as a native and a nurse, she's way too beloved in Kirkjubæjarklaustur to be my sidekick at the winter wedding. Habba vanishes fast. She leaves me to my adopted parents and an awkwardness that deepens by the minute.

I am severely underdressed—a black-jean-and-leather-boot combo that will inspire one guest to nickname me "New York." He is one of about five people who will speak to me tonight. Basically, I've invited myself to a small-town wedding in a country with the population of Toledo, Ohio. And worn pajamas.

There is one way to get through this night: drinking. Biggi hands me a Viking beer and I drain it fast. I open the menu and pretend I can read it. *Lundabaggar, Kartöflumús.* This can only go on so long. *Hákarl, Svid.* I take notes in my head about how obvious it is when women feel their most beautiful, how you can see smiles tamped down in their lips when they scurry to the bathroom in pairs. I go to the bathroom myself to jot down notes in a stall. Someone bursts in on me, and not when I'm taking notes. Someone bursts in on me when I'm pulling up my pants.

This is how a person begins to look forward to heinous food.

My first mistake is taking a little bit of everything. It's such an obvious mistake, in hindsight, but by the time our table is called, I'm so desperate to *do* something, and scooping little pale piles of food from bowls is something to do. Besides, the sour food—set out in glass dishes down a white-clothed table—doesn't look all that heinous. There are no placards.

Back at our table, a quick glance at everyone's plates makes clear I've gone overboard. The others have chosen favorites. Four or five favorites. I have no idea where everyone else got mashed potatoes. My plate is straight meat and fish, a palette of the same five colors: faint pink, soil brown, fishy white, formaldehyde, and putty.

Again, the color problem. Just as the palette of Iceland's hinterlands, with its coal-black pastures and gray masses of ice, warns the traveler this is no place for life, the hues of my Viking dinner promise there is no nutrition here. I chase barely green peas around my plate and work up the nerve for herring.

A flakey piece of it lifts upward, tempting in the way a single French fry would. But dried herring is no quick bite. I press my teeth down and nothing happens. I dig in harder, I clench, like a dog at odds with rawhide, and still—nothing. Are my molars even denting? They are not. I set down the herring, give my jaw a rest, and recall that Icelanders once ate their shoes.

Or so claim histories of the brutal 1700s, a century of astounding catastrophe. Natural disasters don't just strike this part of the world; they inspire and layer upon one another. Earthquakes set off volcanoes. Volcanoes melt glaciers. Glaciers flood the land. Ash blocks the light. Winter comes and steals what's left of it. Consider the year 1783. The Earth shakes, ripping open the Laki volcano. Rivers of lava pour over the land, burying farm after farm. It's an outpouring of magma never before seen by living people: 3.5 trillion gallons. This eruption goes on for eight straight months. Its ash cloud dims the world. Global temperatures drop. Crops in Europe fail. Parts of the Mississippi freeze. The Nile shrinks. As far away as Siberia, trees grow less. But in Iceland, things just die. Birds die, grass dies, a year's worth of hay is poisoned. Iceland loses a fifth of its people, and most of the livestock on the island dies. According to one historian, the Icelandic people verge on extinction. This is when people begin eating shoes.

"Nothing will make you sick," Ragga assures from my left, "everything has been boiled and boiled."

Boiled and boiled. Singed of its hair and thoroughly smoked. Buried under stones then hung like laundry. Desiccated, then beaten to a pulp.

Directives in the Viking cookbook sound authored by someone terrified of her ingredients. Most verbs are synonymous with "to beat" or "to break down." The whole endeavor is to undo flavor, to dismantle texture, to outsmart poisons, to apply heat and wind and months of time until the result is *something* that can actually make it down the hatch.

To keep Viking delicacies straight, I need a close study of synonyms of "disgusting." "Putrefied" means rotten. "Putrid" means rotting. It also means emitting a horrid smell. "Rancid" means smelling or tasting horrid, as a result of rotting. I am not surprised to learn that the root of it all, "rotten," has Old Nordic origins. Rotten, in this part of the world, is a whole genre of cuisine.

At a more old-school Thorrablot, I might be eating seal flipper, gagging on pig's-head jam, or hiding smoked horse meat under my peas. I am also fortunate that the eyeballs of tonight's sheep are not out on the table, adorning the cooked carcass. But the greatest blessing of the night is that no one has prepared skate. A night-before-Christmas specialty, skate has to rot for a month until urea breaks down the bacteria that would make skate poisonous. The smell is so noxious that most people prepare skate outside.

What can I praise at Thorrablot? Edibility? There's a blood sausage that's more grainy than sinewy and so I say, "That's not bad!" Ragga nods. Alone, I'd spit it in my napkin.

Soon I feel a low-grade nausea. I haven't wretched yet; my body is simply saying no. It says: Do not ever touch that again.

Do not so much as touch that gray jelly thing you just put in your mouth. *Don't*. Very soon, 90 percent of the sour meat and fish wads have been scraped, sampled, and firmly ruled out.

So I do the stupidest possible thing. I send myself back for a second plate. I have delusions about mashed potatoes—that some plain puree could make this all work. Everyone else has them. Everyone else is managing. But the search uncovers too many more edible things.

Poor man's pita bread. Pickled herring. Turnips. Boiled and boiled turnips. I return to my seat with two very full plates of every single thing served at Thorrablot in Kirkjubæjarklaustur. Continuing feels out of the question; so does stopping. Sveinn, the Thorrablot caterer, is collecting plates, but only the empty ones. He reaches over mine to clear everyone else's.

I look down. I look for anything that has yet to repulse me. There's a small putty-colored wad, and my fork lingers over it.

"What's that?" I ask Ragga.

She stops chewing and follows my fork. "Do you want me to tell you?"

There's only one thing on tonight's Thorrablot menu you would not tell a faint-of-heart foreigner about. I shake my head and, before there can be any rethinking, eat my rams' balls.

The room goes quiet. People concentrate on their plates. "Everyone's trying to get through their own personal zombie movies," a veteran expat said, summing up the dark weeks leading to Thorrablot. "They get together and just swallow it down." The metaphor was so perfect. Life serves you puttycolored, near-poisonous shark, and you stomach it. You take it like a Viking.

But that's just not what I see. At the next table over, a blond man who's beaten his family back to the table is painting some bit of sour mystery meat with mashed potatoes with such *care*, such patience, deep in anticipation of that one single bite. And down at the end of the table, there isn't a trace of rams' testicles left on dear Habba's plate.

Habba: I watch her all night—so enthused to be here she can't sit down. Someone tells me later that Habba barely survived a heart attack this year. Her absence would have made this a very different night: the first Thorrablot without Habba. There'd have been an ache in the room that everyone felt. When I hold this in mind—how much time steals from us, and how suddenly—I understand better than ever why people take such care with tradition, preserving what constants we can while time moves unrelentingly forward.

People all over the world do this with heirloom food— the delicious kind. Only Icelanders stick to the rancid. Maybe they know something. Maybe the more pungent the food, the better the bridge to the past. Maybe that's why everyone in this bright hall looks like they'd appreciate a moment alone with the last bites of the disgusting dinner they ate exactly this time last year, and every year, deep in the dark of winter, in this very same room.

A brown curtain parts, and everyone turns toward the stage. Familiar people—the Thorrablot committee, their boutonnieres still on—stand before us, straight-faced, looking like the Icelandic impersonation of *American Gothic*. Slack cheeks, stony eyes, no creeping smiles. They're pretty good actors, turns out. Or just playing themselves.

Finally someone in the audience breaks the silence; he chuckles, inviting another chuckle, enabling another, and soon the whole room is laughing at the miserable-looking cast of Kirkjubæjarklaustur.

"Farmer humor," Ragga says, struggling to translate the comedy, as the actors begin reading scripts, dour-faced. I know she's trying her best, because when men appear in nun costumes, she whispers, "Nun costumes." And when the projector stalls, she tells me, hand curled around my ear, "The projector failed." Just about everything else, apparently, is way too local to translate: "Who's got the better snowmobile and that sort of thing."

I was told before coming to Thorrablot that the comedy portion of the night was basically an open mike for winter misery. But no one's getting up to unburden her heart. It is more along the lines of a wedding roast. What's roasted, in place of a groom, is winter. It's a retrospective, because the worst of the year is pretty much over.

The same held true for me. By the time I got my ticket to Iceland, I'd survived the holiday. I'd looked for recompense in my hollow Christmas: a third fewer gifts to buy—his family was big, and no longer mine. Instead, I wrote them goodbye letters. I'd put it off because it felt like the saddest thing. It was the saddest thing. I did it, finally, in the far corner seat of a subway car: put my head down and wrote holiday wishes that were obviously goodbyes, one right after another, to a mother and a sister and a grandmother I would never see again.

Back home for a Christmas I was dreading, I told my mother in plain language and without any embellishing stories that I was sad. I needed to say this to my mother: the woman who taught me to get out of bed, who trained most of the strength I have in me. Through the fall and into winter, she'd praised me—my motion, my forward lean, my back-to-back dating. She needed to know and I needed to say that I was sad. I was doing Christmas like everyone else but all the while felt a single, simple thing: sad. I am sad, Mother. I can make it, we know I will, but this is winter. I need to call this winter.

Ragga stands up to crack a window, letting a chill waft right in. The banquet hall is heating up with laughter, for reasons

I'm hopeless to know. I do get a clear summary of last year's comedy—Ragga and Biggi had leading roles. The theme, they tell me, was the volcano. I assume they mean Laki—the 1783 eruption that put their tiny, indomitable town on the map.

But Biggi isn't talking about the volcano of lore. He means the volcano that filled the air with ash the year before last—in 2011.

Grímsvötn didn't make world news because it didn't halt global air traffic, as the Eyjafjallajökull eruption had, just one year earlier. Nonetheless, when the Earth opened up by Kirkjubæjarklaustur, it got hard to see the sky.

Biggi was working at a fish farm and got trapped there. The air was so thick with black particles, he didn't dare step outside. Back at their home, grit covered every surface. Every cabinet, every drawer, everything cloth. Ragga was out of town, and when she finally returned and opened up her front door, the first thing she did was cover her eyes. She lifted a hand and covered her eyes again.

The ash would take months to clean. And when February came around, they dressed up, got up on the stage, and made a parody of the volcano that buried their town in black.

"Were you nervous?" I ask Biggi. "For the skit?"

"Yes." Little smile. "At first."

I try to imagine either of my host parents on stage, delivering jokes. It's hard. "Did it go over well?"

"Oh, very well," Biggi says, startled by the question, which tells me it was never a question. It was the end of a year of complete calamity. *Of course* people came into this hall ready to laugh.

Tonight's is about lean times: the town's tightening budget, the fact that Kirkjubæjarklaustur can no longer afford its thermal pool. An actor bumbles on stage, slouching like a nerd, camera dangling around his neck. No one has to tell me we're parodying tourism.

Every summer, when the nights get long and bright, Iceland gets a tidal wave of outsiders. Every magazine I pick up in Reykjavik is full of articles that chew on the dilemma: Can a country so tiny handle so many guests? Will a million hikers and bikers and Northern Lights seekers tread too hard on Icelandic ground? The questions I returned to in Iceland were so drastically different from the ones whispered through the brightest summer on record: *Why so many private helicopters? How could all that wealth be real? How could it last?* It couldn't, of course.

"Is it a coincidence that the history of Iceland seems to duplicate world history, though on such an extremely small scale?" asked Icelandic historian Gunnar Karlsson. "Or is that just the form that stories tend to take, whether fictional or historical: the romantic form of initial happiness, times of trouble and regained happiness?" Perhaps. What doesn't seem a coincidence, though, is that a place where cataclysm is so chronic, where disaster is on repeat, and where every year's seasons fling you from one extreme to the opposite, is so prone to radical, sweeping societal change. Prone, or maybe just practiced.

The laughter is getting *so* loud I beg Ragga to translate. She cups my ear and whispers the story of the foreign couple that rolled into town when there was not a single bed left. Someone in town, eager to make a buck, brought them to an old shipping container. The tourists were furious. The people around me are about to piss themselves.

I give up, at a certain point, trying to follow the plot of the comedy. It's not for me and that feels right. The entire town's in here, in this hotbox of laughs. I think about how some people's laughs make other people laugh. How one hearty, unbridled laugh can change a room. I think about Bryn, about what I'll tell her. That ram went down easy, that she was right about the bright lights, and yes, it was strange for me to come here, alone. And I think of the dark highway, threading east, all the way to Jökulsárlón, the lagoon from the poster, where I still want to go. Bryn says it's too far, impractical for this trip, but I can't give up the fantasy. I want to wrap east around Iceland until the sudden view of a hundred tiny glacial boats catches my breath. I want to see it again but in a different season—this strange pool of blue-tipped wonders that once froze me still.

There's a picture of me, right at that spot, so clear in my memory. I look like another person. Her hair is chopped short—she doesn't yet try to be beautiful—and blows easily in the polar wind. Her squint is hard—she doesn't yet care about wrinkles. I know what's behind that squint, in those slivered eyes. I know she's worried about love, about never fully loving. So much has yet to play out. She hasn't met a man she can love totally. She doesn't yet know she can. Here at the lip of the lagoon, she's hoping, she's ready. She wouldn't mind the wind blowing her right into some new person's fixed life. She wouldn't mind borrowing his anchor.

It's hard for me to look at this person, this squinter, without wanting to tell her things. Love can relocate you and fetter you and change just about every detail in your life. But the work of figuring yourself out: That's yours, I want to say. No shortcuts, no magic answers, no savior suitors, I want to tell her. Like Bryn put it yesterday when she called my hotel and reached a jet-lagged person who had no idea who was phoning: "Sort yourself out and call me back."

From nowhere, his memory sweeps me: Dan. I'm at the foot of Europe's biggest glacier, at a sheep farmers' sketch comedy, and somehow the man I expected to grow old with spreads out over my mind, seizing it all. From nowhere, and completely: There he is. My eyes close. They have to. *Dan.* I can't hold in mind the love and the ruin, the completeness of both, without shutting my eyes. I must look like a person savoring something, lidding the present to stay in some moment.

In a way, I am. Behind that long blink, I let the loss spread out, take up all of me. *All of me*: mind and chest and every vessel threading. The swell comes with awesome force. My eyes stay closed. I cooperate. I wait.

Down by the lagoon, if you lock your gaze on those white silhouettes, you eventually notice the melt. A white talon slides off; a glimmering blade coasts elegantly past it. All of this ice is about to float off. This lagoon is the terminal lake of the great glacier, Vatnajökull. It's a kind of waiting room, where broken glacier goes, right before it glides off and gives itself to the sea.

Black Death should be the end of me. One shot and lights out, hotel bed, hard sleep. I am jet-lagged. My body is full of scraps of farm animals killed last September and Arctic fish caught Lord knows when. My stomach feels bloated and confused. Like it needs to think on all this before formulating a response. Add to this strange brew the unsweetened schnapps of Iceland.

It's made from grain and potatoes. It's bottled at eighty proof. There's really just one way to drink Brennivín: shooting quickly.

I order two: one for me, one for Ragga. This is my way of rewarding my host for all the social pain incurred in bringing me to the dinner table. I've commented twice that rams' testicles weren't that bad, neutral really, like the base of a broccoli bunch, but Ragga deserves better than that. Black Death on me.

The bartender sets down chilled shots of clear liquor in front of us. Ragga takes it down like a Viking; I do O.K. for a second, then shudder like a kid. I don't know if alcohol has ever felt more like poison, more immediately raised the question, why do we do this to ourselves? Imagine cutting a permanent marker in two and sucking out its ink.

Even more remarkable is that after drinking poison, after drinking beer, after drinking gin and tonic, twice, what I still feel, more than drunk, is awkward. I can't leave and get into my hotel without finding Sveinn, who is not only the caterer but the hotel manager. The hotel is full of British photographers, sound asleep. Sveinn locked them up, for fear of drunk Thorrablotters stumbling inside and causing trouble. My worry is this: in the time that it takes to find Sveinn and get that hotel key, someone here will make me dance.

Because every other Thorrablot prophecy has come true. Icelanders warned me that the food would be gray, and the lights would be bright, and the texture would cause me trouble, and that shark was best treated as a cube of stinky cheese. But many people also predicted that a drunk old man would sidle up and request a dance.

A four-man band fills the room with trumpet and tambourine and lyrics everyone seems to know by heart. The dance floor is a mosh pit, then a bruise pit. Men toss around women in high heels like boys tempting their toys to smash. There's a lot of twirling, twirling of people whose reaction times seem a solid beat late. Women fall and get right back up, eyes glistening, mock-slapping their tossers. At one point, Biggi lifts a hand to tap a woman about to topple back into her dance, like a volleyball player at the net. I watch, mesmerized by the violence, the revelry I always opted out of in Iceland.

I never did hoot with the owls that summer. I was up as late as anyone; I was sleeping as erratically as anyone, but I just never let loose. Not in the wild way I heard Icelanders did, late, late into the summer nights. I left bars hours before the bacchanalia ensued, before there was any hitting on strangers, before the legendary fights broke out. I only knew things got raucous from the jagged broken beer bottles in my path up Klapparstígur, ablaze in morning light. I didn't partake, didn't let go, because I was too earnest about renewing, doing, making lists, and also because Reykjavik was a city where everyone seemed to be watching.

I'm feeling safe on the sidelines when Biggi II asks me to dance. He is old, and surely drunk, but also sweet Habba's sweet husband. He needs a partner while his wife dances through the room. There is no way to say no.

It happens so fast. His hand, my rise. We're dancing, in the light, on the open floor. Biggi's got my hands and he's twirling and I'm spinning, and we might even be fluid were the other twirlers not bumping us, were the bumpings slightly gentler. It's like a hoedown with the etiquette of Grand Central at rush hour.

Habba's out here, hopping, hands out, fingers spread, the portrait of glee. Someone starts jumping and Biggi gets jumping and we're all soon jumping, and jumping lets me veer Biggi toward the dense center, where I can jump like a kid, hidden by the others, aided now by the boots. The New York boots! I jump with abandon in boots with the bounce of gym shoes as the band plays a song with one word I can join in singing: "Maria!" It's easy to yell out, right when everyone in the bumping forest does, "Maria!" Then there's a chorus line and we join it and kick hard, "Ma-ria!" and then go back to collecting bruises and shouting in a crowd of people almost done enduring winter.

I sit down, red-cheeked, breathless with the proof that we can rekindle our own fires when the sun forsakes us. And it amazes me, really, that I almost didn't do this. That I came back to Iceland and almost sat this one out.

You do not wake up to spring the morning after Thorrablot. You wake up later than you should and you tell the clock it cannot be. It cannot be that time, you say to Iceland's clock. It is. Iceland never answers, because it always is.

You step barefoot across the carpet and catch a tickle of pink in the horizon out your giant windows and it's gone by

the time you trudge downstairs, and so are all the British photographers, off to chase the Northern Lights.

You find Sveinn manning the desk of an emptied hotel.
He offers you coffee; you drink a pot. You find out how long
Thorrablot went on without you: hours. Of course. You learn
that the cook "passed away in a chair." You know Sveinn
means passed out; nonetheless, the blurring of drinking and
dying in Iceland thrills you.

Outside, the town of Kirkjubæjarklaustur is slow to resur-
rect. The parking lot of the banquet hall is full of cars, their
drivers sleeping hard, still negotiating Brennivín. You climb
into a chilly jeep and ride past a familiar woman on the empty
road. She's from the comedy—one of the funniest actors, a
plain-faced brunette—coming back for her car. Her face is
stony as ever, and she's the last human being you see for hours.

Because you're about to make a wrong turn. Iceland has one
main highway: a "ring road." You amaze yourself by missing
it entirely. Instead you go snaking down gravel roads through
the most barren land ever farmed, where the homes are tucked
low among great swells of dried lava, past barns but no animals, and the sound of your wheels spraying black rocks is the
only noise for miles.

Until the wind. Until winds from what you think is north
gather enough force to gently tip your car, every few seconds,
nudging you toward what must be south. The winds carry
snow. Fat pieces, hardly spaced. By the time you find the Ring
Road, finally, you're in a blaze of sideways snow. When the
wind blows, you are swimming in white. Your hands are on
the wheel, your foot on the pedal, and there is nothing to see
but white. The jeep tips south, and the view erases.

You go as slow as wheels can turn. You slap yourself on the
cheeks. You shimmy in the seat, grip harder. You roll down a
window like someone could be out there, like there's a way to
flag for help, and wet snow pours on your lap. *Idiot.* You are

now soaked. The road is so illegible it makes more sense to follow the purple cartoon line on your GPS screen. You know this land and this winter enough to remember that light will vanish by dinnertime. If you're still on this mountain pass at six o'clock, you'll be out of gas, buried in white and wrapped in dark. You think: *I will freeze out here*.

Is there a way to tell Iceland that you get it? That you hear her? The point, you've got it: Survival at this latitude doesn't mean wading through your winter blues, learning to quit famishing yourself on a diet of green apples. This is the place where *people* almost went extinct. And you came here. You came back here. You asked for a lesson in human survival.

Someone dies on this mountain pass today, but not you. You'll hear about the person who died in this blizzard on the day after Thorrablot, which means you live. You reach the city. You pass through the white fugue toward the red beads of what must be taillights. You pass a sign for *Reykjavik*: a word that means something else to you now. It's the name of the settlement that saved your life.

Indoors, my blizzard story gets little play.

Nobody's much in the mood for a winter's tale.

I want to tell someone that I followed a purple line through a white void, but parked cars cram the glowing streets. Everyone's kept inside.

Only Bryn's boyfriend humors me, wanting all the near-death details. He hasn't had enough drives like that this year, he says, sounding envious. He's the second person to share this concern: This winter hasn't been brutal enough. Can spring lose its power without a true winter first? Do we need to be held down—long and hard—to feel the lift?

But there's a lift that even a foreigner can feel after just three days in Iceland. Gray pillows of clouds break open on my last afternoon and sun slices down, remaking the city.

Down by the lake, where two days ago boys were treating the frozen water like turf grass, diving and sprinting for the soccer ball, no one but a trio of waddling swans dares to tread. The ice looks sure to crack. The difference is written in light.

Light. How could I forget? *Light does not fall evenly on all the world's places.* What pours down on Reykjavik is more than warm and crisp and clear; it's transforming. It gets inside what it touches—the moss on trees, shutters on windows, every letter on every sign. It's light you feel like soft heat behind closed eyelids. Crack light, Floki's light, the bath of sun that beckoned him back to Iceland years after he'd left and said good riddance, defeated by winter.

I stalk this light all over the city, basking in familiar scenes, feelings of everything ahead, the feeling I love more than anything: pure horizon. In that very first inkling of spring, everything's ahead of you—not a single day's been subtracted yet from the brightest season. The promise is in the light. That top-of-the-world light.

Light *can't* fall evenly on all the world's places, because the world tilts. When sun hits the equator, it's a straight beam. At the poles, it's striking at a twenty-three-and-a-half-degree angle. The light spreads; it pours over twice as much space. It stretches in Iceland, and in late winter, it builds. It adds up. Fast.

Just before Thorrablot or just after, depending on when your town throws one, Iceland gets seven more minutes of sun every day. The daily gain in December was just three minutes. In January, it's four, then five. But February is a tipping point: suddenly, seven minutes. Seven plus seven plus seven is twenty-one. Add four more sevens to get forty-nine. A few more sevens and the sun hangs an hour longer above your head.

People must be counting. I can't find anyone who will talk about the dark. "This isn't dark," people say when I try, when I call Iceland dark. "You should have seen December."

I start to test people, asking everyone in my path, all the way to the airport. "How do you handle the dark?" Not even Edda, my ever-clad-in-black landlady, will hate on the dark. I find her wearing a rainbow skirt as bright as a Moroccan souk; her hair is dyed violet-red. "It was a shit year," Edda says, "but it's over now."

Down at the lake, I watch gray windows turn to sun mirrors, long boxes of brightness, holding praise straight up to the sky. I watch one yellow house regain its creamy glory. I stand there and hold it, I bring it far into the mind. I imagine someone in that attic room, drenched in the fresh light of the next season.

My socks are damp and my skin is goose-bumped when I turn in my rental jeep. The man who takes the keys must notice my chill. He tells me I really should come back to his country in summer. "It's a whole new world," he says, repeating the promise one more time. A whole new world.

Colleen Kinder is a writer loosely based in too many places. Her work has appeared in The New York Times Magazine, The New Republic, The Wall Street Journal, A Public Space, The Atlantic.com, National Geographic Traveler, Salon.com, Creative Nonfiction, The New York Times, *and* The Best American Travel Writing 2013. *Colleen is the co-founder of the reading series and online publication* Off Assignment *and teaches for Yale Summer Session in Auvillar, France.*

✿ ✿ ✿

Gratitude Day

Lessons in how to say thanks, but no thanks.

One might think I'd have had the good sense to put a stop to the whole thing before it was too late. Before my heathen ways and exceptionally bad judgment were put on display for the entire village.

But I did not.

A Lutheran-born atheist, I'd lived with the nuns for nearly six months. As a volunteer, I taught English in their girls' secondary school, among other randomly assigned duties. Their compound lay on the outskirts of Dilla, a small town tucked among low, green hills halfway between Addis Ababa and the Kenyan border in Ethiopia's Great Rift Valley. A durable group of Roman Catholic nuns ran the school, kindergarten, nutrition program, sewing classes, and a small clinic on their side of the compound, separated from the Fathers by a rickety old fence.

The sisters were an eclectic mix from all over the world: Ethiopia, Italy, India, Ecuador, Korea, and England. It often seemed the only thing they really had in common was being a nun. Sister Ines, a nurse, was the oldest and nearest, by far, to a saint. But she was forgetful and often caught daydreaming while inventorying clinic supplies or recording TB medication. Sister Igina talked endlessly and authoritatively on every subject, including those about which she could know absolutely nothing, such as the circumstances under which I would meet my future husband (whose name would be Bob, she insisted) and why I didn't have any tattoos. Young Sister Elizabeth, from another part of Ethiopia, ran the kindergarten and liked to crack jokes and make mischief only I could see. While we cleaned up after dinner, she and Sister Igina often snapped dishtowels at one another's bottoms, then covered them in mock dismay, shouting, "That's only for Jesus!" Then they erupted into uncontrollable laughter. Sister Agnes cobbled together homemade *kimchi* out of whatever local vegetables she could find and seemed the only truly sane one in the bunch. They were kind, industrious, and endlessly entertaining. I loved them all.

Well, almost all.

The Mother Superior was a tyrant—a grim-faced, ill-humored, bossy, old Italian tyrant who rarely ventured beyond the walls of her compound but was quick to pass judgment on everyone and everything, inside and out. From the start, Sister Thomasina and I rubbed each other the wrong way. She ruled her domain with a holy iron fist, and suddenly I'd dropped into it—seemingly straight from the great blue sky—and mucked up everything. In her eyes, I was, at twenty-four, hardly more than a child and totally unheeding of her rules. (And undoubtedly a serious liability, given all the kidnappers and other evil-doers she imagined lurking behind every acacia bush.) Only three or four days after my arrival, she announced at dinner that I wasn't allowed to leave the compound after dark, which fell like clockwork at six P.M. every evening. Indeed, venturing beyond the walls at any time of day, really, was frowned upon.

That night in the privacy of my little house, I burst into tears. After mustering up the courage to come to Ethiopia all alone—the idea of which scared me so much I almost didn't do it—I now appeared to be seriously stuck. How would I meet people and make friends? Travel and explore? Experience any part of this country not firmly under Sister Thomasina's thumb? Every evening after dinner the sisters sat around the table to knit and listen to Italian radio until it was time for nightly prayers. I wouldn't make it. Despite the kindness of the other nuns, I would crack with loneliness, and I would bolt. Not for home, perhaps, but somewhere—anywhere—Sister Thomasina held no sway.

But I stayed. And I lied regularly, concocting every benign-sounding excuse I could think of to venture into town (Sister Thomasina couldn't reasonably stop me from mailing letters home or exchanging currency, though her looks of disapproval withered the hibiscus). And I violated my house arrest, sneaking out and making friends anyway. I even managed to drink an illicit beer or two every once in a while. Still, after six months chafing under Sister Thomasina's suffocating authority, perhaps in some dark, rascally corner of my heart, I wanted to get even with her. Just a little.

It all started off innocently enough. It was near the end of the school term, and every year at this time, all the students from the various schools and programs put together an afternoon's worth of entertainment for the sisters, teachers, and clinic staff to say thank you. It was called Gratitude Day, and it took place in the big assembly hall with tall windows, rows and rows of benches, and a proper raised stage at one end. Mobs of cute kindergarteners in purple uniforms sang songs and handed out tiny bouquets of bougainvillea. Classes of older students recited poems, read short essays written specially for the occasion, or performed skits.

A group of my students—young women in their late teens and early twenties, barely younger than me at the time—had their hearts set on performing. For weeks they had begged me to help them prepare a humorous skit to showcase the progress they'd made with their English. But they also wanted something visually entertaining that even those who didn't speak the language could enjoy. And Sister Meaza wanted to be the star. One of two young nuns in my class, her lovely oval face was so saintly and serene the other sisters called her the Ethiopian Mary. It was impossible to say no to Sister Meaza.

So I gave in and taught them the only skit I could think of—funny, with speaking roles, but with a plot and jokes everyone could understand. It was one I myself had performed in a high school talent show years earlier. It takes place in the waiting room of a doctor's office when a perfectly healthy man comes in for his regular physical. After speaking briefly with the receptionist, he takes a seat to wait for the doctor. A moment later, another patient arrives, sneezing violently. He checks in and sits down next to the first man. After a few seconds the healthy man sneezes. Once, then twice. Suddenly he can't stop. In the meantime, the second man's sneezing gradually slows and comes to a halt. He's now just fine and so gets up, says goodbye to the receptionist, and leaves. Healthy Man can't stop sneezing; he's clearly caught whatever Sneezing Man had.

Over the course of the skit, this happens several more times. A woman with a terrible hacking cough comes in, gives it to the first man and then is miraculously cured and leaves. Another person enters, continually blowing a very runny nose. A tormented soul arrives who cannot stop itching and scratching. Our poor fellow contracts every single malady.

Then, finally, a very pregnant woman enters the waiting room, and the man runs screaming for the door. Hilarious, right?

Wouldn't it be funny, I thought, if the protagonist was a nun instead of a man?

The girls thought this was a great idea and the perfect role for saintly Sister Meaza. We spent hours preparing during the days leading up to Gratitude Day. Woinshet, a bright young woman with a thousand-watt smile and bit of mischief about her, would play the role of the pregnant woman.

When the big day arrived, we were ready. Everyone was excited and enjoying a break from the daily routine. The assembly hall was packed; it seemed that in addition to students and teachers, half of Dilla had shown up. And front and center of it all, Sister Thomasina held court, surrounded by the other sisters.

It still didn't occur to me that not everyone in the audience might find all of this quite so entertaining. In retrospect, the past six months being what they were, one might think I would have had at least a worrying thought or two. But even if I did, what could I have done to stop it now? The stage was set, literally.

I was lurking backstage, watching from the wings, when my girls' performance got underway. The sneezing patient entered and the laughs came quickly. Cougher, Nose Blower, and Itcher all came and went, and the audience was clearly enjoying it immensely, clapping and laughing loudly. The performance was succeeding tremendously in all the ways we had hoped. I was so proud of my girls.

Then Woinshet walked on stage, her enormous belly leading the way, her pregnant-woman waddle exaggerated for full effect. The hall erupted as Sister Meaza fled in a panic.

Off behind the curtains, I couldn't actually see the audience; I could only hear them—their laughter, shouts of approval, and occasional whistles. Then suddenly, slicing through the din, came the unmistakable sound of Sister Thomasina's deep booming voice. It reverberated through the hall, the noise of the crowd a mere whisper in comparison.

And then it all hit me like an enormous, angry hippo charging toward the nearest body of water. And hippos kill more people than any large animal in all of Africa.

Oh, God. She's mad as hell. And that's exactly where I'm going.

I panicked and did the only thing I could think to do: I ran from the building.

Then I cowered in my little house, heart racing. My hands were ice cold and my cheeks were on fire. That's what this woman did to me. What was I going to do? It would take about three minutes for the entire town to hear how I had enraged the Mother Superior. How I had totally and utterly shamed myself—not to mention my poor, unsuspecting students whom I'd made complicit in this offensive little stunt. It all seemed so ridiculously obvious now.

I would be banished from the compound—perhaps from Dilla—as dirty and shameful as any sinner in the history of Christendom.

It felt like I sat on my narrow bed long enough for the rainy season to come and go. For the avocados and mangos to ripen and fall from the trees. For Sister Ines to finish her daydreams of the Second Coming. It was probably five minutes.

Then suddenly Sister Igina was outside my door.

"Sara?" Knock, knock, knock. "SAAAA-rah!!" Pound, pound, pound. "*Dove sei?* Are you in there?" POUND, POUND, POUND. I knew Sister Igina wouldn't relent until she found me, so reluctantly I opened the door. She rushed in, a blur of frantically gesticulating hands and swirling fabric.

"Sara, *dios mio*, there you are! What are you doing in here? Sister Thomasina, she is looking for you!"

I bet she is.

"You must come back immediately. She wants to speak with you *subito*."

Oh shit.

"She wants you to perform again at dinner tonight!"

Pause. "Uh, she what?"

"Sister Thomasina, she insists you and Sister Meaza must perform the drama again *questa sera*. The other sisters will play the roles of your students."

I sat back down on the bed, stunned. Turned out Sister Thomasina loved our skit. She laughed so hard she nearly split her wimple.

Apparently what I'd heard from backstage and mistaken as her explosive, red-faced rage was actually the sound of her laughter. I'd fled like a coward for no reason. In my defense, however, I could hardly be expected to know the difference; I hadn't heard her laugh, not once, since I'd arrived in Ethiopia.

We did perform the skit at dinner that night, sweet Sister Meaza again the star. I was the Sneezer and the other sisters divided up the remaining afflictions. Sister Elizabeth couldn't stop laughing as she stuffed a large belly of sofa cushions under a borrowed dress.

I wish I could say that relations improved between Sister Thomasina and me after that day, but they didn't—not in any noticeable way. I left Dilla a few weeks later, as I was always scheduled to do. Perhaps she was sorry to see me go. Maybe she'd even become a little fond of me, despite her best efforts to the contrary. After all, I did make her laugh. But more likely than not, she celebrated my departure by finding a shady spot to put up her weary feet for half a moment, mop her brow, and heave a sigh of relief, momentarily grateful for the lightness of one less burden to bear. Then she undoubtedly pushed herself up, straightened her apron, set her scowl, and got back to work. I doubt Sister Thomasina ever wasted another precious moment thinking of me again.

Well, maybe every once in a while—maybe when she sneezed.

✂ ✂ ✂

More of Sara C. Bathum's stories about Dilla can be found in
The Best Women's Travel Writing 2005, 2010, *and* 2011.
She now lives back home in Seattle with her husband, two young
sons, and dog—an adventure that involves fewer nuns and more
cleaning.

🐾 🐾 🐾

Curandero

She waited, she hoped, and she
put herself in their healing hands.

*I*t was ten o'clock at night, and around us, the shopkeepers were snapping off their lights, stall by stall, until the
whole market was dark, except for the stall where we stood.
Light from bare bulbs fell on shelves crowded with bright-
colored boxes and bottles, giving the impression of standing at
a glowing hearth. Behind the counter, a man carefully sifted
glitter onto fat cylindrical candles.

My friend Mary Ann and I were in the depths of Mexico
City's Sonora Market, waiting for that man. We had been
waiting for nearly an hour, feeling conspicuous and uneasy,
and we were prepared to wait much longer. We knew him
only as "Don Hector." He was a witch doctor, and we were
waiting to become his patients.

Mexico makes fine distinctions among the practitioners
of Don Hector's craft. Technically, he and his wife were
curanderos—healers—people who cure in many ways. They
can issue good-luck charms, remove curses, treat illnesses and
forestall others, nurse the soul with blessings and ritual.

We were in line for one of their specialties—*una limpieza,*
or cleansing—recommended by a Mexican friend we'd met

that afternoon while watching Mayan dancers in the *zocalo*. Drawn by throbbing drums that echoed for blocks around Mexico City's vast central plaza, we marveled at the dancers' faces and costumes. Their profiles, ornaments, and long feathered headdresses could have been taken from a carved stone monument at Teotihuacan or a temple painting in the Yucatan. It was like watching archaeology come to life.

"Are those original dances?" we asked an onlooker. No, the man replied, sounding wistful. Most of Mexico's dances were lost in the Spanish Conquest, so these were modern recreations. But other folk customs had survived, he said. The incense the dancers were burning, for example, was *copal*—the same material the ancient Maya used in their ceremonies 1,300 years ago.

That gave me goosebumps, as the idea of survival always does—survival of belief, of custom, of human threads that can be traced back and farther back, back beyond history.

I'd thought Mexico's original religions had been completely eclipsed, either blended with Spanish Catholicism or reduced—as in our country, as in Europe—to scraps of superstition. Our new friend shook his head and smiled. No, he said, the old ways were still alive in Mexico. Call it folk medicine, call it witchcraft, but it endured, and a lot of people believed in it, himself included.

That surprised me. The man was about thirty, well-dressed, with an educated accent—not someone I'd expect would believe in much of anything. It surprised him too, he admitted. But he'd had trouble with migraine headaches, and modern doctors hadn't been able to cure them. He got desperate enough to try a witch doctor, and the headaches stopped.

"Now I believe," he said. His wonder-worker was Don Hector. ("Don" and the female "Doña" are affectionate honorifics in Spanish, used with first names only.)

Don Hector was someone Mexican people depended on, not someone who put on displays for tourists or, for that matter, who got involved with tourists at all. *Could we be the exception?* we wondered.

"He has a stall in the Sonora Market," said the man. "Ask for *una limpieza.*"

The Sonora was a long one-story stucco building on Fray Servando. Most of it was like any other Mexican market—aisles of fruits and vegetables, ranging from the familiar to the unidentifiable; aisles of cut flowers, cool with scent; aisles that stank of cloudy-eyed fish and blood-clotted meats, and aisles of dried herbs and spices, in bags and bins and piles.

In every market, a few of the spice stalls sell more than spices: peculiar stalks, dried leaves, rattlesnake rattles, animal pelts, bird claws and feathers—things used in cures or curses. What made the Sonora different was that it devoted a whole department to these things: the *herbolaria*, a sort of herbalists' warehouse.

It was dark when we arrived. The whole place looked closed, and we almost turned back. The wide parking lot was empty, except for a litter of corn husks and lettuce leaves and flimsy plastic produce bags that drifted across the asphalt like small ghosts.

But the herbalists' entrance was still open. We asked for Don Hector at the first booth we came to—a tourist's mistake. "Never heard of him," snapped the shopkeeper, a young guy in a baseball cap and undershirt, with gold front teeth that gleamed under the naked light bulbs.

"He's a *curandero*," Mary Ann explained in Spanish.

The young man gave us a sharp look. "There are no *curanderos* here," he growled. Never mind that his own stall was crammed with bundles of herbs, plastic skulls, demon masks, and bottles of scented oil.

We should have waited to ask until we were farther inside, where tourists were less likely to venture. So we moved down the aisle, inquiring every few stalls for Don Hector and receiving only head shakes and silence. Eventually, we must have walked past suspicion. When we said his name again, a woman sweeping her stall smiled and pointed to the last one in the row.

I expected Don Hector to be a wrinkled gnome, draped with charms and chanting curses over a fire. But the man we found looked like a successful California lawyer, or maybe a TV chef.

He was about forty-five, tan and fit as a tennis player, with a neatly trimmed ring of salt-and-pepper hair around the back of his balding head, and a warmly confident smile. He wore a denim shirt with the sleeves rolled up and a matching denim apron. No mystery here, no magic, though he did glow a little: While covering candles in glitter, he'd gotten tiny sparkling flakes on his face, the way a busy cook winds up smudged with flour.

We told him we had come for a cleansing. "My wife does that," Don Hector said kindly, and left off gilding candles long enough to go find her. It took a while. Yes, she would do it, he reported, but at least five people were ahead of us, and we'd have to wait our turn.

The Spanish verb *"esperar"* means "to wait" as well as "to hope." A fellow traveler in Latin America once told me that you couldn't really understand the verb until you'd waited for something so long that you gave up hope. That night, we came close to understanding the verb.

The wait, we decided, must have been a kind of test: Only the sincere would keep standing there, in the darkened market, while Don Hector blessed candles and chatted with clients. Customer after customer stepped up to place orders: candles for a wedding; a blessing candle for a child; a pair

of frog charms, one red, one green, for a young couple. Don
Hector advised them to keep the frogs in their pockets or
purse at all times.

While he worked, his wife—a handsome, dark-haired,
fortyish woman in slim blue jeans—took other customers into
a room at the back of the stall for consultations. Finally, Don
Hector's wife sent her last customer on his way and smiled at
us. Our turn.

"You go first," Mary Ann said, and I stepped past the counter into the space behind—a tiny cubicle, its walls lined floor
to ceiling with candles and rainbow-colored bottles.

Doña Hector stepped in beside me. The floor space was no
bigger than the top of a desk. This close to another person,
one needed either strong defenses or complete trust. It had to
be trust.

She asked me gently, in Spanish, what was wrong. She
was completely serious, and suddenly so was I. I poured
out every complaint I had a Spanish word for and acted out
the ones I didn't know, from my own migraines to frequent
stiff necks and a pinched nerve that made my right hand
clumsy.

She listened intently, sometimes asking a question, sometimes gently touching me—my lower back, my shoulders,
the knuckles of my hand—to find out, as a physician would,
whether this place or that place hurt.

Then she called Don Hector in, and they discussed my medical problems. They concluded I needed a special *te-ita*—little
tea. She listed the herbs she wanted, and he returned to his
counter to mix them.

"Now," she said, "you want to have a *limpieza*?" Yes.

She called out front for a special bouquet and the egg of a
black chicken. A young girl assistant, whom I hadn't noticed
before, quickly handed them in: a raw egg with a brown shell
and a nosegay of fresh-smelling green leaves bunched around

a single white daisy and a red carnation. It looked like something a winter bride might carry.

La Doña chose a small bottle of pink liquid from a shelf above her head, sprinkled a few drops into my hands, and told me to rub it over my face and hair. It reminded me of glycerin and rosewater.

Then she picked up the bouquet as if it were a whiskbroom and began to sweep me, stroking my body with the flowers as if dusting a precious relic—first one side, then the other: head, neck, throat, breasts, both arms, both legs, the soles of my feet.

While she swept, she murmured. I expected an incantation, but this was a prayer—a long whispered speech that my *curandera* spun around me like a thick web. Over and over, she asked the Virgin Mary, Jesus, and all the saints to help and protect me.

She swept and murmured for a long time, and I closed my eyes and relaxed under the soft strokes of the bouquet. The process was somewhere between a caress and massage. It was long and startlingly sweet.

Just as I was deeply lulled by the sweeping, la Doña pressed the bouquet hard against my eyelids, and I jumped. "That you may not see evil," she said. She put her hands over my ears next: "That you may not hear evil." Then she pushed the bouquet against my lips. The leaves felt cool, and I could smell the sharp fragrance of the flowers: "That no calumny come from your mouth."

When she had swept me spiritually clean, she laid the bouquet on the floor and instructed me to trample it, crushing the flowers and scattering the leaves.

Next, she picked up the egg and, still praying, passed it over me, working from head to toe, making tiny crosses with it on my forehead and above each breast. I understood that whatever evils remained in me were now entering the egg. The idea pleased me.

Finally, she gave my arms a little squeeze. "Good," she said, the way a mother might after combing a daughter's hair. I knew we were done.

I had been given half an hour of intense, concentrated, professional attention aimed at healing both body and spirit. I felt refreshed, at ease and cared for. No wonder the old ways had survived, I thought; they made you feel better. They helped.

"How was it?" Mary Ann asked as we traded places. I paused, feeling speechless.

"Great," I finally said, knowing that the word didn't come close to the truth.

Out front, Don Hector presented me with a big yellow plastic bag full of what looked like salad—different shades of chopped green leaves, segments of horsetail rushes, clumps of corn silk. My prescription. I was to let it dry—only in the shade—then take a handful of it, add it to boiling water, and drink the resulting tea in place of water every day for a month.

The price for everything—cleansing, *te-ita,* and all that time—was six dollars. At home, it would have required visits to at least four separate professionals—a doctor, a pharmacist, a shrink and a priest, all at once—and cost as much as my round-trip airfare.

As we made our way back through the dark aisles of the Sonora Market and finally stepped into the empty street and the cool night, we agreed that we both felt calm and good. But it was more than that. "Cleansed" seemed a suitable word for it.

I lugged the yellow plastic bag of damp vegetation across Mexico for the next ten days, opening it each night at my hotel and fluffing up the contents, hoping it would dry better. The salad changed colors, but it didn't dry. I did get one pot of tea out of it; it tasted like a cross between licorice and mint. Then I accidentally left the bag on a sunny windowsill for an afternoon, and it began to rot.

I had briefly considered trying to take it home, though I knew a U.S. customs agent wasn't likely to believe my bag of mysterious leaves was homeopathic medicine. But now that it was turning into compost, I abandoned the idea. Still, I couldn't just toss it into a wastebasket—that seemed sacrilegious. Finally, I made a decision, and I think Don Hector and his wife would have approved.

There was a little fireplace in a corner of my hotel room, already laid with kindling, so on my last night in Mexico, I lit it, pulled handfuls of the fermenting leaves from the bag, threw them into the flames, and watched the sweet-smelling smoke drift up the chimney. It reminded me of the incense in the *zocalo*, rising to heaven, like ancient prayers. Whether the magical healing would last, I didn't know, but for that little while, all my pains and problems were rising with the perfumed smoke, and I felt at peace.

Catherine Watson is an award-winning travel writer, editor, photographer and writing coach. A national pioneer in voiced travel writing for newspapers, she was the founding editor of the Travel Section at the Minneapolis Star Tribune *and was its chief travel writer and photographer from 1978 until 2004. Watson teaches college-level workshops in travel writing and memoir, most recently for Ghost Ranch at Abiquiu, New Mexico. She has also taught for The Loft in Minneapolis, the University of Minnesota's Split Rock Arts Program, the Madeline Island School of the Arts in Wisconsin, and Brown University's summer writing programs in Pont-Aven, France, and Segovia, Spain. Her work has appeared in fourteen anthologies, including* The Best Travel Writing 2008 *and* The Best Women's Travel Writing 2009, *both from Travelers' Tales, and* The Best American Travel Writing 2008, *from Houghton-Mifflin. She is the author of two collections of travel essays,* Roads Less Traveled: Dispatches from the Ends of the Earth *and* Home on the Road: Further Dispatches from the Ends of the Earth. *Both were Minnesota Book Award finalists. Nationally, her awards include the top two in travel writing, the Lowell Thomas Travel Journalist of the Year and the Society of American Travel Writers Photographer of the Year.*

♨ ♨ ♨

Call Your Mother

No seriously, call your mother.

*A*t every turn in the dimly lit cave, criminals faced their sentences. Thieves were frozen into ice blocks; drug traffickers grilled on red-hot rotisseries; kidnappers impaled on trees of knives; porn possessors sawed in half; and classroom cheats meticulously disemboweled. But there was one piece of the action I wasn't able to make out through the cluster of young families who'd stopped for a good, long look. And I could hardly grudge them their presence: We were, after all, in a theme park.

Picture *It's a Small World* with set design by Hieronymus Bosch, and you'll start to get an idea of the *10 Courts of Hell*: a detailed tour of the sinner's afterlife, and the centerpiece of Singapore's Haw Par Villa. This sprawling mythological playground—created in 1937 by the brothers behind the Tiger Balm analgesic empire—is a rhapsody in dioramas, each an ode to Chinese history, legend, or virtue.

But it wasn't just any old virtue drawing those families into the cave the day I visited. Once the parents in front of me began to disperse—along with the kids they'd been hoisting for unobstructed views—a stark lesson in filial piety emerged from the shadows. Actually, what emerged was a special place in hell for the *un*filial: Here in Court Four of the underworld, disobedient offspring were being ground to a bloody pulp between boulders. Under the supervision of masked demons.

Filial piety. The virtue of obeying, revering, and caring for one's parents. I'd certainly heard of it—and knew it was big in Confucian circles—but I'd never seen a place so steeped in it as Singapore. Granted, Confucius's homeland had to be a worthy rival, but during my only trip to China years earlier, the language barrier was too high for me to grasp even beginner-level family politics.

Not so in Singapore, where English is an official language—and where even a visitor who considers herself a fairly decent daughter starts to doubt her devotion.

No sooner had I exited that Hell cave than I hit the park's 24 Filial Exemplars diorama. And there, among other goings-on, a pretty young woman made of plaster was guiding one of her milk-filled breasts into the mouth of her sickly, white-haired mother.

"Never in a million years, ma," I whispered apologetically to no one—as my mother was fast asleep on another continent at the time.

I should say in my defense that I've rushed thousands of miles to my mom's bedside more times than I care to count. Since I left my childhood home in Arizona in the late eighties, first for college, then life, on the East Coast, the woman I love most in the world—my sweet, twenty-minute-message-leaving, letter-to-the-editor-penning, mystery tune-humming, compulsively stranger-befriending mother—has given me a whole series of sickening scares.

She's been hit by a car. She's been felled by viruses. She's been invaded by tumors. And though my sister, who's always lived closer to home, has borne the brunt of the emergency response, my routine of jumping on planes and praying not to hear the worst upon landing has grown entirely too familiar.

Still, as I gazed upon that Singaporean sculpture, not only couldn't I imagine breastfeeding my mom, I hadn't even *called* her lately. Normally, I phoned home from wherever I turned up on the planet, but between the almost unnavigable time difference and crazy itinerary on this trip, I resorted to quickie emails instead.

Clearly, that sort of behavior wouldn't fly in Singapore. When I asked a local friend about the whole breastfeeding-your-own-mom thing, she told me she knew someone who'd done it. The model daughter in question had an ailing mother who'd heard breast milk was the best medicine. And in the name of filial piety, the young woman obliged.

"I understand that it goes against Western sensibilities," said my friend, in response to my obvious discomfort. "But so does a lot of what we do to be filial, whether that's living with our parents until we get married, giving them an allowance, or taking them on holidays—though I've failed miserably there compared to my sisters."

Sibling rivalry writ large! Who's the *most* filial?

Indeed, a Singaporean movie, *Filial Party,* poses that very question—not to siblings, but to contestants on a fictional reality show. "They go to the extremes to be filial!" touts the must-view trailer.

Taking filial piety even further, many locals—some Buddhist, some Taoist—literally worship their parents. Or their deceased parents, anyway. The resulting offerings are so multitudinous, the uninitiated mind boggles, as I discovered when I wandered into an ancestor worship supply shop.

There, amongst the overflowing shelves, was anything a departed soul could possibly desire, from three-piece suits to iPhones (or Galaxies, for any dearly departed who leaned

Samsung). Of course, all these items were made of paper so they could be burned in offering. In fact, one woman I chatted up at the store said that her brother—having just acquired his own deluxe massage chair—decided to buy a paper version for their mom, who would surely appreciate being as pampered in the afterlife as he was on Earth.

With that, I was officially guilt-stricken. When had I last gotten something for myself that I loved so much, I thought my mom should have it, too? (That this massage chair was made of paper and *just* big enough for Barbie's Dreamhouse was beside the point.)

Filial piety was now all I could see, whether in the Singaporean papers, where pundits explored the troubled economy's impact on filial duties; on TV, where politicians condemned "the outsourcing of filial piety" to retirement homes; or in temples, where ancestral tablets filled entire pagodas. The question tormented me at every turn: *Was I a good enough daughter?*

Needless to say, I called home the second I touched down at JFK.

My mom answered, and I sensed immediately that something was wrong. Turns out, she was extremely sick with bronchitis, and had been since the day I left for Singapore.

"Why didn't you tell me?" I demanded.

"I didn't want to ruin your trip, sweetheart," she answered.

And as I inwardly vowed to henceforth seriously step up my filial-piety game—I would call more, write more, visit more, dote more, do whatever I could for the remainder of my days, with the notable exception of suckle her—I could almost swear I heard Confucius say, *told you so.*

Abbie Kozolchyk is the author of National Geographic's The World's Most Romantic Destinations—*a book that includes*

no *Confucian theme parks, but does include an Incan spa, a Sami sleigh ride, and various gateways to the Mayan underworld. Taking a page out of her own book, she's just followed her heart to California after a twenty-five-year career in the New York magazine world.*

❧ ❧ ❧

A Country Tradition

The worst was not over.

To a Hungarian, *palinka* is an elixir: it facilitates digestion, staves off an emerging cold, or—as was this case—bolsters the kill. I had dreaded the shots of *palinka* nearly as much as the death of the pig. Fortunately, I knew to throw it back in a gulp. I was still sputtering from the first shot when Dini poured a second.

With two shots behind us, Zoltan muttered, "It's time."

Dini grabbed a sledgehammer and sharp knife while the other men selected a pig from one of the pens. I moved to an area behind the barn and stared out at the farmland. A frigid autumn night had left a thick coating of frost. The sun dawned—a smudge of pink smeared across a drab, gray sky. A moo from a disgruntled milking cow pierced the silence. The farm smelled dank and musty with a strong whiff of manure. This smell reminded me of the dairy farms I had grown up near in New Jersey. The pig squealed in a God-awful pitch as the men pulled it from the pen. Then Dini raised the sledgehammer.

I didn't move to Central Europe to kill a pig; that idea came later. After a three-decade career at a global tech company, one morning my manager phoned and asked me to relocate to Bratislava, Slovakia. My husband, Pat, and I had three grown children. I was restless in my suburban life and bored with my job.

"Why not?" I said, agreeing to move across the planet to a city I had barely heard of and never visited.

Most of our friends asked, "Where's that?" Others asked, "Why?" One woman scribbled *Bratislava* on a scrap of paper and pulled it out whenever we saw her, "So when do you move to . . . one sec . . . Bratislava?" Our children thought we were crazy.

A few months later, Pat and I settled into an apartment near the pedestrianized old town. Locals described buildings as coated in "a communist pallor," but we found a charming maze of cobblestone streets lined with Baroque palaces, freshly restored to their original pastels and adorned with plaster flowers, curlicues, and shells. The one built for Maria Theresa was bubble-gum pink. In the main square, a buttercup-yellow clock tower anchored one corner opposite a mint green coffee shop.

At first, it felt like a European vacation, until the time came for a vacation to end, and we stayed. My focus shifted from classical music concerts in restored palaces to the concrete-block housing complex that scarred a mile of the Danube riverbank. Communication gaps lost their charm. (After hours spent selecting furniture for our apartment one day, we couldn't arrange delivery. Another day, a waiter threw his hands in the air and yelled, "No English!" when we tried to order.) This was my home now. And if I'd been looking for a challenge, I'd found one.

Though I wasn't exactly homesick, I did miss aspects of my life back in the United States—especially the evenings I'd spent volunteering, teaching English to immigrants who faithfully attended every class, even after long shifts as hospital aides or construction workers. They had shared their goals: being able to communicate with their children's teachers; making their English-speaking children proud. I loved helping them, and when we moved to Bratislava, I lamented relinquishing the position. So when I was asked to teach conversational English to my Slovak colleagues, I pounced on the chance.

I started each Monday class with the same ice-breaker: "What did you do this weekend?" Since most of the students were twenty-somethings, their answers usually involved partying with friends or visiting family in their home villages. But one day, a typically quiet man yelled out, "I killed a pig at my grandmother's house." Normally, my students sat mute while I cajoled them to speak, but the pig-killing anecdote ignited a torrent of stories punctuated with laughter.

I forced a neutral expression as I internally debated whether this was the coolest—or most disgusting—story I had ever heard. My meat always came wrapped in white paper, like a gift from my butcher to me.

"Let me get this straight," I asked, "You've all done this?"

They nodded and explained that the event was known as a *zabíjačka*.

"Could I attend one of these?" I asked.

"Doubtful," they frowned. "It's a country tradition."

This, I realized, this kind of cultural exploration, deep and real and undoubtedly disturbing, was why I had moved here—to stretch myself beyond a career that had become rote, to experience a place so different from suburbia. And difficulty only enhanced the allure. But when I asked our city friends about the *zabíjačka*; they rolled their eyes. One chided me, "Julie, please, don't believe all Slovaks raise pigs in their backyards. That's *so* old school." I felt silly and questioned my motives: Ugly American? Cultural observer? Weird mid-life crisis? One doubt nagged. *What if the class had exaggerated the pig-killing story?*

Then one autumn day, I was walking past a restaurant we frequented and saw an advertisement in the window for a *zabíjačka* dinner special. I pointed at it and pulled my husband inside. As we balanced precariously on tall bar stools and dined on the advertised pork platter—ribs, spicy sausage, and a slab of head cheese—our youthful waiter explained that the pig-killing season had started. I asked if he'd ever participated in one.

"Of course," he said. "My grandmother raises a pig in her backyard every year."

"What's happening?" I asked Pat after the waiter left, waving a rib in the air for emphasis. "Half the country swears this doesn't exist while the other half brags about it."

I didn't know what was true. All I knew was I had to find out—by attending a *zabíjačka*.

But by then, eighteen months had passed, and before I could find out, I was asked to relocate again, this time to Budapest, Hungary. We packed up and moved. And within days of pulling into the Budapest train station, we found ourselves living in a place where no one even attempted to deny or hide the tradition: there were pig-killing tourist excursions and pig-killing team-building exercises and pig-killing community events in town squares. In Hungary, I learned, it was called a *disznóvágás*. I saw the word everywhere, in loud pink-and-black print, on flyers in windows and tourist pamphlets scattered in coffee shops. Sometimes the letter "ó" was replaced by a pig snout.

But attending one of these staged events interested me not in the least. It seemed akin to eating at the French pavilion in Epcot Center and believing I had dined in Paris. No, I decided. If it were going to happen, I would need to be accepted by a family and invited as their guest.

At work, I began mentoring a young man named Abraham with spiked chestnut hair, perpetual chin stubble, and

Hollywood good looks. One day he invited Pat and me to join him at a street festival. We watched folk dancers and sipped red wine produced in backyard vineyards and nibbled on *lángos*—fried bread smothered with sour cream, cheese, and garlic. Another weekend, he drove us to a massive hilltop abbey visible for fifty miles where we sampled the Riesling made in the adjacent vineyards by monks for more than a thousand years. A few months later, we ventured to a small town with him to attend a handball game, a ridiculously fast sport played on a basketball-style court with no apparent rules other than a frenzied quest to whip a six-inch ball into the opposing team's goal.

I can't remember when or why I began calling him Abe, but that weekend he admitted to me that he hated when colleagues used the nickname. "But it's O.K," he assured me, "that's what my family calls me. You're family."

Finally, one afternoon in the early fall when we were eating burritos in a dive near my apartment, Abraham mentioned that pig-killing season would begin soon at his girlfriend's family farm. "I was hoping you could join us," he said.

I was so overwhelmed that for a moment I couldn't speak. My assignment in Hungary was scheduled to end in a few months, and I'd begun to accept that I might never experience a pig killing. In those early, off-balanced days in Bratislava, I had latched onto this event as the standard bearer for the weirdness of our new life. When friends asked what Central Europe was like, I would respond, wide-eyed, "They kill pigs in their back yards," as if that single event encapsulated everything. Yet after longing for this invitation for three years, here in the moment, I realized the friendship it implied meant much more than the event itself. I'd grown to love this young man like one of my sons.

"Yes," I buried my face in my hands. When I looked up he was laughing. "Yes!" I said again.

Pat and I arrived in the village of Komárom by train one evening in November. The tiny station was dark except for a tight circle of light from a single incandescent bulb. In the blackness, I descended the train steps, unable to see the Danube River five paces from the tracks. Abe and his girlfriend, Brigi, were waiting under the dab of light. They drove us to our room above a combination bar and pool hall. For eleven dollars we got a soiled carpet, threadbare curtains, and a set of twin beds, one of which tilted on a broken leg.

The next morning, Abe arrived shortly after six o'clock in a wood-paneled station wagon identical to the one my mother had driven in the seventies. He had warned me that no one in the family spoke English. But before I could select a suitable greeting from my ten words of Hungarian, Abe's father, Zoltan—an intimidating giant in an olive-green military jacket—stepped out of the car, crushed me with a hug, and kissed both my cheeks. Abe's six-year-old brother sat in the far back of the station wagon and giggled when he learned this was my first pig killing. "It's my fourth!"

During the short drive to the farm, I tried to calm myself. The promise of a full day of work and celebration with family and close friends enthralled me, but the thought of the pig killing itself terrified me. I breathed deeply, assuring myself that the worst part would soon be over.

At the farm, we met the rest of the family and repeated a round of hugs and kisses before convening to the pig barn. There, we huddled in the corner and were joined by a farmhand and Brigi's stepfather, Dini, who possessed none of the menacing features—bushy black brows, sneer, exceptionally long teeth—that I somehow associated with a Hungarian pig killer.

With a boyishly round face that crinkled into a grin, he doled out a clear, strong-smelling alcohol from a Jim Beam bottle and said, "My friend made this from fruits. Apricots, I think." I recognized the drink as *palinka*, a Hungarian brandy so strong it burns from the lips to the belly.

And then, after downing two shots each, it was time to kill the pig.

Years ago, I studied veterinary medicine in college: castrating piglets, drawing blood, operating on dogs. I'm not squeamish, but back then I coped with death as a necessary advancement of my medical studies. This felt different. Primal. I braced myself—pushing my hands deeper into my jacket pockets and crinkling my toes inside my boots. Had I grown soft? Or worse, did I feel more civilized than this family, coming from a place where I could create a comfortable distance between myself and the meat I consume? Whatever the reason, I'm embarrassed to admit that when I saw the sledgehammer rise, I turned away.

I heard sounds of a tussle and a bone-crushing thump. Then silence. From start to finish, perhaps a minute had transpired. I turned back to survey the scene; the pig lay at the edge of the dirt driveway surrounded by a broadening crimson halo. The farmhand held a bowl under the neck and did his best to gather every last trickle of blood.

Abraham rushed over. "Are you O.K.? I hate that part. It's why we drink the *palinka*." He looked shaken, and I realized no one enjoyed the kill.

"I'm fine," I said, looking up and smiling weakly. The worst was over, "Why did we save the blood?"

"Oh, that's the best," he grinned, "We cook it for breakfast."

The worst is not over.

As I looked back at the pig, I paused, reminding myself to burn this image into my brain: a discarded wheelbarrow rested on a pile of straw, a corrugated tin garage sheltered a pair of tractors, a trio of cows peeked out through slates in the barn. Just then, a man pulled into the farmyard on a bicycle to pick up a bottle of fresh milk at a stand that stood not ten steps away from the pig. He glanced at it but didn't flinch.

Dini carried a bucket of warm water and a shovel from the barn. Then Zoltan and I began preparing the carcass. We burned the hair with a blowtorch, scraped off the charred follicles with the shovel, and scrubbed the skin with a brush until the pig shined as if sculpted from butter. An hour later, my back ached; my hands smelled like smoked bacon. I glanced at my watch. It wasn't yet nine A.M. Finally, Zoltan and Dini hoisted the pig onto a makeshift table in the middle of the driveway. But when Dini raised his knife, he froze mid-air, scowled, and let loose a stream of Hungarian. This was more like the face I had expected from a pig killer. Abraham, noticing my confusion, whispered into my ear, "Dini said he would not eat this pig. It's too dirty."

"Tell your father I'm scared of Dini right now," I said.

Abraham laughed. "He is, too."

Zoltan and I grinned at each other as we redoubled our scrubbing in order to remove the tiniest tufts of hair and smudges of black. We became pig-scrubbing conspirators and budding, if unlikely, friends—we had grown up thousands of miles apart and shared no common language. Through gestures and Abraham's help, however, we had formed a bond. When Dini returned and reexamined the pig, I held my breath until he nodded his satisfaction. Then Dini began the butchering: lopping off the legs, pulling out the organs, and throwing them into a barrel of boiling water. Most of the pig, Abe explained, would be turned into sausage. "It goes further that way." Dini tossed the intestines onto the grass, and a dozen or more cats scampered from neighboring farms, hissing and commencing a feeding frenzy like lions devouring a freshly killed wildebeest.

The men carted hundreds of pounds of meat down concrete steps into a room that was equal parts basement and kitchen: farm contraptions, piles of tires, bottles of wine and *palinka*, a case of sports trophies, and mountains of soda bottles, washed and ready to be reused as milk bottles. There were four or five immaculately scrubbed tables, a meat grinder, and an old stove.

The men dumped the meat onto an industrial-sized table in the center. I grabbed a cutting board and razor-sharp knife, exhaled, and watched my breath form a cloud in the cold air. We would work all day in a natural refrigerator that smelled like a musty butcher shop. Dini set aside the ribs and loin to sell, split the feet for soup, and rolled up a sheet of fat like a yoga mat, which Abraham grabbed and tucked under his arm.

"What's that for?" I asked.

Abraham smiled. "Zoltan will make Christmas cookies."

"Of course," I laughed. "Lard."

When I grabbed my first chunk of meat, I shuddered at its warmth—a crude reminder that moments ago, this pig had been alive. I forced the thought from my mind as I worked beside Dini, Zoltan, and the farmhand. Buried in the heap of warm meat, my hands began to thaw.

Dini pulled off a piece of skin, salted it, and held it out to me. "It was cooked by the flames," he explained. I declined, raising my bloody hands as an excuse. He shrugged and popped it into his mouth.

All day, we worked, dicing parts I would have deemed inedible—brains, ears, jowls—and dumping the pieces into a plastic sleeve to congeal into head cheese. I cubed and ground the remainder of the pig, added spices, and pressed the mixture into intestinal casings to form sausage, while Dini shouted instructions: "Stop! Start! Move faster! Move slower!" And, "Pull the casings over the nozzle like you are pulling on a condom!"

But when I turned the handle too quickly, splitting open the casing and grimacing in embarrassment, Dini only smiled and motioned with his hands: *Slow down. Gentle.* Eventually, we developed a rhythm. When he winked at me after we created section after section of sausage, I felt tired—and proud. At the end of the grueling 12-hour day, 100 pounds of sausage hung over steel poles or lay spiraled in snail-shaped helixes on the table. I could have taken the waste home in a sandwich bag: the eyes, the bladder, and the tail.

All throughout the morning and afternoon, friends and family stopped by to place dibs on the sausage, and each visit provided an excuse to pour another round of drinks. Zoltan filled the glasses and shouted, "A toast to the Americans. They are good *palinka* drinkers!" Pat and Zoltan wrapped their arms around each other and threw back the shots.

"How many is that?" I asked Pat.

"I've lost count," he replied, as he massaged the bridge of his nose with his thumb and forefinger. "Five. No six. No. No idea."

We took three breaks during the day to eat meals made from various parts culled from the pig: a meaty-bone soup served over noodles and a selection of our sausage—blood, organ meat, and kielbasa. There was a homemade pickled salad put up during the fall harvest, as well as freshly baked bread. I devoured the soup, kielbasa, and salad, while pushing the blood and organ sausages around on my plate. The organ sausage tasted like my mother's fried liver, a weekly meal I dreaded as a kid. The blood sausage was black and gooey—foul, unlike anything I had ever eaten. I cringed. Still, as I contemplated this sausage, I was struck by how honorable it felt to consume every morsel of the pig.

The men huddled at one end of the table to analyze the sausage.

"They are happy," Abe whispered in my ear. "Sometimes the spices aren't right, and the sausage is ruined. But today, it's good."

The scrambled blood breakfast turned out to be my favorite meal. All the chairs in the house had been dragged around a harvest table, which was set with a pile of mismatched glasses, plates, and cutlery. In the center, on a platter, awaited a pile of brownish-red mush—the cooked blood—with a texture like scrambled eggs but no discernible odor.

As we crowded around the table, Zoltan told a story. "When I was a boy, we gathered every weekend in the winter to kill a pig. We divided the meat and each family took home their share. We did this because we had no refrigeration."

Though Zoltan and I were the same age, I couldn't relate to the life he described. I felt overwhelmed, emotional. I breathed deeply to keep from crying.

Abraham, misinterpreting my expression, said, "Add salt. It will taste better. If you can't eat this, we'll make you something else."

"No," I said, "This is fine."

The day, I knew, was never about killing a pig—at least not entirely. It was about the way food brings us together. It was about the way our common need for nourishment lowers our guard. I thought back to all the dreaming I had done about this event. I thought about what it meant to be here: to be welcomed not as a foreigner, but as a member of a family.

That night, I stood under the hottest shower I could tolerate until every trace of the pig swirled down the drain. Then I crawled into my tilted bed and slept for twelve hours. The following morning, we stopped by the farm on our way to the train station to say goodbye one final time. Our stint in Hungary would end in a few months, and I doubted I would ever see this farm or these people again. I wanted to thank them once more. Dini stood in the driveway carving a freshly killed pig. When he saw us, he waved his knife and smiled.

Julie Callahan lived in Central Europe for four years before retiring from a thirty-two-year career at IBM and selling everything

off to become a full-time traveler. In pursuit of perpetual spring-time, Julie has wintered in Guatemala, summered in Ireland, and salsa danced into a new year in Cuba. Her three grown children wonder how this will end. So does she. In 2015, Julie and her husband spent three months in a closet-sized apartment in Paris, where she attended the Paris Writing Workshop. There, this essay was born. Julie has also been published in Tales to Go, *but this is her first print publication. She writes about her travels at www.theworldinbetween.com.*

ஐ ஐ ஐ

Outsider Again

An identity crisis bubbles up in the hot springs.

I knew it was a breach in etiquette to stare at other bath-ers in the changing room, but I couldn't help myself. All around me, everyone was breaking almost every unspoken rule. When you take off your clothes, you aren't supposed to throw them into a cubby—you place them neatly in the bas-ket with a bath towel draped over it. When you come back, you aren't supposed to spread out and take over the bench or cover the floor with your stuff—you take up as little room as possible, so as not to disturb the others. And what happened to covering yourself modestly with a wash towel when walk-ing around?

"*Shinjirarenai!*" My train of thought was broken by Yuka, my friend undressing next to me. "I can't believe it," she repeated, laughing. "This is so not Japan."

My husband and I had left San Francisco three days earlier to ski in the northernmost island of Hokkaido. Because I grew up in Tokyo and we had also lived there together in the mid-2000s, our trips back to Japan were always a kind of homecom-ing. Usually, we saw friends, hit up our favorite restaurants, and took at least one overnight trip to a hot springs inn. After a ten-hour flight, there was nothing as blissful as that first bite of sashimi or the first soak in a bath. That was when I slipped out of my American self and became Japanese again.

But this visit to Japan was even more meaningful than usual, because I'd gotten a kidney transplant last spring. My surgery was successful, but the past year had been an anxious one. I was now on a regimen of strong immuno-suppressants that made it easier for me to fall sick. Food poisoning or a stomach flu could knock me out for a couple weeks. Even something as simple as dehydration was a big deal. In the first six months, I'd visited the emergency room twice.

Before my transplant, I had loved traveling. I'd been every-where from Greenland and Iceland to Bhutan and Rwanda. A map on the wall in my home was covered with white and green pins of all the places I'd visited, the white showing where I had been with my husband and the green indicating where I had gone by myself.

For nearly a year, I'd stuck close to home, aside from short weekend trips or family visits, and I was developing serious cabin fever. I was desperate to feel normal again. I needed to stop being "a transplant patient" and go back to just being me. A trip to Japan was fairly routine by my standards, but it held the promise of more travels to come.

We booked a condo in Hirafu village in Niseko, the region's largest ski resort, and invited Yuka, a friend from Tokyo, to join us. I could hardly contain my excitement. I dreamt about the champagne powder on the mountain, ramen and sushi for lunch, and après-ski in the hot springs baths. I couldn't wait to start living again.

Hokkaido was just as I imagined it to be, with the regal Yotei Mountain overlooking vast farmlands that produce some of the country's best vegetables and dairy products. At a hotel nearby, we stopped for a soba lunch. But the minute we entered the village, Japan was gone. The first people we saw were two white guys, carrying skis on their shoulders. A couple hundred feet later was a family of Westerners—Dad was trying to help his two little kids from slipping and falling on the sidewalk. We passed by group after group of Westerners. As we neared the main part of town, my eyes grew wider. Every shop and restaurant sign was in English.

I had known Niseko was popular with foreigners, or *gaijin,* as we called them in Japanese. Some years ago, Australian developers had invested in the area because it was an affordable ski destination for Aussies who didn't want to spend the money or time to travel to North America or Europe. What I hadn't expected was an Australian colony in the middle of Japan. Where were the Japanese?

At our rented condo, a young Australian *gaijin* greeted us and briefed us on our apartment.

"Where's the nearest supermarket?" I asked.

"There's a Lawson's around the corner," she said, "and a Seico Mart across the street."

(But those are convenience stores!)

"What about grocery stores?"

"I think you should be able to find most of what you need at these stores."

(Not a chance!)

"I'd actually like to go to a supermarket," I said. "Where would that be?"

"Well, there's none nearby."

(That's impossible.)

"Then where do the locals shop?"

"Well, there's a MaxValu, but you have to drive for fifteen minutes."

All I wanted was to browse a grocery store for the foods I had missed. It was part of my homecoming ritual. I needed to peruse the yogurt aisle, survey the produce stands, and buy some *natto*, the fermented soybeans we eat with rice for breakfast. Why was this so hard?

When we sat down for dinner at a nearby *izakaya* bar that night, I was even more dismayed. I'd been dreaming of sashimi, freshly made tofu, and seasonal fried morsels of seafood and vegetables. Instead, the menu mostly included standard items, many of which you could find in a restaurant in San Francisco, and some of which you'd only see in a cafeteria. Cheese and crackers? Ugh. Edamame? Boring. Grilled shiitake mushrooms and cheese? Double ugh. The best dish was the fried chicken. We may have been in Japan, but this wasn't the Japan I'd traveled so far to reach.

Now, a day later, we were at the local public baths, and Yuka and I were the only Japanese.

As I took off my sweater, I snuck a peek at a brunette sprawled on a changing bench taking a nap *au naturel*. The sliding door rattled, and I glanced at the tall blond woman striding in from the baths, barely covering herself with a towel. In the corner, two young Australian girls were laughing and chattering about their evening plans. One was pulling on her jeans. The other was still in her bra and thong as she rifled through her belongings in search of her pants. Their towels were strewn around them. Their cheeks were pink from the steam.

I struggled to make sense of the scene. The rows of old plastic baskets in cubbies to put our belongings, the Japanese sign informing bathers of the health benefits of the water, and the electric fan to cool us down—they were all familiar items that reminded me of the public hot springs my parents had taken me to when I was growing up in this country.

But I had also expected to see older Japanese women with their granny underwear hidden under their carefully folded elastic-waist pants in their changing baskets. Or rosy-cheeked little girls asking their mothers if they could get juice on the way out.

Feeling off-kilter, I quickly removed my clothes and made my way to the baths outside. I found a corner to myself and sat down. Breathing in the cold evening air, I was comforted by the familiar smell of sulfur.

As the days passed, I felt increasingly disoriented. At the cafeteria at lunch one day, a young Japanese girl behind the counter asked me in English what I would like. At first I was offended that she didn't recognize that I was Japanese too, so I replied in Japanese. When she responded in heavily accented Japanese, I glanced at her nametag and was embarrassed to realize she was Chinese.

My head filled with questions. Was I to presume everyone was a foreigner here? Was fluent English a requirement even for the Japanese? Should I be speaking in English or Japanese? What did you do if you didn't speak English?

Because of my father's job, I had moved back and forth between Japan and the U.S. three times growing up. As a child, I constantly struggled to fit in. Attending school in Japan was particularly difficult because there was so much pressure to conform. My American accent during English class won me no friends. "A clever hawk hides his claws," a teacher once said, as if I should pretend I couldn't speak English.

As an adult, I learned to embrace my mixed cultural background and prided myself on being able to deftly navigate both cultures. Now, however, my old identity crisis was playing out in front of me like scenes from a movie. I didn't know what language to speak. I didn't know what was appropriate anymore. I felt like a foreigner in my own country.

Meanwhile, Patrick and Yuka were enjoying themselves immensely. My husband's world evolved around food, so every day started with a discussion of which Hokkaido specialty he wanted to have for lunch. "Should I have *ikura-don* (salmon roe bowl)? Or maybe an *uni-don* (sea urchin bowl)?" he'd muse aloud. "Or maybe I could have an *uni-ikura don*!"

Yuka found the foreignness of the town endlessly fascinating. "*Omoshiroi*," she would say (fascinating!) as a tall, broad-shouldered Kiwi fitted her for skis at the rental shop. Or after a conversation with a Malaysian couple who had spent the last seven years skiing in Niseko. Or standing in the middle of a sea of Australians in the lift lines.

To Yuka, Niseko represented a more international Japan. "This place would be so great if you wanted to study abroad, but couldn't afford to," she said for the umpteenth time, sipping hot coffee during a mid-morning break. "It's good for Japan, don't you think?"

As if on cue, a young Japanese cafeteria employee stopped by to see if we needed anything. Her minimal make-up and conservative ponytail were indistinctive, but her un-Japanese mannerisms caught my attention. She made direct eye contact with us when she spoke, smiled easily, and was unfazed by our curiosity about her background. She told us she'd just returned from a work-study trip in Canada, and she was working on the slopes while she awaited a visa to live in Australia.

Perhaps this *was* a sign of a new, changing Japan, one in which neither the cafeteria worker nor I had to identify strictly as Japanese, or American, or something else. A place where we could just be ourselves. And if it wasn't yet, perhaps it *could* be. Or *should* be.

I felt ashamed that I had inadvertently adopted the stereo-typical closed-minded Japanese perspective that tormented me when I was growing up. Not everything had to be done the Japanese way.

Later that evening, in the dressing room of another hot springs bath, I was tickled by the rules posted in English that were at once foreign and Japanese—foreign because they stated the obvious, Japanese because it was so like them to assume foreigners didn't know anything about public bathing.

"No bathing suits," said one.

"No photography," said another.

Another poster illustrated the steps of how to bathe—wash your privates before you take a dip, and don't put your wash towel in the bath. A picture of a boy swimming was crossed out with a big red "X." I smiled, thinking about my seven-year-old nephew in Chicago, who would totally try to swim in the bathtub.

Yuka and I removed our clothes and made our way outside to the bath. As I sat down in the water, I sighed. We were all alone, surrounded by tall banks of snow that sparkled in the moonlight. The steam rose from the baths as the faint smell of sulfur wafted up our noses. I ran a finger over the scar running down my belly and checked to see if it had faded any more since the last time I looked. It was still visible, but less so. The area was only slightly darker than my skin. If I looked at it from the right angle, parts of it disappeared entirely.

"*Kimochi ii*," I said aloud. "It feels so nice." I was finally in Japan. And I was healthy. Life was good.

A few minutes later, I heard splashing and looked up to see Yuka wading over to a bunch of rocks near the wall separating the women's baths from the men's. "Patrick!" she called out loudly to my husband. "Can you hear me? Are you there?"

After hearing no response, she tried again. "Paaaatriiiick!"

I tried to stop her, but I was laughing too hard.

As she prepared to climb on the rocks so she could peek over the fence, the sliding door connecting the outdoor and indoor baths opened, and another bather entered. We both slunk down, chagrined. But something in me had lifted.

Yukari Iwatani Kane is a former staff writer for The Wall Street Journal *and the author of* Haunted Empire: Apple After

Steve Jobs. *She teaches at the University of California, Berkeley Graduate School of Journalism. Though she has spent most of her career writing about technology, her real passion is travel, and she writes about it whenever she can. Her biggest adventure thus far is a six-month around-the-world trip she took with her husband in 2014, after she was diagnosed with late stage kidney failure. Yukari's most memorable moments traveling: nearly drowning in an ice-cold dive in Iceland, teaching an impromptu fifth-grade class in a Bhutanese village school, and getting slapped in the stomach by a gorilla in Rwanda.*

✍ ✍ ✍

Waning Moon

Aloha also means goodbye.

There was a good chance my father would die while we were in Waikiki. Two days before our departure, my brother had called to tell me my father had been checked into the hospital. He had pneumonia and was semi-catatonic.

I did not cancel my plane ticket. I imagined how this story would be told. "She couldn't be bothered to change her plans to see her dying father, to attend his funeral."

It wouldn't matter that my failure to attend was not based on geography. I would not have boarded a plane from Seattle, either, but it is a much easier, uglier fiction from Hawaii. From my home in dark, wet Seattle, I could be sad and broken, but in Waikiki I would be ridiculous, playing in the ocean, shopping for bright aloha shirts, sitting in open-air cocktail bars, while the rest of the family was grieving. I decided to act as though I did not care.

I contacted a handful of friends to let them know that my father was dying and I was leaving, with my husband, two visiting cousins, and the weight of impending grief for ten days on the island of Oahu. "If you are of the praying sort, would you pray for my dad's easy passage? And if not, well, this is happening and I won't be attending the funeral. You're good friends; I wanted to tell you this."

Then, I packed my suitcase and took the night flight to Honolulu. We checked into our vacation rental and walked down to Kalakaua Avenue, the lively party street that runs parallel to the beach. I stood at a crosswalk next to a massive Hawaiian guy with a bracelet of spears tattooed around his biceps.

"People in Waikiki are crazy, man. They walk around looking at their feet." He was talking to a couple of punk-rock *haole* kids. I looked over and smiled at him, and he smiled back. "They need to look up. Me, I'm a moon guy; look over there at that big full moon. Beautiful."

On December 29th, our second morning in Waikiki, my father passed away in a veteran's hospital in Tucson, Arizona. It was very early. After I got the news, I dressed, woke up my husband, and then, I walked right into the ocean. I looked up. The moon was low in the sky, bright, and still so full.

The water was not cold and I could not feel the weight of my clothes at all.

You can walk through the early morning streets of Waikiki shivering like a wet rat in your soaking street clothes and almost no one will look twice. Only an old Japanese man will laugh at you right there on the sand, will walk right up to you and say something you do not understand because there is a roaring in your ears that is not the ocean. He will smile and bow slightly, and you will notice his high-waisted khakis, his oversized glasses, his fanny pack, his striped golf shirt, his sturdy athletic shoes. A few blocks away, a skinny black homeless guy will see your bare feet and say that the sidewalks are cool at this time of day. A security guard will raise an eyebrow, briefly, but will do no more than nod as you enter the building, a trail of salt water dripping behind you.

Everything is in sharp detail, the texture of the side-walk, the slight gray fuzz on the homeless guy's dreadlocks, the white stripes on that navy blue shirt, those puffy white sneakers like over-risen loaves of bread. How is it no one sees the biggest thing: that your father has died and you are in Waikiki, not going to his funeral?

There are two synagogues on Oahu, but they are not in Waikiki proper. There are a number of different kinds of altars: a statue of Duke Kahanomoku, the great surfer; a statue of Gandhi. Behind a guardrail, some *pohaku* stones that signify great mythical healers. There is a Catholic church, and there's Diamond Head, a glittering peak to the south that stands over the city like a spire. I wanted to make some kind of offering, but I did not know what to do or where to make it.

Instead, I talked to my brothers, to my best friends; I traded emails with my aunt (my father's sister, the last of three siblings) and one of my cousins; none of them judged my choices. "Do what you need to do," they all said. And I stood on the balcony, staring at the ocean. I thought about getting back in the water, but the city was too bright, too loud, too crowded.

I paced in our tiny rented apartment. I got in and out of bed and I ate cereal from the box and I stared at the blue ocean horizon. As though it would fix something, I contacted the local synagogue and asked that they say the mourner's Kaddish, a Hebrew prayer for the dead, for my father. Then, I pulled the sheets over my head and fell into a heavy sleep for many, many hours.

It is hard to buy a condolence card for a person with whom you have a difficult relationship. In Waikiki, it is even harder. Buying postcards is a snap; they are three for a dollar on nearly every street corner, but condolence cards are much rarer. I had imagined something simple, a photo of the ocean on a plain card in which I could write my barest thoughts, but everything was a festival of color, a riot of red hibiscus, a row of perfect hula girls, reproduction photos of Waikiki's grand hotels before the skyline was choked with the sand colored high-rises that line the strip today.

We ducked in and out of convenience stores and cruised the stalls at the International Marketplace; all the paper goods screamed of pineapples and surfboards and good times.

"Post office," said one woman, but it was Sunday and the post office was closed.

"Supermarket," said another, and there, between the birthday cards and thank you notes, we found a row of sympathy cards in pastel colors expressing sincerity and graciousness in kind little platitudes.

They were all wrong. "For you and your family . . ." they said, but what if you *were* the family? "In this difficult time . . ." they said, but the difficult time didn't start today, it was last year and the year before and the entire decade before that. There was no card to express my mix of anger and sympathy and hopelessness.

I settled on a tri-fold cream-colored card with roses on it, the colors unlike the turquoise of the ocean. I tested my thoughts on the back of the supermarket receipt and handed it to my husband for review. "Yes," he said, and I wrote inside the card and sealed it. I wanted to send it out as soon as possible, before I gave in to the temptation to explain myself.

I had not talked with my father for just over a year. The last time we'd spoken—in person—he did not know who I was. When I said goodbye, I knew I might not see him again, and that he was lost to me for good.

I had stopped speaking with my stepmom perhaps six months before that last visit. As my father declined, her language became accusatory and insulting, and the tension that had always existed between us increased. My brothers and I worked together to find ways to help my father, but nothing was good enough. The support programs we found wanted too much information, the money we sent was insufficient, why did we need my father's medical records, what good would they do us? My brothers continued the struggle, but I dropped out, leaving nothing but a weighty silence.

That void meant I could not find a physical voice, but acknowledging this loss—our shared loss—felt required. A condolence card to your father's wife? So remote and wrong, but to talk with her on the phone seemed as impossible as standing in the same room. Written words from a distance were all I could manage.

I wrote that I was sorry and sad about my dad. That I genuinely regretted I could not be there for the services. That I hoped she might find some peace now, with the last years of his difficult care behind her. I avoided saying the reasons for my absence were not financial or geographical or temporal, but messier and personal. I sealed the card, put a stamp on it, and wrote my father's last address on the envelope.

I wanted to want to book a ticket to Tucson. I wanted to be home in Seattle, in my house with my sadness. I wanted to go to the local bar with my friends, to order a round of scotch for everyone and to toast my dad, to have a wake to his spirit. I wanted to see through to a time when my anger would be gone; when I would accept that the thread that ties my dad's life to mine does not mean our lives have to turn out the same. I wanted to want to pretend everything was O.K. and to enjoy my time in Waikiki, to go to Duke's and order a giant pink cocktail with a triangle of pineapple and a turquoise umbrella stuck in it.

But whenever I left the apartment, I was spiky with grief. If someone stood too close to me, it hurt, and I was afraid it would hurt them, too. On Kalakaua Avenue, hawkers handed out flyers for activities, paced wearing signboards—discount cruises, shooting ranges, dinner specials. In a fit of self-indulgent drama I imagined doing this myself. I would slap a handful of red Xeroxed papers on my palm and hand them out, just like the Filipino ladies, to tourists on the strip. The tourists would turn them over in their hands, flabbergasted upon reading, "My dad died and I'm not attending his funeral. It's complicated." Perhaps I could have them translated into Japanese, too.

Traditional Jewish burials are austere affairs. A plain pine box, a simple brief ceremony. Cremation is discouraged by more conservative sects; the body is sacred, a gift from God, and should go back to the earth from whence it came. Some believe in the resurrection of the dead with the arrival of the Messiah. There is an enormous cemetery on the Mount of Olives in Jerusalem, supposedly where this resurrection will begin. I heard this story many years ago on a tour of Jerusalem—the Messiah will enter through the now-sealed Eastern Gate and the dead will rise and follow him into a new age, into the City of Peace.

I thought this was creepy. Looking out over the hillsides of stone coffins in Jerusalem, I imagined a kind of zombie apocalypse rather than a glowing army of our departed at their finest. If we need our bodies for the afterlife, in what state do we rise? At age twenty-eight, strong and with the energy for a great future? At fifty, our knees going out, with a sort of confused acceptance for the world around us? Or in the state at which we die, old and worn, or taken too soon by disease and fate? There was no peace in this for me, though I suppose if you believe in the Messiah and you want to follow him through the gate into The World to Come, you need a vehicle—your body—to get you there. No arrangements had been made for my father's remains, but were it up to him, had it been in his power, I think he would have chosen the Mount of Olives, chosen to follow the Messiah into Jerusalem.

On a previous trip to Oahu, I had gone swimming in the ocean early in the morning. While floating in the shallow protected surf, I talked with a local guy who told me he had released his mother's ashes off the seawall behind us. I decided then and there that I should like to be cremated and cast loose here in the middle of the Pacific. What better funeral than to become one with the ocean and all its life? To swim with the ancient sea turtles, and the fish with complicated names: the *panuunuhu*, the *humuhumunukunukuapua'a*. I wanted to be one with the ocean, not with the earth; I wanted the expansiveness of the Pacific, not the enclosure of a box in the ground.

Because of the time change between Hawaii and Tucson, while my dad's funeral took place, I watched the sun rise over the Pacific from the balcony of our rental. The sky was a blaze of burning orange. The sun appeared above the horizon, a glowing ball of red and then, before it lit the morning sky, it set the surface of the ocean on fire. The color was nothing like the rosy gravel and sage cactus of the Tucson desert where my dad would rest until the resurrection came to lift him. Or for eternity, whichever came first.

I am a modern woman, a product of the internet age. Sensible friends talked me through the first days of my father's death, but I also wasted too much time on the web consuming common wisdom about death and grief.

There were forums where embittered stepchildren asked about their legal rights to a dead parent's estate. There were articles about the stages of grief, and more articles debunking the stages of grief theory as bullshit, saying that everyone's situation is different and personal. There were advice columns

in which survivors asked, "Do I have to go to the funeral?"
Dozens of commenters answered, "You have to go, of course
you have to go." and dozens more replied, "You should do
what feels right for you in this time of grief. Don't let anyone
tell you what's right."

It was all inconclusive; I could not see myself in any of it. I
turned off the laptop and went to buy a smoothie with ginseng
and gingko because maybe they are good for stress, or maybe
not, depending on what you read. The smoothie had fresh
papaya and pineapple, too, and I drank it while watching a
woman sweep sand from the sidewalk back onto the beach.

Waikiki is an artificial beach, it should not be here. In
former years, sand had been shipped in from Australia; now
it comes from a sandbar offshore. If left entirely to natural
devices, Waikiki Beach would disappear. This woman with
the broom, with the sharply defined muscles in her brown
arms and a determined grimace on her face, was Sisyphus,
forever returning the sand to the beach where it did not
want to be.

On New Year's Eve, Waikiki was to light up with fireworks.
I knew I could not bear the crowds on the street. Instead, I
ate a thoughtless dinner in our room and, around 9:30, fell
into a very deep sleep. I dreamed of snow, of helping a friend
move. We were putting stuff in her car, but also, I had to carry
some things up a snowy slope and someone would meet me at
the top. I trudged up the hill, leaving my first batch of objects
at the top, and then I went down to fetch some more. But night
was falling, and the snow became blue in the twilight. When I
returned to the top the second time, I was in the wrong place
and everything was gone.

I woke to the roar of fireworks and crowded streets below.
The wind had blown away the rain front from the afternoon
and the sky was clear. Craning my neck over the balcony

rail of our forty-third-floor apartment, I could see the bright explosive lights, spidery white chrysanthemums, a pink spiral, neon colored dancing scarves. People were cheering and screaming and blowing conch shells in the distance. Someone shouted "Happy New Year" from a nearby rooftop.

When it was over, my husband kissed me, saying nothing, and went back to bed. I stayed outside and looked away from the water, up into the sky. The moon wore a halo, and a slice of its silvery light was gone.

Pam Mandel blames her time as a high school exchange student for her incurable desire to be somewhere else. She's written for Thomas Cook, Lonely Planet, Afar, Sunset, World Hum*, DK Eyewitness Guides, the* San Francisco Chronicle*, and dozens of travel websites, some of which are still online. Despite having been to all seven continents, she still thinks there's a great adventure to be had just down the road. Pam lives in Seattle, Washington, with a rescue dog named Harley. She plays rock-and-roll ukulele with her band, The Castaways, and she will always share her dessert. Find out what she's up to now on www.nerdseyeview.com.*

ANNE P. BEATTY

🍃 🍃 🍃

Rich Country

She found riches in places known for poverty.

During monsoons in Nepal—when Shree Gograha Secondary School, where I taught, was not in session—
I would visit an elementary school in the area, which was
housed in a cramped concrete building half a mile from Shree
Gograha. I did not particularly like to go, but its principal,
S. Niroula, had asked me, and nothing feels more useless
than being a Peace Corps Volunteer on vacation. Once there,
while he talked pedagogy, I mostly ate snacks: boiled water-
buffalo milk, instant noodles called Wai Wai, and white bread
smeared with warm ketchup. At least three times a visit, we
drank tea.

Between snacks I visited classrooms, more as a guest
speaker than teacher. At home I would have been just another
twenty-something, but here, where I drank tea with the men
instead of working fourteen-hour days like most women, I
was a celebrity and expert teacher by virtue of being an American. The students fired questions at me that reflected their
education system's emphasis on rote memorization: *What is
the national bird of America? What is the national dish of America? What is the national dress of America? What is the area of
America?* They asked me how there could be no water buffalo

in America if it was such a rich country, and whether if they went to America their skin too would turn white.

Sometimes S. Niroula marched into the classroom in the middle of this barrage and asked the eight-year-old students who I was.

"Annie," they would say in unison, having been forced to memorize my name the day before.

And what country does she come from?

"America!"

And America is a very what country?

"Rich!"

And I, a sweaty white woman in Teva sandals, always nodded.

After my two years in the Peace Corps, I moved to Los Angeles to teach at a public high school. *Why do you want to teach here?* my students in South Central asked, sensing something self-serving in my professed altruism, perhaps suspecting even more than I did how much I craved outsider status. They seemed to be asking: *What is it that you came here looking for? How do you think it will change you?* I openly admit that joining the Peace Corps was a selfish act, but I've never admitted that a similar motive spurred my move to L.A. Maybe that is because what I gained in L.A. was not pleasant, not a nose ring or another language or the imprint of blue hills undulating before me. What I gained in L.A., even more than in Nepal, was an uncomfortable recognition of the kind of American I am.

My students in Nepal had known all the Hindu gods, the latest Bollywood songs, when each type of mango ripened and the best way to eat it. My students in L.A. knew which streets were red for Bloods and blue for Crips for miles around. They knew where drive-bys would occur before they happened. They knew who had guns at school that day and what period everything would go down. They knew they would get jumped if they walked down Denker Avenue carrying a backpack, so they rolled up their school papers and stuck them deep in their pockets. Once I asked my ninth graders to define bravery, and a fourteen-year-old wrote, *One time when I knew my friend was brave was when he killed a person.*

Our school was in an older, established neighborhood that looked innocuous to my untrained eye. When I parked on the residential street across from the school for my interview, I thought, "This is South Central?" The sun shone there. The stucco houses were painted cheery shades of peach and aqua. Later, when I started teaching there, I began to notice the bars on all windows and doors, the fifteen-foot spiked fence enclosing the teachers' parking lot, the bulletproof glass on the drive-through window at the nearby Taco Bell. In the morning, traffic backed up for an hour because many parents would rather have their children miss first period than walk through the streets. Once I had taught there for a year, I knew that most of the surrounding streets and a few corners of the school had been the scenes of drive-by shootings, because they had all happened since I'd arrived.

My future husband also taught at the school. He and I traded anecdotes and paraded versions of them in front of friends who never ventured near South Central. One night he told a group of us this story: "So I'm in the middle of class, and Raylon just stands up and starts walking around, acting crazy. I, of course, tell him to sit down and be quiet. And he says, 'Man, you always telling people to sit down and be quiet! I bet you go to your mama's house and tell her to sit down and be quiet!' Which was funny, you have to give him credit. So then I say, 'Well, Raylon, except for a few similarities, you and my mom are very different people.' That gets a laugh, too, but then Carlos pipes up and says, 'What are the similarities?' I say, 'Well, you see those letters shaved into the side of

Raylon's head? My mom's got those, too.' And Raylon goes, 'Yeah, I saw her getting 'em done down at the barber shop, and I thought, yeah, that looks tight. I'ma do that, too.'"

We laughed, and a lawyer friend said incredulously, "That is so witty! These kids are so smart. Any one of them could be a lawyer."

"Yeah," we agreed glumly, staring into our drinks. "They're smart all right."

And they were. They were witty and clever and observant, keen readers of people. They were survivors, and survival had taught them a lot of things. The problem was that so few of the things they knew would help them make any money—and they all wanted to make money.

Their Life Skills teacher began the semester by asking how many of the students wanted a big house. What about a nice car? Jewelry? Swimming pools? These kids who might be evicted from their family's apartment at the end of the month but sported $140 sneakers raised their hands. The teacher made them write down specifics, exactly what they wanted to own when they were thirty. Then he had them draw it. Where would the house be? How many rooms? What shape for the swimming pool? What kind of cars? With what kind of rims?

When he had them good and salivating, he asked how they expected to acquire these things. Blank stares and silence followed a few jokes about a gold album, or the NBA.

"Things are what these kids want," this teacher explained to me with an evangelist's enthusiasm. "When they realize that whether they get these things or not is up to them, their grades and their actions, then you start to see real progress. You start to see behavior change."

I stood silent, skeptical.

There are two words in Nepali that mean love: *maya* and *prem. Maya* is the kind of unconditional love a parent has for a child, whereas *prem* is romantic love. But neither word can refer to objects, only people. In Nepali, you could never say that you love books or rice, or gold rims or swimming pools, only that you like them very much.

Everywhere I have taught, my students feel sorry for me. In Nepal, they wondered how I could possibly go to the bazaar wearing a *maxi*, the long housedress Nepalis wear as Americans might a bathrobe. They asked what I paid for everything—my bag of lentils, my bicycle, my made-in-Nepal Goldstar sneakers—and clucked with dismay at how I'd been cheated, though all of it seemed cheap to me. I didn't understand Hinduism; I could not keep Ganesh and Hanuman straight; I insisted that a temple could not be both Buddhist and Hindu, but should be one or the other. *Oh miss*, they laughed at me.

My American students pitied me because I never went to the club, didn't eat meat, and was obsessed with whether people took off their hats. When I mentioned one day in class that I didn't have a TV, Juan, stricken, said, "Do you have a *phone?*" as if I might be Amish, or just very, very poor. He offered to take up a collection of black-market, federal-free lunch tickets to buy me a TV.

In both places, I hoped to be seen as more than a sightseer. In Nepal, I saw myself as a certain kind of American, one who had joined the Peace Corps with no grand notions of changing the world, only herself. Nepalis did not deal in these distinctions. I was an American, and my belief that I could shrug off that status was only another sign I did not understand how privilege works. Similarly, I'd thought showing up in South Central every day would prove I was a certain kind of white person, but being white and middle class there marked me as an outsider worthy of suspicion and disdain, a far cry from the curiosity and adoration I had met in Nepal. My place in

American society, which was immediately visible to my students, I saw at last with new clarity.

When my students in Nepal and L.A. asked me why I'd come there, my answers sounded sanctimonious and simpering. *I wanted to see the world. I wanted to give something back.* The truth stank of ingratitude. When I played Barbies as a child, nearly all my games involved packing their clothes—fake fur coats, tiny plastic heels—into the pink Corvette, driving it twelve feet across the rug, and unpacking everything against the opposite wall. Looking back, I can cast this game as indicative either of the incipient traveler, always on the move, or the quintessential American, obsessed with amassing inventory. Maybe both are true; maybe neither. I never told my students that despite all I'd been given, I had felt a great emptiness and left home to fill it up.

My eleventh- and twelfth-grade students at Shree Gograha biked to school or walked or took the city bus, which had no doors. The girls wore burgundy *kurta surwals*, long tunics over pants with shawls draped over their arms. They carried washcloths to mop their brows in the heat. The boys wore olive-green dress slacks, white button-down shirts, and ties. They held hands—boys with boys, girls with girls—and sang or chatted as they walked. Many of them lived in Biratnagar, our city of 230,000, but some came from surrounding villages. One student, explaining how he had come to the city to study from a tiny village, wrote, "My father sold his water buffalo so I could come to school."

The school's name, painted along the top of the building, was flanked by a tilted swastika on one side and the Star of David on the other. Eventually I learned these were ancient Sanskrit symbols of health and education, respectively. The school was built of whitewashed concrete, with different lengths of rebar protruding from the flat roof, suggesting another level might be added any day now. There was no electricity. Before class we pried open heavy wooden shutters to let in the light. All eighty of my students stood up when I entered the classroom and *namasted* me in unison. When I asked them to read aloud and do group work or perform skits, they politely refused, the girls hiding behind their pilled washcloths, the boys studying their notebooks.

"Please, miss," one boy finally said. "Write a summary of the story on the board and we will copy it to study tonight."

"Don't you want to read the story together and talk about it?" I asked.

They shook their heads.

After class, these silent students gathered in the school-yard to clap and sing show tunes from Bollywood films, hips sashaying and wrists flicking under the dusty leaves of the mango tree. The girls brought me candies wrapped in squares of fabric. The boys brought me home to meet their mothers, who fed me plate after plate of rice and lentils. My students showed me where to buy flour for the best price and combed henna through my hair to redden it. When we parted in the bazaar, they left as one large group on their bikes, smiling and waving goodbye, everyone, it seemed, friends with everyone else. At Christmas they gave me hand-lettered cards with messages like, "May Santa Claus bring you the eyes of Lord Buddha."

The nationally mandated curriculum required that I teach *The Great Gatsby* to these students who barely spoke English. One day I said to them: "At the end of chapter eight, Nick is standing in Tom's yard. Gatsby is also there, waiting for Daisy. So, at the end of the chapter, where is Gatsby?"

No one answered.

I repeated: "Where is Gatsby standing?"

A full minute dragged by.

"You guys. Please. What is Gatsby doing here?"

At last Dhiraj shouted, "Cooking chicken curry!"

We all laughed, and then I pantomimed beating myself over the head with the book. I said slowly, "Gatsby. Never. Cooked. Chicken. Curry." On the national exam, there would be a question like, "How does Gatsby represent the American dream?" and my students would write: *Gatsby was born to poor farmers and worked his whole life to earn money and move up in society and he became very rich and he never cooked chicken curry.*

In Los Angeles, we read Lorraine Hansberry's play, *A Raisin in the Sun.* A few days into the play, I handed my students this prompt:

In Act I, scene ii, Beneatha tells Asagai that nothing is wrong; she is just suffering from "acute ghetto-itis." In this assignment, I want you to consider what she means by this phrase.

"First, there's the diagnosis," I said. "What does it mean to have ghetto-itis, in plain English?"

"It's being ghetto!" Jakira yelled.

"O.K., well, what does that mean?" I asked. "How do you define being ghetto?"

"Being hood," Rosa suggested.

"You guys are giving me synonyms, but I want you to define it. And remember, Beneatha is saying this is an illness. It's something that's wrong with her, something that's making her feel bad."

"Ain't nothing wrong with being hood!" Laura said. A chorus of students affirmed this, while a second group refuted it loudly.

"O.K., O.K., quiet down! I want everyone to take a few minutes to write down what you think it means to have ghetto-itis. What is Beneatha sick of? Then keep going. Write down the symptoms of ghetto-itis. Think about the characters in the play. What are some of their traits? How do they feel about where they live? And finally, think of some things that would help the characters feel better about themselves or their lives."

I knew the students would do a better job on the assignment if I talked them through it with a real discussion. But I couldn't run a discussion in that class without it veering off track, so most days I asked them to write down their answers instead. The room always felt like a pressure cooker rattling, soon to be hissing. Sometimes we got through the period without an explosion of profanity and anger. Sometimes we did not. When I picked up Javier's paper from where he'd left it on his desk at the end of the period, I saw he had not written anything under "Diagnosis" or "Symptom," but under "Cure," he had written: *smoke more weed!!!*

In Nepal, when you give something to another person, you hand it over with your right hand, your left cupping your right elbow. The sentiment is that you are giving this object with your whole person, no tricks behind your back. The gesture felt forced and melodramatic at first, as loaded as wearing the native dress of another country. It seemed wrong to do it and wrong not to. I did it anyway. I stopped noticing people do it when they handed me a kilo of potatoes, a copy of *The Kathmandu Post*, my change in wilted rupees.

I often listened to the radio while sitting on my cement patio, papered for much of the year with bougainvillea's pink tissue carcasses. The leaves of date palms and banana trees husked in the breeze. I drank tea spiced with ginger and cloves left for me by the daughter of the family whose house I lived in. They were a middle-class Nepali family, one that displayed drawings torn from a Walt Disney coloring book and plastic dolphin figurines on their shelves.

As I sipped my tea, I would watch the street: the hawking-and-spitting group of men out front, the ring of boys holding toothbrushes, the ox cart thumping along on wooden wheels in the dust. Down the road, when the temperature dropped at night, a family began tying shawls of floral rags round the shoulders of their baby goats. These goats clambered up on woodsheds or benches like sentry grandmothers to stare a few inches ahead into the fog.

One morning, a woman in a faded sari balancing a basket of cow dung on her head wandered over to peer at me. I waved and smiled. The woman beckoned me over.

She asked if it was true I was from America, why I was so tall, and if I'd take her back with me. Henna stained her hands in bleeding patterns of flowers, curlicues, and checkerboards. The dust of the dung she had collected to dry and burn as fuel caked her left hand. I told her I wasn't going back for a long time, two years. She dismissed this. *When you do*, she said.

When I came home from abroad, well-meaning friends and relatives asked about my experiences. I relied either on platitudes ("I got more than I gave. The people I met were incredibly friendly and welcoming. They treated me like family.") or statistics ("Many Nepali families live on just two hundred dollars a year. There are no curbs, no sewage system, no public bathrooms, and no trash collection. It is not uncommon to step over human feces in the street."). My well-meaning friends and relatives would shake their heads and say, "Those poor people." Then I would call another former volunteer, and we would talk for hours about our memories, like the time a man-eating tiger was loose in his village and a multi-day hunt ended with it strapped to the front of a bulldozer, orange fur matted with blood. Or my desperation during the festival of the tuber, when I had been invited to so many houses and fed so many potatoes and yams that I resorted to scraping them from my plate into my backpack whenever my host stepped out of the room. We ached to go back. Nepal seemed full of life and community and hope and culture, whereas America was lonely and sterile, devoid of sounds or smells. For a time I clung to this belief, even though it was as simplistic as an eight-year-old Nepali's faith in America's riches.

Now I live back in North Carolina a few miles from where I grew up, in a neighborhood of older houses, where people still sit on the porch and watch their kids bicycle down the street. I teach in a different neighborhood, one of subdivisions that did not exist when I was a child. Most of my students come from money. One summer afternoon, I drive through their neighborhoods and do not see a soul. The new mansions mushroom from thick red squares carved out of the earth by prehistoric-looking diggers. Realty signs dot the landscape. Clubhouses behind gates boast Olympic-sized pools that sit empty, stirred only by the wind. The nets on basketball courts hang limp. In driveways boats float on air, beached in the precious sunlight.

My current students mostly drive more expensive cars than I do. Many of these students feel sorry for me, too. They look at my diplomas and say, like disappointed parents, "You could have gone to med school." They can't understand why a person with options would want to be a public school teacher. These students have different problems than my students in L.A. or Nepal. They are stressed about getting into college. Their parents do not always understand them. Sometimes they cut themselves, or bully each other. Most of them own lots of things—and by now, so do I.

Former students and colleagues in Nepal still write me emails asking how I can help them get to America. I want to write them back, *It's not what you think*. To do so, of course, would be impertinent. How dare I tell them not to come? I am surprised to realize I would rather have been born poor in Nepal than in America, a thought experiment that seems in the end just another luxury. If I had been born in Nepal, surely I too would be trying to get to America. And perhaps I am wrong, wrong about it all, because after years of trying, my Nepali language teacher from Peace Corps finally did get a visa through the Diversity Lottery program and settled in Florida. This man, who is fluent in multiple languages, went to graduate school, and worked for international development organizations, now wears a paper cap and serves coffee at a Dunkin' Donuts—but his son, who is on the honor roll in middle school, will not.

I no longer feel the urge to move somewhere new or define myself as the outsider. This doesn't mean that the dark clouds of want, loneliness, and restlessness never descend on me—only that when they do, I am now forced to admit what both Gatsby and Nick learn by the end of *The Great Gatsby*: There is nowhere I can go to escape the complications of my own identity.

Sometimes I see myself, fifteen years ago, standing in those classrooms of Nepalis, their slender brown hands thrusting notebooks and pens my way. We all wanted something from each other. Instead of agreeing that America is a very rich country, I wish I had told them, *It's complicated.* But "complicated" is not a word I ever heard Nepalis use. Most days I left S. Niroula's school feeling lonely and splintered, my brow knit in concentration as I biked past lolling water buffalo with muddy rope threading their nostrils. Those children in blue-and-white uniforms, though—they left together, arms draped around each other as they balanced on bicycles inches apart, dusty feet in plastic sandals pedaling furiously, their voices rising in song.

Anne P. Beatty is a writer and high school English teacher. Her nonfiction has appeared in The American Scholar, North American Review, Vela, *and elsewhere. She holds degrees from University of North Carolina at Chapel Hill and Duke University. She lives with her husband and three children in Greensboro, North Carolina.*

ᘔ ᘔ ᘔ

I Am Here, in This Morning Light

Was it worth the effort? Was it even possible?

Car doors slam and boat trailers clank by. Couples call to each other. "Don't forget the cooler." "Scrambled or fried?" "Did you remember sunscreen?" My arm reaches from under the sheet and lifts a corner of the makeshift curtain over its bungee-cord rod. Beyond the rear window, past a field of tents, a mist-blurred sun rises over the Florida Bay. I drop the curtain. My palms push against the carpeted ceiling of the van, and my head knocks against a side window as I stretch the best I can on the platform bed. This is my fifth morning in the Everglades' Flamingo Campground. With each dawn, sleep coming and going as light silvers and then gilds the water, I've pieced together a plan of how to be out by myself, floating, in that light. Today is New Year's Eve. By tomorrow, the New Year, I'll be ready. I slip off the bed onto the sheetrock bucket chamber pot.

Dressed, I release all the bungees, roll up the curtains, and throw open the back doors. This late in the morning only a few mosquitoes follow the light inside. I brace on a window latch and dangle upside down to pull breakfast from the food box under the bed. After slurping a mix of boxed milk and protein powder and peeling a grapefruit, I lean over my feet to open the suitcase of writing supplies, always, on every trip, propped at the corner of the mattress. Pad and pen on my lap, grapefruit sections piled on a dishcloth at my side, and I'm ready to decide. A solo, pre-dawn kayak trip—is it worth the effort? Is it possible?

It helps that my camping companions have already left for home. Friends are great, but they want to come with you. Sure, I could say no, but it's not worth the price to be paid in hurt feelings. The first bite of grapefruit sprays over the yellow pad and wrinkles the paper. I rip it off and start new. Friends have hinted that I'm persnickety and set in my ways. Ex-girlfriends have noted this as well. But I do not want things the way I want them just because that's the way I want them. I have reasons. One joy of a solo kayak trip is that I don't have to explain . . . anything. There is no negotiation about where or especially what time. There is no need for my lecture about the difference between nautical and civil twilights and how a pre-dawn launch does not mean you leave the campsite, load the gear, or make a last bathhouse trip at first light.

And it helps that I've paddled this trail over the Florida Bay to Snake Bight before. The first time was years ago, not long after trading in my braces and crutches for a manual wheelchair. I was stronger. I could shove the boat up into the back of my van. I can't do that anymore, but now I have a power chair. It can haul things. Still, all plans have more complexity and less physical leeway. Solo trips don't come together for me as often. I've missed the chance to be silent, notice what is around me, and let tangled, persever-ating loops of thought unravel. I chew grapefruit and look over the now sun-sparked bay. A flock of ibis dip and rise in slow waves as they approach from over the water. They fly into the campsite low enough that people duck. A satin sheen of black wingtips flickers through my field of view.

I click my pen and write "KAYAK TRIP" in capital letters at the top of the page. I circle it.

Some things I've already figured out. The wheeled kayak carrier I have doesn't quite fit, but I'll make it work and drag the kayak to the Marina's ramp with my wheelchair. And then the wheelchair needs to be left out of the way of backing-up boat trailers but close enough that I can crawl from it to the boat. Yesterday, surrounded by the swirl of holiday crowds, I placed myself here and there around the marina until I found a spot. It blocks a bulletin board displaying faded notices about fish species, but pre-dawn means that I'll be gone before anyone can object. Most of the grapefruit gets eaten while I think about the mile to the Marina. I have to figure out if the wheelchair has enough battery power for the job. I reconsider using the van to transport me, the boat, and all the gear. But at five A.M. there won't be any fellow campers wandering by to corral into loading the kayak. I could give up on the early morning launch, lose the light, and not be alone on the water. That scenario repels me, and I'm back to the battery power calculations.

Battery power is elusive and mutable and predictions of it are always flawed. I put that page aside and instead make a list of objects. My wallet, camera, good pen, iTouch, and pain meds need to be removed from the side, front, and back pouches on my wheelchair and left here at the campsite, locked in the van. An apple, the car keys, and sunscreen go in the dry bag. A procrastinating dither over where to list insect repellant pushes me back to the problem at hand. I spit out a grapefruit seed, dry my fingers on the dishcloth, and return to the battery power page.

O.K. The power chair has to be left in the bathhouse overnight for charging either tonight or after the kayak trip. The transfer into my old manual and subsequent push back to the van uses a chunk of my daily allotment of arm strength. Arm strength is also elusive and mutable. After drawing diagrams with directional arrows and route distances, it seems that if I mostly stick around the campsite today, the battery power will hold through tomorrow. This does mean I'll make the recharging trek after the trip when I'm the most tired. So I start a calculation of physical energy with percentages listed for each activity—bathhouse trip (30 percent), launching kayak (20 percent), the actual kayaking (60 percent), getting back in my wheelchair afterwards (30 percent of my remaining energy)—and stop when, as usual, the math says I should never ever even get out of bed. I rip and crumble that page.

The last wedge of grapefruit leaks out the edges of my mouth. I can adjust the kayaking route. I'll hug the shoreline instead of paddling out to Snake Bight. I wet down a corner of dishcloth, wipe my hands and face, and list getting someone to help fit the kayak onto the carrier as a chore for today. Outside my van, people are fussing around their campsites. Now seems like a good time. I sweep up the peel, seeds, and abandoned calculations and drop them into the trash bag hanging from the side of the hydraulics. I extend my stretch into the long reach past my feet for the control switches. The side doors open and the lift unfolds.

On the lawn behind my van, I make a slow show. First, I attach the bowline of the kayak to my armrest and, with a wide sweep of my wheelchair, pull it alongside the carrier. Next, I pause. The circle of other campers, blurred behind screen tents and tinted RV windows, stare. I've spent days turning down offers of assistance with, "No, thanks, I've got it," and receiving in return some variation of, "Well, you're an independent miss, aren't you," from the rebuffed helpers. I'll have to make this show a bit over the top. I lift the kayak as high as I can, but it, as I expected, fails to clear the sides of the carrier. Both topple away from each other and flop onto the ground. As I reach (with a soft, yet dramatic groan) to set the carrier back up on its wheels, there is the sound of a zipper followed by soft footsteps on sandy grass.

"May I help?" The voice is from the Midwest. The man's beard is gray with lingering streaks of blond and has the still wispy look of a recent retiree trying out a new life. The offer is a combination of kindness and boredom, and I appreciate it. Soon the kayak is cinched into the carrier. He's curious, but I don't tell him my plans. Sometimes word will get around and an official of some sort will decide he's required to interfere. Once, in the Okefenokee Swamp, the rangers hemmed and hawed, but knew it wasn't legal to stop me. And I couldn't stop them from sending a motorboat out to check on me. That was the end of quiet and solitude.

I experiment with tying a loop of bowline that will lift the nose of the kayak up, but not too far up, when I hook it onto the back of my wheelchair. We, the kayak and I, make a successful trial tour of the campground. The helpful retiree is back inside a screen tent new enough that folds still crease the nylon. I wave at him as I rattle by. He looks up from his folding chair, from his novel, and gives me a thumbs up. His wife leans out of their pop-up and waves. I go back to the van and rewrite the list in chronological order. Happy New Year to Me. I scrawl the message over the bottom of the page.

At 4:45 the next morning, I let myself get up. I've been awake every hour certain that the alarm won't go off and listening to the weather radio and worrying about the timing of an approaching cold front. I cinch the headlight around my forehead. Light on and I'm reviewing the list. At this stage of a plan, in the moment of execution, it all seems impossible, even transgressive. In an excitement of anxiety and self-sabotage, I will forget, sometimes, everything or neglect, sometimes, that one thing that is absolutely necessary. The list becomes my way forward. It reminds me to move the binoculars, sunscreen, car keys, apple, and cell phone from wheelchair to kayak. It says to go to the bathhouse.

The list does not say to remember the toiletry bag so I don't, but unbrushed teeth will not stop me. The mosquitoes are circling, but I keep in motion. I'm back from the bathhouse at 5:00. The full moon shows a clear sky. The wind is still calm. The trip is a go. The twenty-five-year-old beat-up crutch left over from my walking days and the extra large vinyl barbeque cover are next on the list. I pull them out of the back of the van. With the crutch braced along my armrests, I hold the slipping folds of the cover as high as I can. I'm almost to the kayak when I feel the pull. My front caster wheel has run over a trailing edge of the plastic. I try to back off, but the wheel flips and wraps a layer of barbeque cover into its axle. A side turn tightens the cover's cinch cord around the wheel. No longer caring about the noise, I throw the crutch into the kayak and brace my ribs on the armrest to lean as far down to the ground as I can. My fingertips reach into the wad of plastic and rope. Whatever angle I pull at, there is no give.

This has not psychologically or emotionally, but actually, for real, stopped me. Anxiety flushes into my still upside-down head and pools under my skull. It makes me pant. I have become an immobilized source of carbon dioxide, and the mosquitoes swarm. I beat my ears and swat at my nose and eyes. There's a pocketknife in the wheelchair's side pocket. I sit up in the seat to reach for it, and mosquitoes attack the length of thigh where my pants stretch tight. Finding repellant becomes the priority. I can't remember which list it ended up on. My arm twists deep into the back pouch. My fingers scramble through the leavings of a week of camping and locate the tube between a crumbled park map and a black mangrove leaf. I take off the spray cap and pour it into my hands and rub them down my arms, over my ears, and along the part in my hair where the scalp is exposed. Sure, it's poison, but you reach a certain age and the phrase "long-term effects" has less meaning.

The mosquitoes back off. I finger into the pocket and feel past the earplugs, floss, and under the nail clippers for the pocketknife. I flip out each of the choices and decide on the blade rather than the miniature scissors. It won't cut. I try and try, but it won't cut. I'm going to be here, stuck, for hours, with the mosquitoes, until the campground wakes up. My trip is ruined. I knew this wouldn't work. I feel along the blade, which it seems is an emery board. I exchange it for the real knife. The plastic slices away, but the cord still won't unwrap from around the bearings. I stick the knife into the axle and hack. Strands pop loose, fray, and unwind until only threads are left. I finish the fine work with the scissors, and I'm free.

I becalm myself by studying the list. Once I decide that the umbrella and poncho are to be left in the wheelchair's back pouch in case I've timed the incoming weather wrong, everything is loaded that needs to be, and everything is left that needs to be. I'm ready. I back into position at the front of the kayak and lift the bowline loop onto the wheelchair's handle. It hooks on the first try. The kayak and I rattle past what I doubt are still sleeping campers.

The mile to the marina seems longer than it does during the day. I worry about being late even as I know there is no late except for what I decide. Still, I push on the joystick and increase my speed. When the kayak pops in and out of a gap in the asphalt, I hear a new rattle following along behind me. I stop and twist in my seat. The bowline isn't working itself off the handle, and the paddle hasn't fallen onto the road. I resume the trip at a lower speed, but something still sounds loose. I recalculate and make myself a deal. If I'm halfway before the kayak falls off its carrier, I'll drag it along the verge. That will still leave me enough battery power to get back in the afternoon. I think.

And now there isn't anything else to figure out. This trip might really happen. I turn off my headlight. The moon brightens the pavement with a gray luster and throws the shadow of my caravan along the grass. We continue at a stately pace. No cars pass. The road surface smooths as I arrive. I slow and make a wide careful turn into the darkness under the mahogany trees that line the parking lot. The marina is lit in thick yellow light. I can hear bowlines clang against the dock and smell the salty coolness off the water. I stop at the top of the ramp and review.

The important thing is to not get out of my wheelchair, crawl over the concrete to the boat, and then look back and see the paddle or binoculars or water or dry bag or life vest beside the wheelchair. I position the kayak close to the water. I load and tie down what I hope is everything. I park the wheelchair, perch at the edge of the seat, and think things through one more time. Then I slide down the footrests and drop to the concrete. As my weight is irretrievably pulled down, as my palms and one thigh hit the ground, I hold my breath. This is usually when I remember whatever it is I've forgotten. This morning, it seems, I haven't. And nothing snags or catches as the barbeque cover fits over my wheelchair. The carrier and my crutch tuck neatly underneath. There isn't a rope to cinch the cover with anymore, but I shove the side of the wheelchair with my shoulder until I can anchor an edge of plastic under a wheel.

I've crawled the few feet over to the ramp, and am about to make a controlled fall from the ledge into the kayak, when a boat trailer backs down beside me. They'll be headed out into the Gulf. I'll never see them. "We can help?" they ask. No thanks, I say, I've got it. But as I use the bulk of my torso to hump the kayak down the ramp, I gather enough of my bad Spanish to ask them what time it is. "*Seis en punto*," they report. I'm early. Or would be if there was an early other than what I make it. One more heave and the kayak slides itself the rest of the way down the ramp. The cupping of water around the keel moves under me from stern to bow until I'm floating. I'm floating. I lift my paddle and tilt one moonlit blade into the water.

Out in the bay, the horizon has a suggestive strip of gray—nautical twilight. I paddle toward it. The moon is behind me and when fish jump, the west side of the ripples flash. Cormorants make frantic takeoff shuffles over the surface, and brown pelican dives smack the water. Flocks of shorebirds, too dark and quick to see, snap and hum by my side. The horizon releases streams of red and pink over the surface. I paddle toward them. Beside me, the water galumphs into a swell and drop that presses against the boat. I decide it was a sea turtle. As clouds reflect into the now pink water, I try to center myself in the rose glow between the sky above and the sky below. It seems to be an optical impossibility. No matter how hard I paddle, the reflections are always not where I am.

The kayak slides through the passage between Joe Kemp Key and the mainland before sunrise. Farther out is the channel to Snake Bight, a cove within a cove where roseate spoonbills roost and below them, on the mudflats, reddish egrets dance around great white herons. My paddle treads water and holds my boat in place as I think that Snake Bight is not that much farther, that the incoming front won't kick up the winds for hours yet, that I'm here and should just go for it. I also remember that I'm pushing to my edge already and that this isn't a marathon. And finally I remember that I am here, in this morning light, on this bay where no direction is second best or less than.

I paddle twice on my right to turn the boat north and close to the mangroved shore. Still, I keep watch to the east. When gold shows through a gap in the horizon's cloud bank, I turn my boat toward it and stop paddling. This is the first sunrise of a new year. I think I'm supposed to wish for something. Probably it should be love and not writing career success. So, do I just straight out wish for a girlfriend? Do I really want one? Or is it better to wish to give love, to be capable of love, to accept love. Maybe it shouldn't be just a girlfriend. Maybe it should be a wish for love in the world—a peace on Earth sort of thing. I'm quoting out of cheesy affirmation books. I stop thinking the best I can.

The sun's lowest curve is still attached to the horizon. It pulls taut and pours orange light over the ocean too bright to look at straight on. Dawn has been wished to for all the years anyone has existed to wish. "Love" I say. The sun will know what to do with that. I put the paddle back in the water and turn north again. My vision smears into wavering black circles with glowing coronas—images of the sun in negative. As the spots fade to gray, the muscles around my eyes relax. Beside me, the shadowed greens of the high mangrove wall squawk and flutter. My pupils regain their size, and cormorants, great blues, and brown pelicans become visible in the twists of branches. Under the lowest prop roots, on a bird foot-sized lift of mud, a night heron is preening her wings.

The tide is leaving and somewhere along here the water will run out. But these are full moon tides so I get farther than I would have thought possible. At the place I think of as the secret cove, I hold my paddle above the surface and drift toward the opening. Mosquitoes are its first defense, but my clothes are saturated with enough residual repellent to deter all but a few dozen. I don't go any farther, but I don't leave. I haven't been here in years, and still the birds startle out of their hiding place in the same species order as they always have. The roseate spoonbills are last. They fly over my head, rippling scarlet to salmon in the new light, pale cherry in their watery reflections. They disappear into a white strip of beach in the distance, and I follow them. The mangroves recede to reveal marl-gray beaches where I imagine crocodiles lay their eggs. My keel bumps onto the raised edge of mud left by a tidal creek wandering out of the trees. This is as far as I go. I put my feet up on the sides of my kayak, lean into the seat, and scan the distance with binoculars. What has seemed to be a beach becomes a hundred white pelicans. The roseates are sprinkled among them. I put down the binoculars and stretch my arms high over my head. Breasts lift, a spine loosens, ribs spread wide.

As if there's been a signal, rafts of pelicans lift, extend their nine-feet width of wings, and fly toward and then past me. Other flocks—ibis, sanderlings, cormorants, the roseates—go by. They follow the change of tide. I should follow them. I put my paddle in the water, and it sinks into a stir of mud. My boat has been left behind. I rock my body against the kayak seat and take careful backward strokes. The paddle edge only skims the surface until the keel sucks loose, and the rasp of muck underneath me lessens. When the water deepens and the current turns the boat, I rest the paddle on my knees and let the tide pull me home.

At the point of land before I turn back west, I see another kayak. A woman is paddling. Is this my girlfriend, already delivered? We pass, nod, say good morning. She tells me there are dolphins around the corner. I can tell she's Canadian. That would mean a big commute. Well, she'd have to move down to Florida eventually. I'm not leaving my own home. Which is pretty small for another person. She'd have to get her own place. We continue past each other. Around the point I see the dolphins. The two of them stay close and touch each time they huff and rise. I watch until they leave for open water.

The marina is awake now. Boats motor out of its entrance and up the channel. The sandbar in front of the Visitors Center is above water and crowded with birds. I paddle through the sea grass meadows toward them. On the far side of the sandbar, a ranger is leading the early morning bird walk from the lawn along the sea wall. I hear him say reddish egret and see tourist binoculars raise and point at me. I rest into my backrest and pull out the apple. In front of me the egret lurches through the crowd of white pelicans and black skimmers. It jerks a wing open and shut as it searches for food. I eat my breakfast as the tide lowers and more wading birds arrive to poke into the almost-exposed surfaces for clams and worms. I tuck the apple core into my shirt pocket. I'm ready to go back.

The wheelchair is still there. This is always a relief. But the ramp is different. Low tide has made it a long, steep way to the top. This was not in my calculations. I paddle hard, lean back to lift the bow, and ram as far up the concrete as I can. No more than the tip of my bow sticks. I rest. My muscles are wobbly from the trip. Lots of people pass by. They can't tell I use a wheelchair so they don't stare except in envy. I imagine. I rest and think about how I can do this. There will be crawling. And it will be in front of people so I'm less likely to feel comfortable or even be allowed to collapse flat out on the concrete partway up. I'm gathering myself to get started when a Spanish-softened voice asks if he can help. I don't even wonder how he knew I needed help. It is not the man from before dawn. "Yes," I say. "Can you pull the kayak up the ramp a little?"

Two heaves and I'm at the top of the ramp, past my wheelchair, and have to laugh and wave my arms and say *"sufficiente, gracias, sufficiente."* I roll off the edge of the kayak and over to my wheelchair. Usually in front of people I scoot on my butt. Somehow I imagine that it looks less weird, but rolling is easier on my arms. And really, being stared at is being stared at, so today I roll. And I do that thing where I remove myself. The people around me blur, my hearing diminishes, I

look no one in the eye. It is as if I'm alone. Four full revolutions
over the concrete that my hips will feel by tomorrow and I'm
alongside my wheelchair. I fish the crutch out from under the
cover and use it to flip the plastic up and over. And now for
its main purpose. I put the life vest on the concrete, twist on to
it, and raise into a shaky kneel. I slip my arm into the crutch
and angle it out from the chair and make sure the tip is stuck
into a crack before I put my other hand on the wheelchair
seat. I take a breath and lift, except that I don't. Some weight
comes off my knees, enough to make me topple to my butt,
but that's it. While I'm leaning against the wheelchair, panting
and working harder to ignore the milling crowd, I decide the
crutch angle is too steep and my body should start farther out
from the seat. I might only have the strength for one more try. I
reposition and concentrate. No one is admiring my grace, but
I do get the edge of one butt cheek on the seat. That's enough.
I pull and lift until I'm centered. With one finger I push the
power button, the controls light up, and it is only now, now
that it's done, that I'm certain that this trip is possible.

Once the carrier is perched alongside the kayak, I let myself
notice the world again. I smile at the crowd around me. I try
to yank the kayak onto the carrier, and, of course, fail. But it
works.

"Need some help?" I believe he has a German accent.

"Yes, thanks. The carrier needs to be positioned under
where the seat is. Great. Now, let's wrap the straps in front
of the seat and I'll lift the bow while you tighten the heck out
of it. No, tighter." I might be sounding bossy, but really, why
waste his or my time? We're done just as his group of people
start offering suggestions. Germans, definitely. I thank them
for their help.

"You are the expert, are you not?"

I'm not sure which of them says this, so I give a general-
ized bland smile and think, "Yes, I sure am." I lift the kayak

into place behind me and turn in a wide sweep toward the campground.

The road is now full of RVs, trucks, minivans, cyclists, and people walking with binoculars strapped to their chest by harnesses. The kayak and I get thumbs up, waves, smiles. People yell, "Happy New Year" at me. I wish I had a picture. I know I'm looking dang cute. This could get me that girlfriend. Sure, my shirt gapes over an ancient, stretched-out bra and my hair is spiky but not in a stylish way. The zipper on my pants twists off over a hip, and I'm not sure I've been remembering about deodorant, but I know from experience that after kayaking, when I'm this tired, my face beams some sort of feverish, angelic glow.

After unloading and reassembling my gear, I lie on my bed with the back door open to the Florida Bay. I've showered. My power wheelchair is in the bathhouse charging until morning. I'm on my bed until I leave to go home tomorrow. I take anti-inflammatory drugs. I don't think about food since I'm too tired to reach into the food box. I listen to the weather radio. The front is moving down the state. Tomorrow is going to be close to freezing. Right now, around me, the air is the warmest it's been the whole trip and the mosquitoes are encouraged. Before I have to cover up or close doors against them, the first signs of the coming storm arrive. I lean over to the lift controls and open the side doors. Wind rushes through my van, blowing the mosquitoes away, and I can feel change on my bare skin in the curls of sharp air that swirl through the humidity. People from away are lighting grills for dinner. People from Florida gather their gear, close windows, and take down awnings and screen tents. I leave the doors open to the gusts until the last moment. It comes suddenly, the rain. With a flip of the switch, I shut my doors and watch campers scurry. I am self-contained until morning.

ও২ ও২ ও২

Sandra Gail Lambert writes fiction and memoir that is often about the body and its relationship to the natural world. Her writing has received Pushcart and "Best of the Net" nominations, and among the places it's been published are New Letters, Brevity, The Weekly Rumpus, Arts & Letters, the Alaska Quarterly Review, DIAGRAM, Hippocampus, *and* Water~Stone Review. The River's Memory *is her debut novel. She lives in Gainesville, Florida, a home base for trips to her beloved rivers and salt marshes.*

∂❀ ∂❀ ∂❀

Heartbeats on Teshima

What better way to celebrate being alive?

The day before my fiftieth birthday, I had lunch with my friend Susan. We were in her office at the university where she teaches full-time and I teach part-time.

"I wonder if I'll get cake this year," I said.

"I've stopped eating sugar," she said. She was in the middle of a detox.

"Yes, I know sugar is bad for you, but I still want a birthday cake."

The year before, my family and I had gone out to dinner to celebrate, but there had been no cake with candles. My daughter had been angry on my behalf. She wanted cake, too. This year, however, I was having a "big" birthday, as my American friends and family said. Fifty was a milestone. I'd been on this Earth for half of a century, and I wanted my birthday to be special.

On my brother's fiftieth birthday, my sister-in-law threw him a surprise party. A month earlier, one of my friends had taken a trip to New York City to celebrate her fiftieth. I remembered that another friend's boyfriend had once taken her on a hot air balloon ride to celebrate turning a year older.

Susan and I were the same age—her birthday was a couple of months ago. She, too, was married to a Japanese man; he was currently working in another city. We'd met when our sons were first graders at the same elementary school, the only two kids in their grade with foreign mothers.

"Remember, people don't celebrate birthdays in Japan the way Westerners do," she said. Her husband had sent her an email to mark her fiftieth.

"Yes, I know," I said, trying not to expect too much. I knew I wouldn't be getting a ride in a hot air balloon, but a cake didn't seem too much to hope for.

We ate our lunches. Afterward, Susan produced a box of old CDs and invited me to take whatever I wanted. She'd just finished reading that Japanese book about housekeeping, and she was getting rid of whatever didn't spark joy in her heart.

Being reminded of all of the cleaning I needed to do made me a little grumpy. I decided I wouldn't do any housework on my birthday.

The next morning when I woke up, there was cat vomit on the floor. I had to clean it up. I made French toast for breakfast. When my sleepy children came to the table, they didn't say anything about my birthday. Neither did my husband. I decided to wait and see if they'd remember on their own.

I washed the dishes, did laundry, and swept the floor. O.K., so I had done a little housework, which was good, but I wasn't going to cook for the rest of the day. I spent the next few hours reading and writing and browsing websites. I came across the website for Teshima, a small island in the Inland Sea, where a French artist had been collecting heartbeats. The recorded heartbeats were then integrated into an art installation. I was intrigued.

Around five o'clock the telephone rang—it was my husband. *Maybe*, I thought, *he's calling to say we're going out to eat.*

"*Moshi moshi*," I answered.

"Hi," he said. "I won't be home for dinner. I'm going out with one of my former students. He just passed the teacher's exam and we're going to celebrate."

I was silent. How could he have forgotten? I thought about waiting to see how long it would take before my family remembered my big birthday. Maybe it would be days, weeks, even months.

I couldn't wait that long. "Today is my birthday," I finally said.

"Oh, no!" He apologized, but didn't offer to change his plans. "We'll celebrate tomorrow."

I hung up the phone. I was no longer expecting cake.

If I wanted to do something special for my birthday, I'd have to plan it myself. Because of the time difference, it would still be my birthday in the United States the next day. And I didn't have any classes to teach. I decided I'd go to the island of Teshima and record my heartbeat. What better way to celebrate being alive?

For my fiftieth birthday dinner, I ordered a pizza, and the kids and I ate it with leftovers. When we were finished, I told my son, "Today is my birthday, so you can wash the dishes."

A wave of guilt crossed his face. He agreed without complaint.

While he was cleaning up, I went for a walk in the light of the full moon.

My husband finally came home, bringing gifts he'd hastily purchased at a nearby mall. He'd gotten me running shoes with bright pink laces and two small bottles of lip color from the expensive shop that sold natural cosmetics. One of them was fuchsia, like the shoelaces. It wasn't a color I would normally choose. I thought it was gaudy, especially for someone my age, but I said "thank you."

I told my husband I wouldn't be able to celebrate my birthday with him the next day. I was going on a trip, and

I wouldn't be home in time for dinner. He'd have to cook it himself.

"Where are you going?" he asked.

"Teshima," I said. "I'm going to record my heartbeat."

"By yourself."

"Yes, by myself."

The day after my big birthday, I put on both my brand new sneakers with the fuchsia laces and the matching lip color. Yes, I decided, it was gaudy. So what? The famous Japanese artist Yayoi Kusama wore a bright red wig and dresses with huge polka dots. She was over seventy years old.

I took a bus to Takamatsu, walked to the ferry terminal, and bought a round-trip ticket to Teshima. Although we had just suffered through a long hot summer, the early autumn weather was perfect. Not too hot, not too cold. Fleecy white clouds floated across the azure sky.

I was the first one on the pier.

"Please wait," the young captain said.

I nodded. As I looked at the small hovercraft, I wondered if I would be the only passenger. Gradually, though, people began to gather. Most were young, which I found ironic, since few young Japanese people wanted to actually live in the remote areas of Japan. Because of the art, however, the islands were now becoming "cool." I spotted young Japanese couples and a foreign woman with a nose ring. Her male companion carried a huge backpack with muddy boots dangling from it.

A few minutes before departure, we were allowed to board the ferry. I sat next to the window. A middle-aged Japanese man and woman in suits took the seats in front of me. They carried binders. Where were they going? From the map I'd picked up, it looked as if the island was mostly made up of farms and fishing villages.

When we arrived at Teshima, I rented an electric bicycle and set out to explore. I rode past a small grove of olive trees. The green fruit was almost ready for picking. Soon I came upon the Sea Restaurant. Many of my fellow ferry passengers had already stopped here; their rented bicycles were lined up in the parking area. I decided to stop, too.

"We're very busy right now," the waiter told me. "It will take awhile."

"That's O.K.," I said. "I can wait." Part of the restaurant was inside the long low building. I could see through the glass windows that it was mostly full, but I didn't care. I wanted to sit on the terrace anyhow, where I could gaze at the sea and the humps of green islands in the distance.

I settled down in a lawn chair and pulled myself up to a table.

When the waiter came by, I asked for the daily special and a glass of white wine.

Soon the tables on the terrace filled as well. Three tables down, a group of Americans talked loudly. At the table to my right, an American couple sat thumbing their smart phones. At the table to my left, a Japanese couple did the same.

The waiter brought my wine. I took a sip, listening to the Americans three tables away.

"Did you go to the Issey Miyake store?" a woman asked.

A white ferry sailed past. I saw a fish leaping.

"I'd look like a mutant," another woman said.

A butterfly fluttered up above.

". . . sort of like a heartbeat," a man was saying.

The waiter brought my lunch of sea bream and crusty multigrain bread. The food was beautifully prepared and delicious, the red and orange of the vegetable sauce set off by the pure white dishes. I finished my lunch, paid my bill, and hopped back on my bicycle.

The island was quiet. I imagined the people who lived in the houses along the way were out fishing or working on another island. After I'd pedaled awhile, I came upon a few cows lazing in a terraced pasture. Farther along, farmers harvested rice. I wondered if they enjoyed looking at art, and what they thought of the many foreigners who visited their island.

Finally, I came to the reception office for the Teshima Art Museum.

Seeing my face, the Japanese man at the desk began to speak in English. He handed me a map, also in English. "Walk along the path," he said, indicating a sidewalk that curved into the forest. "After a few minutes, you'll arrive at the art space."

As I strolled through the woods, I caught glimpses of the harbor below. A young Japanese man stood waiting in a clearing. Just beyond him was the art space, a white oval structure that resembled a tent, or maybe an alien spaceship.

"Please take off your shoes," the man said, even though we were outside in the woods. "Once inside, be careful of the water and the balls on the floor."

"Um, O.K." I sat down on a bench and unlaced my sneakers. I put them in a cubbyhole, along with the shoes of the other visitors.

"Please be quiet," he added.

I walked softly onto the concrete floor of the "art space." Through oval windows on each end, I could see trees and sky. A couple of ribbons hung from the curved ceiling, swaying in the faint breeze. Here and there was a puddle, alongside smaller blobs of water. Suddenly, one of the smaller blobs began to morph into a snake shape. It squiggled toward a larger puddle and joined it. I wasn't sure what made the water start moving. From time to time, I heard an ambient sound like chimes, or water dripping from somewhere. Maybe sound caused the water to flow and flagellate. At any rate, it seemed to be alive.

I walked around, trying to make sense of this art space. White orbs the size of ping-pong balls were positioned on the floor. The water seemed to interact with the balls.

Sounds from outside entered the space. Crows cawed. An insect crawled across the floor, it too becoming part of this work of art. After a few minutes, I went back outside, careful not to step on the balls or the moving water, and laced up my shoes again.

Back on my bike, I followed signs to the beach, parked my bike, and stood on the shore for a moment listening to the waves lapping upon the sand. Then I went down a jungle path until I reached the rustic weathered wooden building that housed Christian Boltanski's "Archives of the Heart."

A young woman sat behind a desk. She explained that I could record my heartbeat if I wanted to, and it would be added to the archives. Or, I could just enter the art space.

"I want to record my heartbeat," I said.

She smiled and directed me into a small, private room where there was a computer and a stethoscope. I read the instructions in English and typed in a simple message: "I'm here on my fiftieth birthday. I'm happy that my heart is still beating. It's good to be alive."

I pressed the stethoscope to my chest, above my heart, clicked on "begin," and waited forty seconds without moving while my heart went "*ba BOOM ba BOOM*." When I was finished, I returned to the reception area. The young woman prepared a CD of my heartbeat for me to take home as a souvenir. "Now you can listen to your heartbeat," she said. The rhythms of my heart had been added to those of more than forty thousand other people.

I opened the door to the "Archives of the Heart." The room was dark except for a single light bulb hanging from the ceiling. The walls were covered with mirrors. The light pulsed in time to the percussion of heartbeats. Some were loud, like thunder. They sounded like drums, those hearts from all over the world, from people of many ages, everyone so alive.

I headed back in the direction of the ferry terminal. On the way, I stopped at the foot of a trail leading into the woods. According to my map, a sculpture was at the end of the trail, but it was blocked off by a chain. A sign said "closed." I noticed, however, a couple of bicycles parked there. Someone had apparently gone into the woods. I looked around, wondering if I'd been mistaken. Maybe the artwork was down a different trail. A few minutes later, a young Japanese couple emerged from the woods. The young man told me the owner of the bicycle rental shop had said it was O.K. to go down the trail in spite of the sign.

"It's muddy, though," he warned. "Be careful."

I followed the stepping stones into the forest of pine and bamboo. In Japanese gardens, stones are placed irregularly so visitors must think about where to place their feet. This trail was the same. I had to pay attention to my steps so as not to slip. I held onto the bamboo guardrail as I climbed higher up the mountain. At the end of the trail, there was a clearing with a smooth white sculpture centered on a green concrete area. It looked as if the white stone was floating in a pond. I peered at the sculpture from different angles. Elaborate spiderwebs were strung between bamboo trees. If I gazed at the sculpture through the scrim of spider silk, the webs became a part of the art, too.

I was only a couple of minutes' walk from the road, but alone in this place, surrounded by greenery, I felt removed from civilization. Bird songs and the sound of rushing water filled my ears.

No one was around when I emerged from the forest. I climbed back on my bike and rode toward the village.

I had heard that olives, rice, lemons, and strawberries grew on the island. I wanted to try the strawberries while I was there. I came across a small café selling crepes, smoothies, and other sweets. I hadn't ordered dessert at the Sea Restaurant, and I'd been cycling all over the island. It was time for a break.

Sitting outside with a cup of coffee and a strawberry crepe, I watched some of my fellow ferry passengers ride by on their rented bikes. The sun was lowering in the sky. Before I left, I bought a strawberry roll cake to take back to my family. It was my birthday, after all, and I still hadn't had cake.

A couple of hours later, after the ferry and the bus and a short drive in my car, I arrived at home. My supper was on the table. I ate with my son, who was also late getting home. I showed him photos I'd taken of the island cats gathered at the port, and of the café I'd discovered with pop art décor.

"What was your purpose in going there?" he asked me.

"To see the island," I said. What other purpose did I need?

We finished our dinner, and I cut cake for all of us.

Suzanne Kamata is the author of four novels, including The Mermaids of Lake Michigan, *and the editor of the anthologies* Call Me Okaasan: Adventures in Multicultural Mothering *and* Love You to Pieces: Creative Writers on Raising a Child with Special Needs. *She received a grant from the Sustainable Arts Foundation in support of her mother/daughter travel memoir,* Squeaky Wheels, *which was also named Best Novel/Memoir in the Half the World Global Literati Awards.*

ERIN BYRNE

ॐ ॐ ॐ

Reconnaissance

So. You have a wonderful view but no
way into the prospect. I have no wings,
you mutter, depressed, but your looking
outside the senses is a fire that kindles the body.

— *Jelaluddin Rumi*

I stood in the alcove knowing she'd called me here, but
I still had no idea why. What did she want with me?
Hadn't I come here every day for the past week, waiting for
her to speak? She'd reclined in her jewel-encrusted bed, silent.

The fact that she had been dead for more than fifteen hundred years was no excuse.

A church is normally the last place I would look for answers, but on a recent trip to Paris, I had entered the white sculpted-stone cathedral of Saint-Étienne-du-Mont and walked down the right side admiring the stenciled intricacy, like cut-out snowflakes, of identical spiral staircases that met in a high bridge across the middle of the church. I stopped to light a candle for my mother who was ill and my father-in-law who had recently died, and kept walking to once again end up in front of this stone reliquary under a latticed ironwork design in the chapel of Sainte-Geneviève, the patron saint of Paris.

I had repeated this scenario every day for the past week.

The previous week, I'd made the horrid discovery that my grounding force in Paris, *Winged Victory*, was away at every ancient-girl-statue's version of a spa vacation, having her cracks highlighted, her marble massaged and, as she had no arms, probably just a pedicure. I shuddered at the memory of the gunmetal gray partition denying me access to her just when I was desperate for her counsel. During my last few visits to Paris, I'd also had the utterly absurd feeling that she was trying to shoo me away, to toss me from the nest, and now that she was gone, I was stung by rejection.

I'd tried everything to comfort myself, but the sneaking suspicion that *Winged Victory* was just a statue slid into the realization that Paris, my elegant refuge, was in many ways a city like any other. I had noticed tents pitched by the side of the freeway on the way in from Charles de Gaulle airport, pickpockets appeared to lurk everywhere, and the city seemed seeped in smog. Sabrina, my closest American friend in Paris, who always appeared in front of me whenever I thought of her, was out of town, and my other friends were either gone or busy.

I was plagued by the conviction that I needed a mystical connection with some sort of sisterly figure. Over the past few years, I had come to take such illogical hunches seriously, as signs that needed attention, so there I was, right where my sixth sense of intuition had led me.

But Sainte-Geneviève couldn't be for me. I was not religious, had only recently become comfortable wandering into cathedrals, and knew nothing about her.

I left the church and, glancing at the Pantheon's dome catching the sun on its curve, went the opposite way, down the hill toward the bookstore to find a book about her.

Geneviève was born in A.D. 420 in Nanterre, in northern France, the daughter of a simple shepherd. As a girl, she often attended her father's flock on Mount Valérien. When she was eight years old, two bishops visited Nanterre and happened to inquire whether she might want to become a nun someday. As soon as she said yes, her mother said no. In what was surely every thwarted eight-year-old's guilt-laced fantasy, Geneviève's mother was struck blind on the spot.

Geneviève had many visions and dreams of saints and angels, and, like Jeanne d'Arc would nearly a thousand years later, this peasant girl followed her inner signals. All she had to do was bide her time until she could enter the church. After both parents died, at age fifteen, she went to live with her godmother Lutetia in Paris and became a nun.

In 451, when Attila the Hun approached to conquer Paris, Geneviève upbraided the cowardly men who wanted to leave town. "Wait. Hold still. Don't move. Just stay inside your homes," I imagined her saying. The men stayed, and the barbarians abandoned their quest and went off to conquer Orléans instead.

Geneviève also performed exorcisms and other political and garden-variety miracles, led prayer marathons, and was an intermediary with kings. Her enemies conspired to drown her in a lake of fire (always the aim of zealots through the ages) but she had fans as well: Saint Symeon the Stylite, a fifth-century celebrity, saw Geneviève in a vision and wrote her a letter, which must have thrilled her.

Geneviève seemed like a rock star of a saint. On my repeated trips to her home in Saint-Étienne-du-Mont, chapel de Sainte-Geneviève, I noticed the stained-glass windows with scenes of her curing her mother's blindness like a good girl, enduring a nightmare about Hell in preparation for her mission, distributing bread to Parisians, and patiently relighting a candle blown out by a devil. There was also a statue of her holding the keys to the city, and of course, the shrine that housed what was left of her remains.

Geneviève was buried, at the request of France's very first king, Clovis, next to his wife and him. Her shrine was venerated and visited so often that a series of churches were built to accommodate the crowds. She became increasingly popular when miracles began to be attributed to her. In one case, in 1129, an epidemic, *le mal des ardents*, a blazing, pestilent fever with "a violent inward heat," had killed off fourteen thousand victims in Paris. This burning sickness was halted when the shrine containing Geneviève's relics was carried to Notre Dame Cathedral. The little structure next to Notre Dame, now the treasury, was named after her. The following year, the pope declared a feast day for her, and eventually her shrine was moved to the New Church of Sainte-Geneviève.

Then those philosophizing free-thinkers of the Revolution secularized the church and renamed it The Pantheon, and in 1793, melted down Geneviève's shrine. They hauled up her remains and held a public trial of her bones, the pile of which were found guilty of "participation in the propagation of error" and were burned, like a pile of sticks, on Place de Grève, now Place d'Hôtel de Ville. Her ashes were tossed into the Seine.

What remained of Geneviève's body was ultimately collected, and these relics were placed in a sarcophagus tombstone that was covered in a lacy, gilded ironwork design and kept in Saint-Étienne-du-Mont, this gorgeous church with the delicately carved interior, a perfect home for her to finally rest after all her ordeals.

It was this humiliation of her very remains, her bones, that most struck me. Geneviève had been through the ringer, even after her death, and seemed capable of becoming my advisor. Compared to her, *Winged Victory* had had it easy, just sailed over from the Greek island of Samothrace missing only her head and arms. Geneviève, although in pieces, was one tough gal. I'd likely remain intact, but felt sure she could offer me a pointer or two.

I noticed copper plaques papering the wall of her chapel. *Reconnaissance*, they said. *Reconnaissance, Sainte-Geneviève.*

Reconnaissance, I thought, like a reconnaissance mission, must translate to mean seeking. All the people who commissioned the plaques had been seeking, just as I was. But what was I seeking? And why did I need Sainte-Geneviève? I tried every combination of reasons.

Perhaps some strength for my upcoming trip to Morocco. I'd spent the winter grieving—and helping my family grieve—the death of my father-in-law, working with my frantic father trying to find medical care for my ailing mother, and missing deadline after deadline for writing publications. I was in no mood to be in Morocco, an ancient place that sizzles with spectacular intensity and zaps every sense in the body.

Maybe as a dream amnesiac I needed this patroness's ability to remember her dreams, or her quick hand at curing her mother's ailments? None of my guesses seemed accurate.

Geneviève's story bolstered me during the week in Morocco—every time my spirits flagged or a snag arose, I thought of her squeezing her eyes shut and ordering the devil out of a writhing figure, or bolting upright in her nightshirt, hair disheveled, from a nightmare of burning-hot Hell, or of her bones igniting like kindling. I saw how small my troubles were by comparison.

Her bones, her bones, her bones, I thought. My bones were strong, I could feel them. Not one had ever been broken, and I imagined them, white and marrow-filled. This gave me energy, but it wasn't enough; I was an automatic marionette moving as if someone else were jerking the strings.

I returned to California, with plans to go between Seattle and the Bay Area throughout the summer and finish my book by July. I would make this deadline, I vowed, and do a few other things as well. In May I planned to write two chapters of the book, resume work on a novel I hadn't looked at in months, and finish a chapter of that to take to a literary conference I'd been invited to attend. I'd spend four days in Calistoga at the conference. I also planned to begin accepting submissions for an anthology about Morocco I was editing, and write an entire screenplay for a short film. It was a lot, but I knew I could do it if I kept my pace.

The puppet danced faster and forgot about her saint-sister.

At the Napa conference, a well-known author worked with me on my chapter. I outlined all my projects and she gawked at me. "Girl," she drawled, "you got too much goin' on."

I inwardly flared. I could do it, I knew I could, if I just accelerated everything.

The conference was invigorating and exhausting, but I returned ready to roll. I Skyped with my screenwriting mentor twice a day, plowed through page after page, dotting i's, crossing t's, met with my editor to complete a chapter each week, and sent out calls for submission for the anthology.

One morning toward the end of May, I shut my computer and headed out the door for my daily walk. On the way out I glanced back at a postcard of Sainte-Geneviève I kept on my desk: a statue in an outdoor alcove, her braids spilling over the folds of her robe, a sheep snuggling her feet. *Her bones,* I thought with a sigh.

I never had figured out why she was my new guide; she'd helped me in Morocco but I knew there was more. I remembered the sensation of rightness I'd had standing in front of her elaborate coffin. My brain picked up the puzzle as I clipped up and down the hills of Sausalito. The church? No, I hadn't found religion. Invaders? No, I hadn't been burglarized. Nightmares, devils, fires, no, no, no.

It seemed by now I should know the reason for the strange affinity I had with this saint. So many burning questions persisted, like an un-erasable chalkboard filled with equations, with permutations of meanings. $x=yz+m2$. As sand shushed through the hourglass, I pondered: What was the value of x, the meaning of y combined with z, the significance of $m2$? My reasoning was paralyzed.

I walked faster, as if I were chasing answers.

A month later, the questions intensified, became crows pecking at my eyes, puncturing my brain. Why, why, why?

For four weeks, I had been strapped in a thick, padded contraption that pinned my arm to my chest. A branding iron of pain sizzled from my shoulder down my arm, from my shoulder up through my head, from my shoulder into my body. I burned with fever, and had no sense of whether I was asleep or awake, dreaming or existing.

I had fallen while powerwalking down a hill that day in Sausalito, found myself sprawled in the middle of the street with such agony screaming from my shoulder that I could not move. Horrified, I saw something bulging in the middle of my arm, shoved my shoulder back into its socket, and crawled to the side of the road. Ambulance, morphine, hospital, morphine, airplane, Seattle.

I had broken my shoulder in a crescent shape in the exact spot where all of the nerves, tendons, everything connected. It shrieked in white-hot pain every second, and the pain doubled whenever I moved because I had bruised some ribs as well. I developed a high fever, an infection.

Wait, came a voice from the back of my memory. *Hold still. Don't move.*

The doctor told me that the pain would be excruciating for two months, that all I could do was keep my arm still and wait for my bone to miraculously heal itself.

I drew on Sainte-Geneviève's reserves of patience, of endurance, of composure while being licked by flames. She reminded me that the rift in my bone would sew itself together on its own and there was nothing I could do except do nothing.

Gradually I began to move. Unable to type with both hands on a computer, I started to write by hand. I found my notes from Paris, from Saint-Étienne-du-Mont.

Her bones. Reconnaissance. So many seeking, like I had been, seeking Sainte-Geneviève.

I remembered this had only been a guess at the meaning, so I clumsily reached across my strapped chest and grabbed my yellow-and-blue French dictionary.

Reconnaissance: recognition, acknowledgment, gratefulness, gratitude.

All those plaques thanking her for her life, her intercession, her healing power. All those different people who had found what they had sought right there in Saint-Étienne-du-Mont in her chapel in front of her iron-laced crypt, who had stopped there and felt peace.

My equation became clearer. The value of a steady pace. The meaning of pain combined with patience. The significance of going to her without understanding why. So often, we do not find the answers we seek at the time we search for them, and we must wait—and sometimes seek outside the senses and slow down long enough to grasp what is offered.

Sainte-Geneviève, I saw now, had been innocent of the Revolution's charge. She had, for me, participated in the propagation of truth.

The fire of gratitude kindled my body.

Erin Byrne is the author of Wings—Gifts of Art, Life, and Travel in France, *which won the Paris Book Festival Award for travel genre. She is the editor of* Vignettes & Postcards from Paris *and* Vignettes & Postcards from Morocco, *and writer of* The Storykeeper *film. Erin's travel essays, poetry, fiction, and*

screenplays have won numerous awards including three Grand Prize Solas Awards for Travel Story of the Year, the Readers' Favorite Award, Foreword Reviews Book of the Year Finalist, and an Accolade Award for film. Erin is occasional guest instructor at Shakespeare and Company Bookstore in Paris and teaches on Deep Travel trips. Her screenplay, Siesta, *is in pre-production in Spain, and she is working on a novel set in the Ritz Paris during the occupation, called* Illuminations. *Erin is host of the LitWings Event series at Book Passage by the Bay in Sausalito, which brings together writers, photographers, and filmmakers. See her work at www.e-byrne.com.*

ॐ ॐ ॐ

Delle Donne

Courage—did she have it or would she need it?

I woke to a riot of birds. My small hotel, hidden from the street behind a tall iron gate, sat in an overgrown orchard of lemon trees. With the help of a little white pill, I'd slept through the jet lag, and lemony sunlight poured through the open windows. It was my first morning in Italy, and I wanted to be happy.

"*Coraggio!*" the woman next to me on the plane the day before had sighed, followed by, "*E perque sola?*" I hadn't known enough Italian to explain why I was traveling alone, so I'd just shrugged and smiled. She'd stared at me for a long minute trying to figure me out. Did she know something I didn't? Was she saying that I *had* courage or that I'd *need* it? She'd scribbled her number in Naples on a scrap of paper and pressed it into my hand, shaking her head. I knew I wouldn't call her; she was too worried. I flashed her my it-will-be-fine face and made my way into the Naples airport. Then I lost her in the snarl of bodies and never saw her again.

The airport had been crowded, the air hot and stale. Neither of the bank machines worked, and the only money-changing booth was closed. As I'd wheeled my suitcase through the crowd and fumbled with my wallet at the broken machines, I felt the darting eyes of single men. I thought about that word, *corragio*, and hugged my shoulder bag close. In line at Hertz Italiano, I finally felt like I'd landed in the right place. I was about to get my prepaid rental car and start my homemade tour of Southern Italy. But when it was my turn, the young woman behind the counter refused to give me a car. I'd left my California drivers license at home.

"But look," I said, waving my International Drivers License. "See! This is *me*. See the photo." I pointed back and forth to my face and the picture. The woman didn't even look at the gray card I shoved across the counter.

"No," she'd told me firmly. "We must see the California license. Without this, we cannot give you the car."

"But International is more important than California, right?" I nodded in agreement with myself. She just shook her head: *No license, no car.* Then she tapped her pen hard on the counter to let me know we were done. I got dizzy and my stomach began to roil; I felt like I was going to faint and throw up at the same time.

This trip had been challenging from the start. People told me I shouldn't go to Italy by myself; I shouldn't drive through the south; it wasn't safe for a woman. I should take a train or book a tour. All of which only made me more determined. I'd traveled alone before, and this kind of trip was exactly what I wanted—time alone on my own schedule without having to attend to anyone else's needs, a gift to myself after thirty-five years of teaching.

I rarely get bored or lonely when I'm by myself. I grew up in a house that was empty all day while my parents worked, and I learned to love the quiet I met when I unlocked the front door after school. I liked the way the rooms felt with no one in them, the way the light filtered in through the venetian blinds in the late afternoons. I'd make myself a snack of cookies and milk and read curled up on the couch or sit at the piano and pick out songs with one hand. When I'm alone, a space opens up that isn't usually there, letting me find myself on my own terms. Traveling alone, staying in small hotels, wandering in the world, gives me that same happiness.

Standing at the Hertz Italiano counter, I saw my trip whisked away from me, saw myself stuck on the ugly outskirts of Naples forever. I frantically dabbed water on my forehead from a paper cup and stammered for help, "Oh no, this is terrible. What can I do?" The sophisticated traveler crumbled as I became my inner four-year-old: "Please, *per favore, Signorina!*" She didn't know what to do with me. A long line had formed, and someone's roller bag was pushing against my legs. I gripped the plastic counter with both hands and begged: "Isn't there someone I can talk to?"

Vincenzo took the young woman's place. His manner was gentle, his voice kind. As he refilled my little cup, he counseled me in his nearly perfect English, "Drink the water, *Signora*. Maybe you would like to go to the bathroom. Don't worry." He made a call to California. Then he drove me to the bus stop, all the while murmuring: "Be calm, *Signora*, you will go to Sorrento by the bus. You will get your car. You must be calm."

Something about Vincenzo reminded me of my mother, restoring my faith in having faith. He didn't give up like the woman behind the counter; he knew that with a little effort, he could make things better. My mother was the same way— she didn't believe in giving up, and as we both got older, she began to show a quiet faith in me. This was odd since she worried about almost everything else. She worried about money and about the state of the world. She worried if she didn't have at least six boxes of Kleenex on the shelf. She worried about why the rest of the family didn't come to see her. She used to worry about me when I was younger, but around the time I became a mom, in my mid-thirties, something shifted between us. She came to the conclusion that I would be fine.

When we moved my mother into assisted care in her mid-eighties, she asked me to hang her pictures. She had a collection of framed art from the house she and my father had lived in for fifty years.

She'd pointed at the blank walls: "I want you to hang the art. You're not afraid."

"Not afraid of what?"

"You're not afraid to do things. You just do them and it all works out," my mother said matter-of-factly, like it was obvious.

If she were still alive before I left for Italy, she would have said, "I know you. You'll do it." Her confidence in me was like a tugboat pulling me forward.

That first morning in Sorrento, shaking off the bliss of the sleeping pill and the thick songs of the birds, I thought about the fact that I didn't have a car or any euros. Maybe I couldn't do this after all. The planning and research and hotel booking I'd done at home had looked so good on paper. I sat up in bed and looked out the window at the green of the garden, wondering how things could go wrong in such a perfect place. I summoned up Vincenzo: *You must be calm.* Across the room, my suitcase was propped open on a velvet loveseat, clothes spilling over the sides, and I thought about how I had only a couple of hours before check out. How would I get to my hotel in Paestum? The train didn't stop there, and a bus wouldn't take me anywhere near my hotel. My room, several hours down the coast, was paid for, and I knew it would be beautiful.

I imagined my mother's face and heard her voice in my head. *You'll do it,* she said. I showered, dressed, and left the singing birds for downtown Sorrento.

The diesel smell and buzzing engines of cars and delivery vans filled the streets, the sidewalks busy with locals running their morning errands. As I walked along the main drag, a dark woman seemed to be shadowing me. She was in her late forties, bone-thin with long, straight black hair. Wherever I walked, she was nearby. We shared an awning when a sudden burst of rain poured down, and I saw that she had nothing but the clothes she was wearing—no shopping bag, no umbrella, not even a purse. After about twenty minutes I lost track of her. But she reappeared at the Hertz office, a plastic hanger of socks in her hand, and tapped my shoulder.

"Perfavore, Signora, due euros. Due, signora." She was standing too close, dangling the socks in my face—a trio of black, blue, and gray—men's or women's, I couldn't tell. Her dark eyes were fixed on me.

"No, grazie," I said, looking away. She scared me, this shadow-woman. I didn't want her stuff.

"Perfavore," she repeated. Her voice had become harder, more demanding, like a brick aimed at my head. I turned my back and pretended to study a sightseeing brochure until she slipped away.

The Hertz people accepted the PDF of my license emailed from home and gave me my car, a Fiat Panda, red and shiny. I drove it out of the tiny cobblestone lot straight into Sorrento traffic, intoxicated by my change of luck. I didn't need that woman's socks, her sad dark need. But a few blocks later, I found myself looking for her. I thought about how she only wanted two euros, how I had my car and she had nothing. I thought about how being poor can make you desperate. But she'd disappeared into the cracks of the city.

As I drove straight into the noise and chaos, I felt dangerously light. How would I find my hotel, where would I park the car? I looked out at the gray-clouded sky. My feet in sandals were cold. I hadn't brought any socks to Italy.

An hour later, a fork in the road and a homemade sign pointed me out of town to the Amalfi Coast road, SS 163, a narrow shoelace strung across the high cliffs of the Lattari Mountains, with gorgeous dizzying drops to the Bay of Naples below. Huge hulking tourist buses appeared regularly on blind turns. I slowed to a crawl, hoping for an extra inch of room to pass. There was nothing else to do but hope—or pray, if you were in the habit of talking to God. I shut my eyes so I wouldn't see the tangled mess of our collision.

What would my mother think of me driving this road alone, my clutch foot cramping and my hands clammy on the steering wheel? She grew up during the Depression, never went to college, and worked nine-to-five clerical jobs her whole life. But she had another life. My mother was a radical. She and my father protested every war that came along. They invited civil rights leaders from Mississippi to stay in our house, marched down Market Street in San Francisco for gay rights, and stood outside Planned Parenthood to help women get safely inside.

My mother was a fighter, but she wasn't an adventurer—and she hated to be alone. When my father died, I reserved two nights for her in a hotel room on the coast with a view straight out to the ocean. I thought she'd love it, but she shook her head. "Oh no," she said. "I don't want to go anywhere. Thank you, but no." She didn't go; she curled up on the couch in their apartment, alone for the first time in fifty years. Being alone in a hotel room was my idea of solace, not hers.

SS 163 baptized me. I let the beauty be bigger than the terror. I eased the cramp in my foot and kept driving until I hit Vietri sul Mare, a small town on a flat stretch of road next to the sea. It was raining lightly, and there were little whitecaps on the water; it felt dreamy, like an old black-and-white film. I found a place where I could park and an espresso bar where I could take a break from the road. Out of the corner of my eye, I watched a man and woman at the bar stir sugar into their coffees with tiny spoons. Standing just as they did at the zinc counter, I stirred in my packet of sugar and then tipped the tiny white cup to my lips. It only took a minute, but it was a perfect minute. It reminded me of sitting on a barstool at home waiting for a glass of whiskey. I could be alone and it was O.K.

You need a high tolerance for chaos to drive in Italy. My tolerance level was low-medium. On my second day on the road, I wrote the words for right and left, *destro* and *sinistra,* on my hands. Drivers sped up behind me and pushed me forward with their horns, through the main arteries of towns and out the other sides. I asked everyone for directions; it took more than ten Italians to get me anywhere.

When I was thoroughly lost, I'd pull off the road to study a totem pole of signs, ten or twelve destinations all pointing in different directions, my AAA map spread out on my lap. By late afternoon, I landed in Rivello, an ancient hilltop town that had sounded good on the internet. It was cold and nearly deserted. I parked the car and walked through a labyrinth of cobblestones, memorizing landmarks to keep from getting lost. Soon I noticed a trail of rose petals along the path—pink, red, and white—dropped in thick bunches across the stones. A wedding? A funeral? I followed the path of petals, only walking where I saw them, hoping they'd lead me to something. The contrast of flowers on stone was startling and beautiful. At the corner of a lane, a woman dressed all in brown—chocolate-brown skirt, jacket, shoes, and the same color hair, dyed, as she looked to be in her eighties—sat on her porch looking down on the street below.

I smiled up at her and said, *"Buona sera."* She answered eagerly, but then immediately began a loud litany of sadness, her words punctuated by wails and cries. I nodded and called out, *"Si Signora"* at intervals, looking up at her as she sat on her straight wooden chair. I thought maybe she was locked out, and I wondered what to do. Then a large cat slipped though an inch or two of open door, so I knew she wasn't crying about something that simple.

"*Ho nove figli. Nessuno viene a trovarmi. Nessuno visita*," she wailed.

I got that she had nine kids and no one came to see her, no one visited. I looked sympathetic, nodded and murmured, "*Si Signora.*" That's a lot of kids to not have any of them stop by.

She continued in the same loud voice: "*Ho dolore terribile.*" She pointed to her neck, her shoulder, her legs.

She had pain, all over. I sighed, "*Si Signora.*" Then I added firmly, "*No capisco,*" I don't understand. "*No parle Italiano,*" I said sadly, which was only partly true.

"*Nessuno! Nessuno!*" Nobody! Nobody! She was howling now.

I raised my voice to get her attention: "*No capisco, Signora!*" But I did understand. She wouldn't be wailing to a complete stranger if she weren't alone, on the Earth or in her mind.

Now and then she'd smile for the pleasure of telling someone, so I stayed looking up at her, repeating: "*Si Signora. No capisco, signora. No parle Italiano.*" But she paid no attention. I didn't know what to do with all this information. I couldn't talk to her and I couldn't help her. I barely knew Italian, and her misery was too immense, too private. I wanted to return to the rose petals and my solitude, something I could understand. Finally, I gave her a heartfelt smile and waved goodbye, murmuring, "*Ciao Signora,*" leaving her in the same spot, talking into the empty street.

My mother regularly came home from work in a bad mood. She'd shut herself up in her room, lying on the bed and sobbing loud enough so we could hear. My father would tell me to go in and talk to her, that I was the only one who could make her feel better. I hated the pressure, hated feeling like I was being thrown into deep water. I was just a kid and I wanted to be happy. Eventually I'd go in. All the shades would be drawn and she'd be in a clump on her bed. I'd sit beside her, put my hand on her back and say I was sorry she was sad. Maybe I cheered her up—I don't remember. All I remember is not wanting to go in.

A half hour later, I took a twisting alley above the woman's house to avoid her. I could still hear her, but she wasn't talking now; she was sobbing into the dusky light. In a film or novel I would have gone to her, put my arms around her, brought her into the house with the slippery cat, made her tea. In life, I skirted her, my heart sore. I felt close to crying—for her, for me, for lonely women who sit in front of their doors with no one to tell.

The next day I drove south through Calabria toward the Tyrrhenian Sea, to Tropea, the name charming me forward. But where had the highway gone? Suddenly, I found myself on a narrow country lane, slamming on the brakes to avoid crushing a three-wheeled cart posing as a car, its tiny chugging engine making it slower than a mule. Fields of corn hugged both sides of the road. Did I daydream through an intersection, another Italian totem pole of long green signs all pointing in different directions? My hands tightened on the wheel and my eyes darted back and forth, looking for a sign or a human being. A few miles into the corn, a little blue marker was stuck into the dirt on the side of the road: SS 16. I was on the right road; it had just gotten smaller and stranger.

Then I saw something that didn't make sense. A very dark-skinned woman, maybe black, was sitting on a chair under a tree on the side of the road. She had on thick makeup, a tight dress, and lace-up, high-heeled boots. I told myself I was having a Fellini moment. A couple turns in the road later, I saw a slender woman with long black hair standing on the side of the road, carrying an umbrella for the sun. She was dressed in tight sapphire blue pants. Waiting for a bus, I thought. More turns, more women: pale, blond, olive-skinned, thin, fat, black, brown. One of them wore nothing but lacy black underwear and heels. Three black women stood together under the shade of a tree; around another turn, two white women sat on kitchen chairs, looking bored. They all wore garishly bright lipstick, rouge, eye makeup, over-the-top sexy clothing. I finally got it: they were prostitutes.

It was hot and bright. High noon. Lunchtime. I always thought this was an after-dark activity. My mind filled with questions: Where did they go—the car, the cornfields, an abandoned shack—and how would they get home to wherever they lived? Plus, it was Sunday and Italy was a Catholic country, home of the pope. I couldn't stop thinking about the women. Who were they? Black Italians? Immigrants working for papers? Where were they from and how did they get here?

I was strangely drawn to these women—the idea of them—a sexual hallucination cropping up in the green and gold of the afternoon. I found myself surprisingly titillated, sweaty from the heat of the afternoon, my legs bare under my thin dress, my thighs touching. I also felt uneasy, and I didn't know why. Then suddenly the road opened up, leaving the cornfields and the women behind. I kept looking for them, but they were gone.

I'd known two prostitutes when I was in college. They were both interesting and smart; they were like me, but more confident and worldly. I met Beth in a psychology class and Carol in a women's group. They weren't proud of being prostitutes but not ashamed either. They fascinated me, but I didn't want to get too close, as though that other life they were living would somehow infect mine.

At different times when I've needed money I've imagined being a prostitute or a call girl. Maybe every woman has. But then I'd think about the way some men smell, their skin and breath, how certain body types repulse me and how I might be hurt physically, alone in a room with a psycho, a woman-hater. I'd also think about how I didn't want it to ruin sex, a place of pleasure and refuge. I remembered both Beth and Carol telling me the same thing: they'd just go somewhere else in their heads and return when it was over. One of them married a john, left the business and went back to school. The other had a boyfriend, a cable-car driver, who, she claimed, accepted her double life. It was San Francisco in the seventies and everything was acceptable.

My parents talked openly about almost everything when I was growing up. My mother told me she'd had more than one illegal abortion and how horrible it was to sneak around and feel like a criminal. Once she'd driven all the way to Mexico. She regarded abortion and prostitution as political issues, women's issues. When I was sixteen, she took me to get birth control; I wasn't even having sex, and I was embarrassed. My mother treated the trip like we were going to the department store for school clothes.

There was almost always something interesting going on in our house. I'd sneak out of bed at night and crouch in the half-dark on the kitchen floor to listen to my parents and their friends. They'd sit in the dining room long after the dishes were cleared, drinking red wine or whiskey, arguing about how to fix the world. My mother lit up when she talked politics. She'd get loud and excited, and then there would be more things to do—put out a mailing, join a picket line, organize a protest. She wasn't the same woman who dragged herself up the stairs at the end of a long workday. For years she did mindless clerical work in offices. Then she trained herself to be a bookkeeper and got a job with a fancy bakery. At the end of the day, she'd drive home across the city, stopping to get groceries for dinner. If it wasn't a meeting night, she'd pay the bills, help me with my homework, keep up with the laundry, and some nights, iron the sheets and pillowcases. She'd smooth the warm sheets with her hands, then fold them into perfect squares, creating order in a world full of problems.

In the late afternoon, I reached Tropea, as pretty as its name. Mildly lost, I wheeled my suitcase down a narrow cobblestoned street and stuck my head into a gift store. Three women stood staring up at a row of ceramic heads of the saints hanging from the ceiling. They turned when they heard me asking for directions in my guidebook Italian, and one of them, the oldest, announced in English: "I know where you want to go." She grabbed the hotel booking information from my hand and continued to stare up at the gaudy painted heads. I noticed they didn't ask about the prices, and they weren't carrying purses. The women weren't buying, only dreaming of buying.

As we walked, the trio introduced themselves: Silvana, Valentina, Francisca. They were warm and friendly, leading me to my hotel just twenty steps away. We entered a cool courtyard and climbed three flights of narrow stairs while they chattered to each other in Italian. I was surprised that all three came along until I saw they worked there. I named it *Hotel delle Donne, Hotel of Women,* because there wasn't a man in sight.

Silvana was blond and handsome with a tired face, missing back teeth, a bunch of kids, and no husband. She was the big sister of the group. When she realized I was traveling alone, Silvana said, "That's funny." I agreed yes, it's funny. Then I added the word "*independente*," so she wouldn't think I'd been abandoned, left by the side of the road. She looked up from folding clean sheets and nodded, like she thought being *independente* was a good thing.

Valentina was the youngest, plump and pretty, with dimples in her cheeks. She took a break from cleaning rooms one afternoon to walk me to a view of the sea spread out like turquoise cloth at the foot of the hillside town.

"*Bello, el mare!*" Valentina said, placing her hand on her heart and fixing her eyes on the sea.

"*Si, molto bello!* Let's go!" I made swimming motions with my arms and pointed down at the blue-green water.

"No, I want," she said, "but I cannot. *Lavoro*—I work—*tutti giorni*. Each day." We looked out at the sea and the perfect slice of sandy beach with its bright umbrellas and people running along the shore and splashing into the water.

"But tomorrow—*Domenica*. It's Sunday. We can go!" I liked the idea of a local girl showing me the beach, plus she loved it so much. I wanted her to have it.

"*No, Io lavoro sette giorni. Lavoro Domenica.*" Valentina shook her head firmly as if to say, that's the reality, lady. I work seven days a week, including Sunday.

Francisca loved literature and wanted to write fiction. She was the most educated and spoke the best English, so she worked the front of the hotel. One night Francisca and I sat at the hotel desk until late at night telling each other about our favorite writers. "Toni Morrison!" I proclaimed. "She won the Nobel Prize."

Francisca responded wistfully, "I haven't read, but I know this name." Then Francisca smiled and said, "Maria Attanasio! Of Sicilia. She is good."

Francisca wrote out a list of southern Italian writers on a piece of hotel stationery in her big schoolgirl print. She had a round doll-like face, bangs and full red lips. She became animated talking about the writers she loved and the stories she wanted to write. But her face changed when I asked about her future.

She sighed and frowned: "In Italy, is very bad now," she said. "This job is not anything, but is all I have. I must give the money to my mother and father." She shrugged.

All day and into the evening the women of the *Hotel delle Donne* mopped the floors and cleaned the rooms. In the morning they cooked frittatas, arranged trays of fruit, cheese, salami, and pastries on the rooftop terrace, and served coffee and tea. By midday they'd cleared and washed the dishes and put everything away. All afternoon they carried dirty laundry downstairs and returned with piles of freshly washed sheets and swept and re-swept the hallways and stairs. Then they took buses to smaller, less expensive towns, back to families, children, housework. Their long days showed through their smiles.

On the nights my parents went to meetings they'd sit on folding chairs in the socialist party headquarters—a large room in a comrade's long flat—drinking coffee and talking politics, organizing protests and demonstrations and trading strategies. I'd be left home with the TV and, as I got older, with my mother's huge Buick of a typewriter. I'd sit alone in the house and type secret manifestos about justice and love. Eventually my parents would come home, tired but happy. At those times, my father didn't worry about my mother; she was as tough, as committed, as he was. She might sigh and say, "Oh that was a long meeting," but I could tell she loved it. She was infuriated by injustice, especially to women. I think she felt that her life would have been different, fuller, if she had been born in another time; she would have had more meaningful work and become "something." As her only child, and a daughter, she couldn't imagine how I would turn out to be less than "something." She might have worried about the world, but I was where she put her faith, and as bad as things might get, she knew I would be fine because she'd made me that way.

The morning I left Tropea, I asked Valentina if she'd help me carry my things down the steep stairs of the hotel. I'd thought about her when I ventured to the beach alone,

swimming in the salty sea and napping in the warm sand. I
saw her often working in the hotel—in the mornings cooking
breakfast and serving our coffee, and during the day carrying
a mop and bucket to clean our rooms. I'd smile and say *buon
giorno* or *como stai* and she'd smile back, flashing her deep
dimples. She looked worried when I asked her to help me, so
I offered to give her some euros. I figured she was afraid of
getting behind in her work. But she refused the money and
stayed with me, walking up the hill to my car.

It was hot and my rolling suitcase bumped awkwardly over
the uneven cobblestones. Valentina carried my shoulder bag,
heavy with books and small jars of spicy Calabrian sauces.

"I go next month to *la scuola for la polizia*," she told me
when I asked the usual, "*Como stai?*"

"*Si?*" I made a face showing my surprise. It was hard to
imagine her as a policewoman; she seemed so wholesome
and soft.

"*Si!* I want!" She nodded her head emphatically and made a
serious face to show me just how much she wanted to become
a *polizia*. "It is very difficult," she added, frowning.

"Then why?" I asked, even though I could guess. She told
me she needed a better job, more money, security. She and her
boyfriend wanted to get married. She covered her heart with
her palm.

When we turned the corner and reached my parking spot,
I saw that Valentina's long hair had come untied and was falling loose around her face, and her clothes were rumpled and
stained. She was only nineteen, and she already seemed worn
out by life. We stopped for a minute in the shade and gave
each other a goodbye hug. She smiled, her dimples perfect
commas. I lifted a runaway strand of hair from her face and
said, "You'll do it."

As she walked away, I mouthed "*corragio*" into the air
between us.

❧ ❧ ❧

Katharine Harer has a horrible sense of direction and a perverse attraction to getting lost. She often goes off alone because no one else likes to travel like this. Katharine teaches English and Creative Writing at Skyline Community College, where she's the Co-Vice President of the faculty union. Katharine has published six collections of poetry; the most recent, Jazz & Other Hot Subjects, *came out in 2015 from Bombshelter Press in Los Angeles. She has recent work in* Miramar, Visions International, *and* Bali Belly *and on the* Baseball Bard, TalkingWriting, *and* Medical Literary Messenger *websites. Katharine reads her poetry in colleges, bookstores, galleries, and cafés and often performs with jazz musicians. Her nonfiction projects include a book about women who played pro ball in the forties and fifties, a travel memoir/literary homage about Pablo Neruda, and personal essays about Italy. Katharine lives in San Rafael, California, with her husband, Bob, their dog, Shaggy, and sometimes her grown son, Leo.*

♬ ♬ ♬

The Storytelling Animal

Who grants the right to represent?

We are in the market square in Djenné, in central Mali. Ali the Griot holds court on a low wooden stool by the pharmacy. He chants:

"The Fulani came from Ethiopia: first the Diallos, then the Sows, then the Bâs. The Bâs had the most cattle, their cows are white, they give the most milk, from that milk comes the sweetest butter."

He chants:

"Do you know Amadou Cissé? His ancestors lived in the bush and herded cows—and this Cissé has no cows, he lives in town, and works as a guide herding white tourists!"

An old man on a motorcycle pulls up to the pharmacy. His *boubou* is starched and very white against the red dust of Djenné's unpaved streets, and the watch on his wrist is golden. He recently had sold his cows to pay the bride price for a second wife, and a television for his city home. The *griot* chants:

"He has nothing now, just his penis."

Passersby snigger. The old man just stands there. No one dares contradict a *griot*, a hereditary documentarian, a descendant of historian-poets who for hundreds of years have preserved and passed down their family bloodlines the ancestral sagas of their neighbors. A *griot* decides whether to keep or broadcast people's iniquities and virtues. His praise and reprimands stoke or resolve conflicts, bestow or retract fame, devastate or strengthen. Only a blacksmith—who uses fire to forge matter out of nothingness—evokes more awe.

The North African scholar-traveler Ibn Battuta, who wrote about his visit to Mali in 1352, found *griots* repugnant, their performance comical, and, in the chapter he titled "Account of what I found good and what I found bad in the conduct of the Blacks," lumped them with sinners: "Other bad practices are the clowning we have described when poets recite their works, and the fact that many of [the Malians] eat carrion, dogs and donkeys." But the Djennénke know better. They submit to the *griots'* fearful poetry because it comes from the very forces that helped shape the universe. They recognize the awesome power of storytelling.

Bruce Chatwin proposed that, as the indigenous Australians' totemic ancestors had sung into being a geographical score at the era of creation they called the Dreamtime, so had the first humans sung their way across the world. The poetry of those first songs, says Chatwin, was the original *poïesis*, creation. In a manner of speaking, it was: the command of complex language may have enabled our ancestors to share plans and gave them the cohesion to strike out of Africa some sixty thousand years ago. Stanza by millennial stanza, we talked ourselves all the way to Patagonia.

That initiatory song is unceasing. It enacts its magic again and again in myriad individual instances of becoming: When a mother names everything to her infant. When new lovers point out to each other a moonrise, a sunset, a freckle as if these had never been seen before. Look! Look! Each story is foundational, each makes the universe afresh. Like a *griot's* testimony, each creates a new world and a new way of being in it. When a writer tells faraway stories, she sings the Other into existence on the page, and every story is loaded with the potential to transform lives, profoundly and at random.

On the surface, my storyteller's work is straightforward. I enter a community, a culture, and cut an unambiguous covenant with my hosts: I will absorb their caring instruction and recount their story to the world. On a planet constantly redefined by the Anthropocene, where avarice and technology rend and throw together landscapes, and megacultures subsume whole ways of seeing, their accounts testify both to our connectedness and to the astonishingly different ways in which we are alive.

On and off for a year, to research a book, I walked around the Malian Sahel with a family of Fulani nomads. The Fulani herd their lyre-horned Zebu cattle on foot, keeping the pace set twelve thousand years ago, when a man first took a cow to graze and committed to life on the hoof. It is a pace as old as Abel. Two thousand footsteps per mile. Twenty to forty thousand footsteps a day. Seven to fifteen million footsteps a year chasing rain in the African savannah, faithfully hugging the routes hewn by centuries of common sense and bad habits, with minor deviations for temporary things—crops, droughts, borders, wars. Every footfall is an umbilical cord that connects the Fulani to the very first cowboys, reminds them of who they are on Earth. Every footfall propels the narrative of being human.

In West Africa, the right to spew blessings and augury is a matter of caste. A *griot* is born into it, anointed a poet in the womb. For twenty years I have been telling stories from the peopled landscapes of the Global South—but who appointed me, a stranger, a storyteller from the edge? The responsibility is immense: I may be the single conduit between my subjects and my audience, their only megaphone. What if no other documents mile after mile the stories of loss and redemption and fear and love Fulani nomads tell round the campfire on ancient transhumance routes? What if no one else chronicles an Afghan village weave, for a year, her woes into the opiated patterns of a carpet, or records, aboard a wooden Senegalese fishing pirogue, the ancient Ahab-like obsession that drives man to test and test again the foremost boundary that divides our planet into the solid and the unfathomable? Everything is at stake.

"You catch the snowflake but when you look in your hand you don't have it no more," an old *brujo* tells the boy Billy Parham in Cormac McCarthy's novel *The Crossing*. "If you want to see it you have to see it on its own ground. If you catch it you lose it." Who gave me the right to package something so magical, and why?

"Things separate from their stories have no meaning," a Mexican hermit priest tells Billy later on. But what about stories separate from their things?

The maddening paradox of representation lies in the innate contradiction between the moral imperative to expose the world's iniquities by honoring the lives these iniquities most affect—and the constant doubt in the right to render something so exceedingly private, to distill it the way one distills an essence. To exhibit it apart from its context. To transpose it onto a different context, my own.

The Fulani measure out the Sahel in yearlong loops. Their sinuous footpaths run from one grazing ground to the next and back. When the Fulani move camp and cattle flow before them in endless groaning herds, their wake smells like sour milk. When they stop—for a few days, or weeks, or months—they dismantle and reclaim the dilapidated reed-and-straw huts of herders come before, adding to these bequeathed shelters temporary embellishments: a blue plastic tarp to keep out the rain, a scavenged clay water jug. The huts smell like sour milk, too. When they break camp again they leave such repurposed homes scattered with crockery shards, torn mats, glass vials of vermicide, ripped plastic bags: tangible exhalations of their passing.

Next to these middens are Fulani graves. They are unmarked mounds of dirt. The nomads' transhumance routes return to them once or twice a year. Most are children's graves: children in Mali die of disease and hunger at the highest rate in the world. When I traveled with them, the migration route of my hosts linked together the graves of five of their children. Now it links seven.

Maybe sorrow charts its own topography, its own distinct story.

Within these amplitudes lie smaller migrations. The twice-daily trek to pasture. The long sweltering walks to market every other day to swap buttermilk for rice and millet. The forage for firewood, the hike to the nearest well. There is rarely time to be idle, but there is seldom a hurry, either. Life is measured, iambic. There is always a moment to stand knee-deep in the river and eat a mango, letting sweet piney juice drip into the current from the elbows and chin, to watch swallows dance in the high blue, to laugh and gossip.

One evening, after the last call to prayer had dissolved in the dusk, my friend Ousman brought his ten-month-old son to sit in the dust at the edge of the circle where his herd stood in dark and breathing silhouette. Ousman told the baby nothing about the cows. He didn't point anything out. He didn't have to. In the bush you pass down the love of animals simply by loving. I thought: This was the truest form of storytelling, of story-learning. It involved no middlemen.

The year I spent with the nomads I was missing someone very much, and my sadness clung to the savannah like wet silk. It contoured everything, created a frame of reference

of its own. As my hosts migrated, in each of their footfalls
I saw a separation. I saw them leave behind loved ones, lovers, their dead. I saw them shape their living within sequences
of holding on and letting go, trying to accept the transience of
everything—and to embrace man's innate impotence to accept
it. My narrative of their journey is an imperfect decoction of
a world seen through my particular tragicomic bird's mask.

Neuroscience explains that such inadequacy is predeter-
mined and unavoidable. It is a function of anatomy. Something
particular—this melancholy song of a milkmaid, that solitary
cattle egret like an enormous lotus blossom descending—stirs
the storyteller's neurons to respond, rebates off the memories
they store. Except these memories themselves are malleable,
unreliable, even possibly untrue. Our brain may even create
them on the fly, in the very moment of the encounter, when
something indefinable in the unique and ephemeral sound-
board of our cortex is strummed just so and resounds. Neuro-
psychologists call such memories, ominously, "false," "ghosts,"
"superposition catastrophes."

In other words, what we elect to see and how we see it is
irrevocably conditioned by our history, our longings, our joys,
the way life appears to us in the specific moment of seeing,
and our impulse to draw connections, identify patterns, estab-
lish syllogisms. The modest call it a coincidence and, virtu-
ously, stop at that. Writers take or create context, then fit life
into it. The result is a story.

It is a paradigm Eliot Weinberger—writer, poet, editor,
translator—describes in his essay "The Desert Music: South,"
about the mysterious geoglyphs on the Nazca plain in Peru.
For almost a hundred years people have been trying to deci-
pher these lines. "The plain mirrors one's own preoccupation,"
writes Weinberger: some see celestial data, others engineering feats, or runway markers for UFOs. Toward the end of
the essay, Weinberger reveals to us what he himself perceives.

"Nazca, empty of the forms of life, was pure description itself: the world turned into writing, with the plain as its page." Of course. He is a wordsmith: he sees a text.

Like most sacred rites, storytelling usually happens at night. This makes sense. It is easier to imagine different realities in a dark void, where nothing distracts the mind and possibilities seem limitless. It is like closing our eyes. Fulani nomads tell stories after dinner, after the campfire has grown cold and the children have jigsawed on thin moonlit mats under their mothers' skirts and grandfathers' blankets.

The nomads are egalitarian storytellers. Men, women, and older children take turns, piecing together new worlds in equal measure from the ornate allegories of Islam and *griots'* incantatory oral histories and ancient animalistic parables that traveled on transatlantic slave ships to become tales about Br'er Rabbit. They populate these worlds with cowboys whose herds spill beyond the horizon, water spirits that feed on human eyes and bellybuttons, spendthrift youngsters who squander their inheritance of cows on women and cigarettes, herders who lose their pasturelands to the intensifying drought or to the global war on terror that is ravaging traditional nomadic routes on the edges of the Sahel.

At the end of each anecdote the listeners click their tongues in appreciation. Then they say:

"Good story. Go on."

My hosts trusted me to convert their intimacies into stories because they wanted people beyond the Sahel to hear about their life. They encouraged me to write things down. They made sure I sketched the right number of teats on a cow's udder. (Four teats.) Maybe they understood that bias was inherent to any narrative. They live in a pre-modern lifestyle, with no access to radio, television, or internet, and they must have learned, over centuries of listening to stories told by *griots, marabouts,* and other nomads, that every storyteller introduces distortion into her tales. Perhaps they even like them for the flaws.

On storytelling nights they would ask that I tell them stories, too—about the emergence of stars, about lands so cold that snow covers pastures for months on end, about human origins. My accounts were improbable, my context strange, my perspective biased. The Fulani accepted all of that as part of the bargain. Their scratchy savannah had given birth to magical realism, and it has room for everything else. They judged each story on its own merit as a map of a new territory, a journey someplace ineffable.

There is a different way to describe Chatwin's idea that people had narrated the Earth into existence. He was a writer and a wanderer, and he envisioned the perfect union of his two passions, a Dreaming-track song. If we fall in love with the world of his distinct creation it is because it surprises us, takes us someplace new, resonates in some insatiable cavern within that forever wants a narrative, to explain things. It strums something that makes us say: Yes. Good story. Go on.

Anna Badkhen writes about people in extremis, exposing the world's iniquities by honoring the lives these iniquities most affect. Her investigation into what it means to live in the Global South has yielded five books of lyrical nonfiction, most recently Walking with Abel: Journeys with the Nomads of the African Savannah, *a book about transience. She also contributes to periodicals such as* Granta, The New York Times, Guernica, Nautilus *and* Foreign Policy. *She is at work on* Fisherman's Blues, *a book of magical nonfiction about the porous boundary between the terra firma and the unfathomable. It is set in Senegal. Badkhen has grown up and worked in the developing world most of her life. She is a fellow with the Tulsa Artist Fellowship in Oklahoma.*

ACKNOWLEDGMENTS

$\mathcal{I}$'m wildly grateful to all the wonderful humans who helped bring this book to fruition.

First, to the women who wrote the nearly five hundred essays submitted this year: Your words lit up my days and evenings and late-late-late nights, and I thank you for going out into the world with openheartedness, courage, and compassion, for seeing and doing astounding things, meeting fascinating people, feeling and learning so much, and then writing down your stories and sharing them. I feel truly honored to have read them all.

To Larry Habegger and James O'Reilly of Travelers' Tales: I continue to be impressed by your extraordinary wisdom, kindness, and excellence, and you have my eternal gratitude for being just plain awesome to work with. Thank you for everything you do for women and travel writing—it's *a lot*—and also for giving me a year off (O.K., two) from editing so I could work on being a mom. Thanks to Susan Brady, too, for all the hard work.

To Dan Prothero, World's Best Boo, for all the pep talks and all the love and all the coffee and all the life I could ever wish for.

To Dolly Spalding, Kimberley Lovato, Marcia DeSanctis, Katie Sperry, Blake Spalding, Meera Subramanian, Vanessa Fernandez, Erin Melcher, and Colette Hannahan, for so much sage advice and invaluable insight. You are the Best, Women.

And finally, to you, the readers of *The Best Women's Travel Writing*. Your faith and support are what keep this collection going, and you have my deepest gratitude, till the end of time.

"The End of Something" by Janis Cooke Newman originally appeared in *Days Like This: Good Writers on Bad Luck, Bum Deals, and Other Torments* in 2015. Reprinted by permission of the author. Copyright © 2015 by Janis Cooke Newman.

"Goodnight, Sweetheart" by Marcia DeSanctis originally appeared in *The New York Times Magazine* in 2010. Reprinted by permission of the author. Copyright © 2010 by Marcia DeSanctis.

"The Bad Place" by Maggie Downs published with permission from the author. Copyright © 2017 by Maggie Downs.

"A Long Night's Journey Into Spring" by Colleen Kinder originally appeared in the *Virginia Quarterly Review* in 2015. Reprinted by permission of the author. Copyright © 2015 by Colleen Kinder.

"Gratitude Day" by Sara C. Bathum published with permission from the author. Copyright © 2017 by Sara C. Bathum.

"Curandero" by Catherine Watson published with permission from the author. Copyright © 2017 by Catherine Watson.

"Call Your Mother" by Abbie Kozolchyk originally appeared in the *San Francisco Chronicle* and on *WorldHum* in 2014. Reprinted by permission of the author. Copyright © 2014 by Abbie Kozolchyk.

"A Country Tradition" by Julie Callahan published with permission from the author. Copyright © 2017 by Julie Callahan.

"Outsider Again" by Yukari Iwatani Kane published with permission from the author. Copyright © 2017 by Yukari Iwatani Kane.

"Waning Moon" by Pam Mandel published with permission from the author. Copyright © 2017 by Pam Mandel.

"Rich Country" by Anne P. Beatty originally appeared online at *Vela Magazine* in 2016. Reprinted by permission of the author. Copyright © 2016 by Anne P. Beatty.

"I Am Here, in This Morning Light" by Sandra Gail Lambert originally appeared in the Fall 2012, Volume 297 issue of the *North American Review*. Published with permission from the author. Copyright © 2012 by Sandra Gail Lambert.

"Heartbeats on Teshima" by Suzanne Kamata published with permission from the author. Copyright © 2017 by Suzanne Kamata.

"Reconnaissance" by Erin Byrne excerpted from *Wings: Gifts of Art, Life, and Travel in France* by Erin Byrne. Reprinted with permission from Solas House, Inc. and the author. Copyright © 2016 by Erin Byrne.

Lavinia Spalding has edited four previous volumes of The Best Women's Travel Writing. *She is the author of* Writing Away: A Creative Guide to Awakening the Journal-Writing Traveler *and* With a Measure of Grace, the Story and Recipes of a Small Town Restaurant. *She also introduced the reissued e-book edition of Edith Wharton's classic travelogue,* A Motor-Flight Through France. *Her writing appears in numerous print and online publications, as well as in tattered, coffee-stained journals around the world. She lives in New Orleans with her family, where she is working on a memoir and becoming an expert in all things oyster.*